Making a Submarine Officer

USS San Francisco (SSN-711)
2nd Edition 2016

By Alex C. Fleming

D1738151

Making a Submarine Officer
By Alex Fleming

Contents

Acknowledgments

Preface

Introduction

Chapter 1: Beginnings
Chapter 2: Qualification
Chapter 3: Problems
Chapter 4: Federal Disaster Area
Chapter 5: Examinations
Chapter 6: Hitting Rock Bottom
Chapter 7: Strange Luck
Chapter 8: Second Chance
Chapter 9: Broken
Chapter 10: The Tip of the Spear
Chapter 11: Collision
Chapter 12: Shattered

Conclusion

Afterword

Glossary

For the crew of 711,
my wife - Mary-Katherine,
and my children - Cheyanne, RJ, and Shiloh

Acknowledgments

I would like to thank, above all, the crew of the USS San Francisco (SSN-711), who taught me what it means to be a good leader and a good person. This book would not have been possible without the review and editorial support of MH, MP, JE, AB, AJ, HH, JH, BC, KM, and many others who read portions of this work. I'm grateful to the United States Navy and the United States Submarine Force for giving me an incredible experience and leadership training. It will define me for the rest of my life. I would like to thank the educational institutions that gave me the tools to succeed: All Saints' Episcopal Day School in Phoenix, Arizona, Choate Rosemary Hall in Wallingford, Connecticut, and the University of Pennsylvania in Philadelphia. The comments of Stephanie Kehrer, Alice Martell, Debbie Leight, and Matthew Morgan were invaluable. My parents Jim and Claudia and my sister Erica have given me unending support and love. I dedicate this effort and its publication to my wife Mary-Katherine, without whom I would never have completed this book.

Author's Note: Parts of this book may be more difficult to understand for those unfamiliar with the Navy. For those readers, I have tried to use relatively few acronyms and to make the writing as accessible as possible. The Glossary defines commonly used acronyms. Readers who want more information about portions of the story, technical subjects, and my background can find it in the footnotes. These provide deeper subject matter for the ambitious reader.

People on a submarine are often referred to by their rank or the position they occupy. You will find this most often with the senior officers: CO (Captain), XO (Executive Officer), ENG (Engineer), NAV (Navigator), WEPS (Weapons Officer), and SUPPO or CHOP (Supply Officer). Enlisted men are also referred to by their job and level, such as EM1 for Electrician's Mate First Class and MM3 for Machinist's Mate Third Class (a First Class is higher than a Third Class). Again, I have tried to keep these to a minimum.

<ins>The Department of Defense and the United States Navy do not endorse this publication, and the views expressed herein do not represent the policy or views of the United States government.</ins>

About the Author

Alex Fleming served on active duty in the United States Navy from 2001 to 2006. He holds an MBA in finance from the Wharton School of the University of Pennsylvania and an MA in international relations from Johns Hopkins University. He works as a management consultant and lives in Denver, CO.

Preface

Failure is a much more powerful teacher than success. In the beginning, I was an idealistic young man who did not know failure. I had endured small mistakes, wrong steps, and imperfect performances, but I had never truly set my heart and mind to something and watched it go completely wrong. My experiences in the Navy brought me to a horrifying and gut-wrenching place in my own mind that made me question my very existence and every value I possessed. My fight was not a physical one, and it cannot be compared to what infantry soldiers face. The submarine battle is a war of the mind and of the overwhelming forces in the darkest depths of the world. This fight brought me face to face with my nightmares and shaped the person I'm today. The important people in my life endured this evolution, and they continue to help me build the person I'm on the other side. I'm eternally grateful for their patience.

The public perception is that the submarine force has less to do now that the Cold War is over. This is the exact opposite of the truth because we have fewer submarines than before, fewer trained crewmembers, and more missions. The versatility and adaptability of submarines mean that we can go wherever we are needed quickly without refueling. The Tomahawk land attack missile (TLAM) is an incredible weapon that submarines can launch far onto land, which was proven definitively during the Gulf Wars. The ability to remain undetected in any ocean makes intelligence, surveillance, and reconnaissance our primary mission.

The number of mission requirements for submarines keeps increasing, and the number of ships keeps dropping. This is a big problem for the fleet and Navy brass because they do not want to turn down any jobs. The money game in Washington means that every service is competing for less funding. Even within the Navy, different service areas have to justify their existence every year, so Fleet Commanders will never turn down a mission even if it puts stress on crews and ships because it gives them ammunition to get more funding for the next fiscal year. These cost concerns drove ships to be home ported in Guam and drive the creation of the schedule.

This book is not a comprehensive history of the USS San Francisco. It is not an unbiased retelling of the events that occurred between September 2002 and September 2005. The story contains my memories, journals, and reflections of life on a nuclear attack submarine. During that time, the ship changed homeports from Norfolk to Guam to Seattle, traveled approximately 51,000 miles, dry-docked twice, and was involved in a near-collision and a submerged grounding.

The secrecy and security of submarine operations means that a great deal of my story involving nuclear power and the ship's missions is heavily abridged to protect America and the safety of submariners out there under the water right now. Wherever possible, I have consulted with my shipmates about conversations and events that involved a number of different people and for the times when I was not onboard. I have attempted to portray the statements of other people in the story with as much accuracy as possible, and if any misinterpretation has occurred, the error is mine. **The Department of Defense and the United States Navy do not endorse this publication, and the views expressed herein do not represent the policy or views of the United States government.**

The five men who commanded the submarine during my tenure led the one hundred twenty crewmembers through a gauntlet of trials that bound us forever and showed us the best and worst of the United States Navy. We went from the shipyard to operations, from dry-dock to the depths of the Pacific, from failure to success, and through tragedy and pain to return home.

Welcome aboard...

Introduction

No matter how long I have been onboard, I still notice the smell. It's a faint, chemical aroma, like sniffing a bottle of ammonia, and it is always present. Sometimes, I allow myself to forget about it and walk around the boat for weeks without noticing, but it always returns. It is in my clothes and my hair and every personal item in the storage pan underneath my bed. The scent returns to me now, as I stand with my back against the wall outside the Captain's stateroom. I'm pressed up against the cheap plastic of the surface behind me, which is smooth and cold. Even with my back against the wall, there are only seven inches between me and the opposite wall, so that every man who passes has to turn sideways and our chests brush against one another. In my case, my stomach is becoming significant enough from my nervous eating habits that it is my widest point.

The hallway is dark, which is normal after sunset, though the hours of daylight have little meaning when we are underwater. The traditions of the service mean that we still turn the lights to red at night, which always seems like teasing to me because there is some normal person somewhere who gets to watch the sunset and have a normal schedule. I stand in the dark passageway, listening intently to the unintelligible sounds coming from behind the Captain's door to my left. White light shines under the doorframe, and a soft red glow comes through the small round window in the door to the control room at the end of the hall on my left. Every few moments, a face looks through to check whether I'm still here because everyone seems to know why I'm waiting. I get tired of seeing the faces and trying to appear calm, so I look at my belt and the bottom half of my blue jumpsuit. My tennis shoes are getting dirty from a year of constant use on the ship, and I remind myself again that I must get new ones when we get back to port ... unless I'm not going to have to get underway again. The thought makes me glance upward, past the polished walls. They are so clean I'm afraid to touch them for fear of leaving fingerprints. It is still hard to imagine the painstaking time taken to clean cheap plastic walls with a fake wood grain pattern and thin metal plating. I focus on the ceiling, which is also false and easily removed to get to the equipment installed above it. The new powder coating is glossy white, but the latches have begun to chip after only a few days. The Master Chief will be furious, and we will probably have to do the job again. It won't surprise anyone, but we will still get angry about it for show.

The seconds tick by, and I try to avoid looking at my watch. I close my eyes and lean my head back on the uneven welds of the frame piece behind me. It's cold, but I've become accustomed to feeling a chill most of the time. I wear a thick brown wool sweater, which scratches at my neck and smells like it's as old as the boat. Washing repeatedly and dry cleaning did not fix the smell, and it's just another sign that the marks of being on a submarine are hard to remove. I shut my eyes tighter and focus on the sound. We are deep and going fast, and my head on the frame piece feels the deep, throbbing vibration of the engines. The throaty noise is complimented by the fans. There is a ventilation duct above me, and the fans that push the chemical-smelling air around the ship hum constantly. It is so much a part of our consciousness that the first thing we notice in many emergencies is the fans coasting down. I shift my weight slightly back and forth, from my heels to my toes, as I feel the ship rocking with the slight rudder corrections. It must be a new helmsman at the wheel to be correcting so hard at this speed. The more experienced drivers correct their course so smoothly that you can hardly feel the turns. The rumbles and hums and shifts are the heartbeat of the ship, and they calm me with their familiarity.

I jerk out of my reverie as I hear someone on the stairs to my right. The messenger climbs up a staircase from the deck below, a dim glow outlining his form. I don't need to see his face; I know his body outline, gait, and voice well enough. A voice is all I need to identify someone on this ship, especially the messengers, since they are the first voice you hear through the curtain when you wake up. He gives me a brusque nod and whispers, "Excuse me, sir," as he turns sideways and passes me, heading for control. People glance through from control to see whether I'm still there as he opens and then silently shuts the door. I'm back in the darkness.

Suddenly, light floods the hallway as the Captain's door opens. The Executive Officer steps out, and even though I'm blinded and cannot see his face, I can sense the solemn expression from the outline of his features. He tells me that the Captain is ready to see me, and I walk into the doorframe and straighten my back as I knock twice on the already open door. A pinched and abrupt voice tells me to come in and close the door. I turn my shoulders sideways to fit them through the doorway and step into the cabin, silently latching the handle behind me.

The Captain's cabin is the only space on the whole ship that one person has for himself alone. A safe and a desk are built into the left wall, which faces aft. The electronic equipment is affixed at seemingly random intervals, almost like every new screen or gadget had to be put in where it could fit at the discretion of the occupant. The far wall has a bed, which is normally folded into the wall, but since it is night, a mess steward has opened and made the bed, something that is done only for the Captain. There is a bookshelf with a metal restraint that prevents the contents from pouring out, and the forward wall has the door to the bathroom. I'm standing against the thin plastic separating the cabin from the hallway, and to my right is a mirror with a sink that folds out of the wall. I have to concentrate to remain standing at attention and not glance at myself in the mirror to see whether I'm pale. The calendar on the wall in front of me stares back: September 2003. The new month's picture is of a submarine on the surface leaving Pearl Harbor. I wonder whether there were officers on that ship with my problems. The ceiling of the room is solid in places, with patches of blue vinyl snapped over other rectangles. The Captain sits at the desk a few inches in front of me, typing on his laptop. I know better than to speak, and I stand tense, waiting for the inevitable explosion.

Paul Lovpock closes his laptop and folds up his desk before turning to look at me. He rotates his chair and gazes over the thin-framed glasses that rest on his sharp, beak-like nose. It is hard not to look at the shiny gleam from his bald head, so I try to keep my eyes unfocused, aimed at the ugly wood pattern on the far wall. Finally, he crosses his arms and speaks.

"Mr. Fleming, you are broken as a leader and I don't know how I'm going to fix you." His words sound like a sneer, without any visible facial expression.

I listen with exhaustion and defeat after the worst twelve months of my life, and I wonder whether any job is worth this pain. I try to think of something to say that will not make the situation worse, but no thoughts come. It's like my brain is gridlocked. Only thirty months ago, I had been commissioned as a Naval Officer after graduating from the University of Pennsylvania with an honors degree in physics and Russian. I was eager to join one of the most elite groups of officers in the Navy. But now, I'm close to a nervous breakdown. How could my path have led me to the point of being fired and assigned to a desk job for my remaining three years in the Navy?

Chapter 1: Beginnings

July 2002

I'm sitting in a small hotel room at the Susse Chalet on the Naval Submarine Base in Groton, Connecticut. The walls are cheap, pastel pink with ridges of rapidly applied cloth wall covering. An indescribably boring watercolor painting of birds and a lake hangs on the wall behind me. Students of the Submarine Officer Basic School are required to live here for the three months of their transient life at the base. I'm watching a DVD on my small computer after a long day of extraordinarily boring lectures, most of them longer than eighty PowerPoint slides each. My mind wanders as I contemplate the journey just a month ahead to Guam, a place I know very little about. I only know that it is far from anything I have ever seen. My phone rings and I hear the first voice from the USS San Francisco:

"Dude, are you drinking beer every night?"

"Um ... yes," I lie, but it seems the right thing to say.

"Awesome, enjoy it while you can, because once you get here, life starts to suck." The voice on the other end belongs to Mike Harven, an officer who has been on 711 for about a year during the end of a refueling. Though he sounds cheerful and funny on the phone, he also strikes me as very negative, which sets off internal alarm bells in my mind about my destination.

Mike continues, "Well, I'm not actually your sponsor; he is at Engineer's school. But we were looking through his box and found your letter. So we thought we would give you a call and see what was up." Every Navy command assigns a sponsor to each newly reporting crewmember to answer questions and assist in the transition. My orders came in March, and this phone call is my first contact. My original sponsor, Chris Falcone, is away from the ship at a three-month school to qualify as a Nuclear Engineer Officer. "Thanks," I reply. "So what's the wardroom like?" I have a million questions, but this one seems best because the collective group of officers, called the wardroom, is what's going to determine my quality of life for the next three years.

"Dude, it is a crazy bunch. The new Captain is kind of strange, but he hasn't been around long enough to get a bead on him. The XO is a tyrant, a screamer, but he gets the job done. The ENG is an idiot. Most of the time we have to keep him out of trouble. He'll tell us to do things and we'll be like, '... ENG, you can't do that.' But he listens most of the time, so he is manageable. WEPS and NAV are both new, but they seem pretty cool. The NAV is incredibly smart. As far as the JOs (Junior Officers) go, we're all pretty disgruntled since we've spent the last 24 months in the shipyard getting our asses kicked by the man." I think "the man" probably refers to Naval Reactors, whose representatives are notorious for their forceful and antagonistic monitoring even in the training pipeline.

We talk for a few more minutes about when I'm arriving and whether I've heard anything about Guam. I tell Mike that I requested Guam, but only as a second choice.

"That was stupid; I hear the place sucks," he replies.

I get his phone number, and the conversation ends on a rather ominous note:

"Have fun while you have the chance, man."

I sit quietly, going over the news in my head. It must be odd to find someone so negative? I'm an optimist, and I'm excited to get out of this endless training pipeline and to the fleet. Mike must not be representative; there's nothing to worry about. Ever since September 11, 2001, all I can think about is making a difference. This outlook is common among my classmates, but only those who have never been in the Navy before. The prior-enlisted guys look at us with something akin to fond pity, like dogs that have been accidentally blinded but yip and jump nonetheless (Note 1).

August 2002

I jump into the sleek silver SUV that pulls up in front of the hotel at Submarine School, and I meet Matt Priests for the first time. He's a Submarine Officer Advanced Course student, while I'm here for the Basic Course, and he is going to be the Engineer for most of my time on San Francisco. I have heard that the Engineer is important in every young officer's life, so I'm nervous about meeting him. I email him to set something up, and he replies that we should have dinner up at the Mohegan Sun Casino since the food there is good and he can teach me to play craps. He sounds cool over email, but you can never tell until you meet someone in person.

Matt is built like a middleweight boxer and carries himself intensely on his 6'1" frame. His nose is crooked from an injury obtained fighting at the Naval Academy, and he has potent eyes that seem to capture you when he talks. I discover that he has just completed his MBA at the Wharton School of the University of Pennsylvania, the same university I attended as an undergrad. He's not happy about going back into the Navy because he's a finance genius and had several job offers that he had to turn down. Instead, he's paying the service back for his school time and heading off to take the worst job in the submarine force. He explains that he fully expects to have no life for the next three years. This will be especially hard for his wife Diane and their son, who is only four months old, but he is not too worried about them because there is a strong Latter Day Saints community on Guam.

I tell him about my background and he's very excited, but he wonders why I got into the Navy instead of going straight to graduate school. I explain my desire to serve and the need to pay for college. He just shakes his head and chuckles at me, like he pities my foolishness. He tells me candidly that he thinks a submarine is going to be pretty tough for a guy like me. Matt thinks my creativity will make me different from most of the guys, and it'll be hard to stay interested in the more boring aspects of the job. He tells me that he's looking forward to working with me, but there's something he wants me to be prepared for.

"Alex, I'm going to be your boss. I'm going to work with you the best I can, but there are some times that you're going to hate me. I mean you are really going to HATE me. I'm going to turn your life upside down and put you through incredible amounts of pain. This will be necessary for the operation of the ship.

"I like you a lot as a person, so I want you to remember one thing – Nothing is personal. If you take things personally on a submarine, you're going to become frustrated and eat yourself up inside. Everything that happens, you have to do your best, but don't let it get to you. Remember – Nothing, none of it, is personal; it's just the job."

September 2002

I'm walking out of the National Gallery of Art on the Washington National Mall on a beautiful Wednesday afternoon after Labor Day weekend. The sun is warm and comforting, as vignettes of fall in DC play out in front of me: A family having ice cream, tourists taking snapshots of the Capitol, an outdoor concert, and two joggers. Despite the gentle breeze, nothing can change my sense of anxiety. I'm excited to get to my first command next week, but I'm also nervous about things I've heard. As I walk down the steps, I'm stopped as a group of 400 men and women in red dresses run down the street in front of me. I smile at the odd things you see here, and it doesn't occur to me for a minute that I will be a member of that particular international group in three months' time.

I walk slowly back to my sister's apartment in Foggy Bottom, where I'm crashing for a few days, enjoying the sun as I go. My email is full of the usual daily spam on my return, but there's one message from my submarine role model. Commander Mark Ginda is the officer who convinced me to join the submarine force, and I've asked him for advice on my first few weeks on the boat. As I read his message, I'm developing my strategy. Commander Ginda's advice is to hit the ground running and complete my first qualification in two weeks to set the standard that I'm someone who pulls his load. My energy and excitement increase as I plan and fantasize about the impact I'm going to make. I'm sure that I'm going to be the best officer they've ever seen. If the standard is two weeks, I'm going to do it in one. I'm a hard charger, and I'll set the new standard. I'm jerked from my thoughts as my cell phone rings.

"Hello, is this Alex Fleming?" says a nasal, pinched voice. I answer.

"My name is Mark Sheklund; I'm a JO on the San Francisco, and I guess I'm your sponsor." This is the first time I've spoken to him, and I'm reporting next week.

"Where are you right now?" he asks, without any preliminary small talk.

"Crashing at my sister's place in D.C.," I reply with a questioning attitude.

"How soon can you get here?" he asks urgently.

"Well, I guess I could drive down tomorrow. Why, what's going on?" I'm disappointed at losing a week of vacation after a year of 12-hour days studying nuclear power.

"The XO is on a rampage this week, and he just reviewed the school requirements. He saw that we need an officer to go to Non-Dive Supervisor School in Hawaii next week, and you're it. You learn to run dives without actually getting to go to dive school." My mood immediately improves on the prospect of a trip to Pearl Harbor.

He continues, "Yeah, we were all sitting in the wardroom arguing about who got to go, and he settled it by giving it to you, so everyone is pretty pissed." My spirits drop right back down at the thought of every single officer resenting me from the beginning.

"Well, I'll pack up my stuff and be there tomorrow afternoon. Where is the boat?" I reply nervously.

"OK, you come to Norfolk Naval Station, and we're at Pier 3 at the far end of the pier on the right. We're right across from the USS Jacksonville. Get here as soon as you can." I'm surprised how fast plans change, but I get a strange feeling that this is only the beginning.

"I'll be there tomorrow." My anxiety from earlier in the day becomes stark fear as my stomach drops into my foot. A tingling sensation in my mind tells me I should be more concerned about the symbolism of this change in plans, but I shake it off. It's probably nothing.

Thursday afternoon, the following day

My Ford Bronco makes record time down Interstate 95 and then off an interchange to a very well-patrolled section of Virginia highway. The road signs are easy to follow as I drive toward the Norfolk Naval Base, one of the biggest bases in the country. It's a humid and sticky day, conditions better suited for the jungle. The reflection of the sun on the asphalt seems to intensify my nervousness the closer I get to the base. My summer whites are hanging in the back of the car, ready to put on as the required uniform for reporting to any command. I've been on reserve bases before, but this place is so huge that I'm astonished by the sheer acreage of the parking lots.

I change into my whites in the bathroom of the Naval Exchange, my pitifully small "starter set" of ribbons on my chest showing my inexperience and lack of qualification. I drive through the gates to the pier area and complete two laps of the whole base before finding Pier 3, which has six submarines moored. I begin to sweat in the synthetic white material before I even get out of the car as I debate what to bring onboard with me.

I grab my bag with my personnel files, medical and dental records, and orders. With a deep breath and a prayer, I walk toward the pier. I pass a loading dock at the end of the pier and an older chief with a huge, bushy mustache salutes and stops me.

"Looking good, sir. It's good to see a JO not straining his whites with his stomach." I weigh 195 pounds at six feet tall, and I'm very proud of maintaining it over a year of studying. I'm unsure of the proper response, so I smile and reply, "Thanks a lot, Chief. Don't have too much fun there." He smiles and points me down the pier. I guess that he is on the San Francisco and expecting me.

I continue down the pier past a swarm of activity, people loading and unloading all manner of food and supplies. I understand very little of it, but my instinct is to stay out of the way. I pass several sailors who smile at me as they salute, as if they know exactly what this fresh Ensign is doing on their pier. I begin to feel like I'm on a walk of shame, intended to humble me. After dodging a few more trucks and cranes, I see the USS San Francisco for the first time (Note 2).

September 5, 2002. 1420 hours.

It's identical to every other submarine at the pier, but there's something dirtier and older about it. An accumulated pile of pigeon excrement crusts the entire flat surface of the rudder. The seawater laps at the black hull, but inches of green sea growth are visible just below the waterline, reminding me of a Chia Pet. Most of the large sail structures sticking out of the top of the other submarines are smooth and well painted. Ours appears to be covered in rusty scaffolding, with several holes open. The rust patches extend over the whole ship, though a few dirty sailors are painting a small patch of the deck. The sight does not thrill me.

I walk up to the brow of the 711, which I know only by the banner since there are no identifying marks on the ship. It is a small wooden shack at the end of a rough and dirty metal walkway that crosses to the ship. People walk back and forth, but no one gives me a second glance as they go about their business. It's not what I expect based on my very short experience on the USS Pasadena, but this boat is just coming out of a long time in the shipyard, so maybe it's normal.

The seaman standing watch on the brow looks at me with a barely concealed grin, and I have a feeling that I'm fulfilling some cliché without even knowing it. I look closer at him. His name tag says "PETERSON," and he is tall and skinny, with puffy black hair and thin-framed glasses. His voice has a decidedly middle-American twang. I tell him that I'm reporting aboard, and he takes my ID to make the required deck log entry: "1420 hours, Ensign Alexander C. Fleming USN, reported for duty." He asks me if I know who is meeting me, and I tell him it's Lieutenant Junior Grade Sheklund. I wait as he calls down on an old-looking metal box that brings images of the Second World War. He's attempting to get me an escort; since I haven't been "read-in" to security yet, I cannot walk around the boat alone. For 20 minutes, I wait and make uncomfortable small talk in my whites, now developing unsightly sweat marks.

I'm tired of waiting, and the Petty Officer who comes from below decks wearing a gun belt and carrying an old clipboard says that he cannot find Mr. Sheklund. I stop the next crewmember to walk across the pier, whose name is Brown, and ask him if he can escort me onto the ship. He responds in a very odd tone of voice but with a puppy-dog-like enthusiasm that tells me it's not very often that an officer needs something from him. I shrug off the feeling because I just want to get onto my new ship.

I climb down the ladder into the command passageway and immediately discover the first problem of being on a submarine: you're always in the way, no matter where you stand. Submarine passageways are wide enough for only one set of shoulders; if two people pass each other, they have to turn sideways, and their chests still touch with both backs on the wall. At the bottom of the ladder, I immediately cause a roadblock because I don't know which way to go. Several people give me nasty looks as I finally follow Brown down the steep ladder one more level. We walk aft past an endless stream of people staring at me; I'm apparently the fresh meat for the grinder. The hallways are crowded with equipment affixed everywhere. Lockers and boxes hang in every space, and I feel surrounded on all sides. There is no wasted space.

We dodge a closed conference room full of people, the wardroom, and I discover that I can't stop without stopping all traffic. I look to the port side of the ship and slip into a tiny space with crates piled everywhere and machinery covering the walls. I ask Brown where I can find the officers. He runs away for a minute and then comes back, very much like an eager dog, to tell me that they're in training in the wardroom. I convince Brown that it's safe to leave me in this small closet room alone, watching the passageway traffic, and that I'll wait here for training to be over.

I find a bench among the boxes and sit down. There are several sharp metal valves above me and two large safes to my right with frayed and scratched warning signs. I touch the cold metal table to my right, and I realize that this must be a medical space. There is a very well-used aspirin dispenser, an electronic thermometer, a defibrillator kit, and several green oxygen bottles on the wall, along with piles and piles of medical files. The supplies piled around me are half unpacked, and I think I may be intruding, but no one tells me to move. Constant traffic goes by in the passage in front of me. People stop to use a small water fountain that is recessed into the wall, but never for more than a few seconds. The scene reminds me of a crowded river that's full of fish and the only way to stop moving is to get out of the flow. I try to relax and lean back, but my head will not fit above a piece of piping, and I have to cock it to the side.

I sit quietly, watching people go by. A few people talk to me, but the conversation is brief and to the point: "Are you the new Ensign?" "Yes" "OK, welcome aboard." I realize that it's not because they're mean. Everyone is polite, but they look busy and intent on their job. I'm now a NUB (Non-Useful Body), or an Oxygen Consumer, on the submarine. I will be ignored except for the most basic courtesies until I can stand a watch, fill a billet, or get something done that takes a load off someone else. I don't think it's out of spite; it's just efficiency. I don't deserve any energy input until I can give something back. Thirty-five minutes of this type of interaction move slowly, but mostly I'm left alone until I look up to see a man in blue coveralls and a brown, high-collared "submarine" sweater. He walks from across the passageway and steps into the small space, and I stand up to meet him.

"Hi, you must be Ensign Fleming. I'm Paul Lovpock. Welcome aboard." I realize with a jolt of nerves that this is the Captain. He stands four inches shorter than me and is a small, compact man who looks like a college professor. He's bald except for a ring of graying dark hair and has a pointed nose that strikes me as very bird-like, holding up his round-frames glasses. Commander Lovpock moves with his upper body slightly bent forward, like he's leaning into his walk. His accent is standard American, with a slight nasal tone, though he stresses different words in sentences than I would expect. He moves with his arms locked straight at his side in an almost robot-like posture. He poses a series of rapid-fire questions:

"So, Mr. Fleming, where did you go to school?"

"The University of Pennsylvania, in Philly, sir."

"Great, and what was your major?"

"I was a double major in physics and Russian," I reply.

"Russian, wow, do you speak it?"

"Yes, sir, I lived there for a semester."

"Good, well, you got here just in time for Officer Training in the wardroom." It's now 1550. Apparently, officer training starts at 1600. "Well, welcome aboard."

"Thank you, sir." Then he's gone off down the passageway before I even see where he's going. I stand for a moment, feeling strange about my first encounter with my new boss. I can't place the feeling. He'ss just … strange. I shake off the sensation; it's probably just jitters. I grab my bag and make a dash across the passageway into the wardroom. The experience reminds me of crossing an eight-lane road on foot. I get to the wardroom passageway, also known as "officer country," and knock for the first time on the door of the place that will be my lounge, office, and home for the tour.

The wardroom is a space 10 feet wide by 14 feet long centered on a ten-seat dining table that doubles as a conference table. The sides of the room are covered with couches that allow people to sit in a ring around the walls. The couches and chairs are covered in a blue vinyl material that squeaks and makes odd noises as you move. The head of the table is the only chair with armrests, and it's the Captain's chair. No other person will ever sit there under any conditions. The other two walls have bookshelves and a door into the food service areas. There are no pictures or plaques anywhere on the walls. The room strikes me as harsh and stark, like a hotel room without character. I suppose it could grow on me, but for now, the strangeness is hard to overcome.

Officers begin introducing themselves in rapid succession. I don't remember a single name, though I do recognize Mike Harven and Mark Sheklund. Harven is a 5'10" blond Florida native with a huge voice and infectious attitude that brings laughter to any room. His medium build is apparently fueled by a love of beer, and he wears small, black, oval-rimmed glasses. Sheklund is a skinny, slight man with dark hair and glasses who reminds me of a younger version of Alan Greenspan. He has just qualified in the engineering plant and has an air of intelligence that can only be gained by months spent bent over technical manuals. I'm beginning to realize that I'm the only officer onboard who does not wear glasses, which is the side effect of smart officers in the Navy whose eyes make them ineligible for aviation.

I'm welcomed with a reserved enthusiasm, and I take a seat on the far side of the room where I can watch everyone and see the wide flat-screen television on one wall. I answer questions quickly, with most of the attention focused on my Russian experience and family background. I feel like I'm on the witness stand of a murder trial. The fact that I have a 20-year-old sister draws a large amount of attention in a way that amuses me, and I promise several people introductions.

I turn my head as a bear of a man storms into the room with an intensity that seems to push people out of the way. Kevin Jorges, the Executive Officer, is 6'4" and has to duck to make his way through the submarine. He has wavy blond hair that's just turning grey at the edges. The notebook in his hand is tattered and well used, and even as I speak, he does not make eye contact. He falls into the chair at the Captain's right hand and nods, barely hearing my words. He chuckles at me as I finish my speech and begins reading out of his flip-book, which I quickly realize is the notebook of choice for the officers. He has a checklist, three pages long, and it takes him 10 minutes to give "tasking" to each of the officers. There is light banter, coupled with a list of jobs that fly out seemingly at random.

The officers joke with the XO, and he barks with fake anger. He responds to them with a shake of his head and whispers, "You mother-fuckers." Everyone seems to get along well, and the lecture begins as a harried-looking man with black hair and intense eyes stands at the end of the room over a laptop and begins talking about battle group operations. I look closer and realize that his face is young, but his eyes are dark, suspicious, and intelligent, like someone who's seen more than other people his age. This must be the Navigator. Most of the material is new to me, but the others seem to be bored and disinterested. The Navigator, giving the training from a long PowerPoint presentation, talks without looking at his notes and has interesting background stories about every point in the lecture. I'm astounded by his sheer volume of experience as I wonder about his background in the Navy.

The training ends after fifty minutes, which is an hour by Navy training tradition. As everyone leaves, a pinched-faced officer with a diver insignia sits down at the table and regards me. He is tall as well, but his glasses are bigger and his face has odd proportions. His ears seem disproportionately large, and his voice jars me with its rudeness.

"So you get to go to Hawaii instead of me. Thanks a lot." Martin Sprocket establishes himself with an arrogance that jumps across the table at me. "I'm the Ship's Scuba Diving officer, so we don't need a non-dive supervisor, but the XO," he says, checking to see that the XO is gone, "will not fucking listen to me."

"Umm ... ok, sorry about that." I'm unsure how to respond in the face of blatant hostility since I have to work with this guy for a long time.

"Well, have fun and learn something because, as soon as you get back, you're doing all my bitch paperwork in the diving division." He gets up and leaves without any more small talk. I turn to the officer sitting next to me, Mike Harven, who laughs and says, "Don't worry; he's always been an asshole." It is very little comfort. Then Sprocket comes back through the door and asks if I have my coveralls with me. He wants me to walk through a battery-charging lineup, which I cannot do in my whites.

"I need to get you qualified so I never have to do one again," he says to explain his logic. I'm eager to get started on being useful and compensate for my Hawaii trip, so I go out to my car and get my coveralls. The first qualification any officer gets is as the checker of a battery-charging lineup, an entirely unpleasant job that involves crawling around in very small places for an hour and hopefully not getting sprayed with battery acid.

Later in the evening, I drive to downtown Norfolk and have dinner at a TGI Friday's while my mind races at a thousand miles per hour thinking about my new co-workers. I'm trying to escape to a place of familiarity, and a chain restaurant is the first thing that catches my eye. The officers seem like a tight-knit group, but I feel a bitterness and almost painful sarcasm about everything. It's like I'm looking in on a group of survivors that have brought each other through by will alone. I remember many stories about being a junior

13

officer in the shipyard, and I wonder whether this is the result. I'm still excited and optimistic, and I've completed my first practical factor (the battery charge) during my first two hours on the submarine. I want to set the standard and get qualified fast. I've never failed at anything, and I see no other option but to throw myself into this challenge. I will show all of them.

I run around like crazy doing a million errands and getting checked in at medical, dental, and squadron. My paperwork says that I'm in Virginia but supposed to be in Guam. The ship has already passed the effective date of the homeport change, but it is months from actually moving, and the issues that have to be dealt with 7,000 miles away are causing incredible trouble. I'm not getting paid correctly, but I have a credit card that can take the slack. I hear rumors that several people are in the same situation, and apparently moving a ship to the other side of the world creates big pay problems. Right now, I'm just concerned with getting my orders written on Friday afternoon so I can fly to Honolulu on Saturday. They come in at 1655 hours.

I spend one week learning about dive medicine, coaching divers, safety procedures, and the basics of Navy diving. It's a low-intensity school, which means that the classes are usually done before lunch and the exam is open book. I do learn a lot, and I'm determined not to be useless when I return. I enjoy my interactions with the dive school instructors, who truly love their jobs, and I fantasize about coming back as a scuba student. The time in Hawaii also gives me time to do an ambitious amount of drinking and dancing every night for six days, with the idea that I'll have plenty of time to relax on the plane home. I return to work convinced that submarine life is all sunny trips to Hawaii, but I have a hunch that the routine is normally much more mundane.

I see the first evidence of that as I arrive at work on my first Monday back. The schedule apparently moves according to a document called the Plan of the Day, which is posted all over the ship. I scan it in the morning, trying to read as people keep pushing me out of the way, and I think that the Officer/LPO Call at 0715 is probably the first thing I have to show up for. I walk into the crew's mess five minutes early, and the seats are already taken. It's clear that I'm at the bottom of hierarchy, standing packed like a sardine in the corner of the room.

The crew's mess is a space about twenty feet wide and twenty feet long with five tables covered with the same blue vinyl material. Poorly padded bench seats accompany each table, and the front of the room has a steam serving line for feeding the crew. The galley is quiet now as all the senior people onboard stuff in for the morning meeting. Almost 40 men are packed into every free space of the room. I study everyone as the Master Chief begins to talk. It's clear that there's an order to it, even if it's hard to pick out. Each department has a different table, and the head of the department always gets to sit down. The Chiefs come next, and they have the power to demand a seat, and then the leading petty officers squeeze in where they can. The big departments have bigger tables. The very junior officers and lower enlisted people have to stand in the corner of the room and hang their hands on the pipes that run along the ceiling. The far wall has the same fake wood pattern, but there is also a plastic imitation of a colored glass window, with a picture of the Golden Gate Bridge. The Executive Officer and the Master Chief who helps the Captain run the ship (COB, for Chief of the Boat) stand in the front of the room and guide the meeting, asking questions and giving out tasking. This XO has a quick temper, and he yells often, causing me to jerk with surprise. The faces in the room seem used to it for the twenty minutes of discussion that follow.

I barely keep up with what is going on as people talk in shorthand and acronyms. People seem free to speak up with a concern even if they are not a high rank, but they are allowed to talk because of their knowledge and competence. This is the military, but the meeting makes me feel like I'm in a meritocracy. I hang my hand on a ventilation pipe and stay very quiet. I'm sure this will all make sense to me sometime, but for now, I'm just confused. I feel like I'm playing catch-up.

Just as my mind begins to wander, the XO turns toward me, barking, "Fleming!" I catch some amused looks from the room as I jump out of my skin, my cheeks flushing with embarrassment.

My first job as an officer is to investigate a case of unauthorized absence. This duty is traditionally divided between officers and chiefs in a rotation and involves gathering statements and providing an evaluation of whether certain charges have merit. I'm excited and honored to have such an important job, not knowing that it happens all the time. I decide that I will get the job done better and more thoroughly than anyone before. I begin to find my way around the ship by trial and error, hitting my head so often that it begins to bleed. I feel like I'm being watched and evaluated everywhere I go, like some kind of new zoo animal, and no one is quite sure what to make of me.

My walks around the engine room and forward compartment begin to show me one thing; I'm being tested. I walk around a corner to a call of "flying squirrels in the engine room," and find myself immediately facing more male genitalia than I can imagine. I respond by shaking my head, laughing, and walking the other way. This seems to be the right answer, since I have the feeling the guys are trying to see what gets me angry or annoyed. I make the absolute mistake of mentioning to another officer that I don't like being called "Flemwad." This spreads throughout the ship within an hour, and I find myself being called that at every turn. Someone calls my nuclear power school instructors and finds out my nickname, "Red Monkey," for the stickers I have on my notebooks. I feel like people are going out of their way to push my buttons and see what I'll do. The only solution I can think of is to not talk, finish my investigation, and bury my head in a book. I continue to find my way around and discover that the way to get things done is not through the officers or chiefs but the second-class petty officers. These men are the movers, shakers, and get-it-done guys who show me my way around my new job. Just as I begin to feel like I'm getting settled, it's Friday.

I learn that I'm going to another school off the ship, this one in Dams Neck, Virginia. This time, I'm learning to operate the computers that run tactics and coordination for the Navy, and I have a companion. Mike Vasquez arrived a few months before me and is closest to me in qualification and rank. We set off together to the beach on the other side of Norfolk and spend a week becoming friends. Mike is an incredibly intelligent but very laid-back guy. His black hair would be bushy if he did not have a receding hairline, and his thin face matches his tall and very wiry frame. He has an ironic and sharp sense of humor, and over the week, I learn about his odd path to the Navy through college, work, and the Peace Corps in Africa. He is much older than I'm at 29, and his "coolness" and strange sense of humor appeal to me, along with our shared love of beer.

Every time I think I'm headed back to the boat, I get sent to another school. I realize that I'm useless to the ship because I cannot stand a watch. When I go to the boat to study, the junior officers encourage me to leave as soon as possible and take the time off while it lasts. I ignore them, thinking they're joking, and continue to sneak aboard during my free time to get signatures. I spend five out of my first seven weeks in schools, and I begin to realize how late the boat is becoming. We're two months late on our departure, and all I see of the XO and CO are frantic efforts to get the ship put back together, get a technical installation done, and get to sea. The feeling that we're always behind begins to set in, coupled with the fact that many people don't want to leave Virginia. I get all this in passing, as I'm sent away from the boat as much as possible.

Time passes and the problems build up. None of the crew is getting paid correctly, since we are not in Guam, nor are we technically in Virginia. Families move away and leave married men to celebrate life without their wives around. Cars are shipped and people are forced to walk around the city. The bachelor quarters attempts to make all the officers pay for the extra months in Virginia, and we have to get an Admiral to intervene to stop our $1,400 hotel bills. I have only one bag with me, in preparation for leaving, so I spend a lot of time away from the hotel. The stress builds as it becomes clear that the Navy has no idea what's going on with the Guam paperwork, and things build up in the "deal with it when we get there" pile.

The families in Guam are sending mixed signals about the island. The housing has not been lived in for years, and the support staff is very small. Some of the wives are having such a stressful time that it's driving them to drastic action. One officer's wife divorces him while we sit in Virginia, sending him into a spiral of angst and depression. Children's school plays and sports are missed. The crew, which has been shore-bound for three years, is suddenly ripped away from all they know and being sent to a place that has not home-ported submarines in 20 years.

Mike Harven sits me down one day and tries to explain what's happening. Crews in port lose proficiency and formality (Note 3), becoming more like civilian workers and less like sailors as they fix the boat. Knowledge is lost, and it takes time to rebuild, time that the Navy doesn't have because we're behind schedule. People in the stratosphere of Navy leadership have decided that there will be submarines in Guam, and we have no choice but to execute. The "Guam Train" has left the station, and we need to hurry up and get on it. The officers are trying to go through the safe learning curve, practicing skills they've all studied and done on other ships a few times but now must be executed daily.

The intensity ramps up to a peak as we reach 10 weeks of delay leaving Virginia. Repairs are nearing completion, and even though we can't make everything work, the powers above ask every day, "When is San Francisco going to leave?" I find my time is best spent staying out of the way, doing random jobs for the XO, and keeping my head in the books, which keeps everyone off my back. My interactions with the crew are very limited, since I can't fill any jobs yet, so I'm mostly ignored.

The pressure builds until every day is one crisis after another. I'm determined to qualify battery-charging line-up quickly so I can make myself useful, and I focus on that. One of the other officers is so jaded that he rarely gets excited about anything. His divorce has pushed him so far into depression about Guam that he's "shut down," doing the absolute minimum to execute his job, with no enthusiasm or passion for the work. The officers are roughly divided into two groups – those who've shut down and are getting out of the Navy or submarine force and those who are "Dig-its," who like the job and will come back to be department heads. I learn that calling someone a Dig-it is considered an insult because it means he enjoys the pain of being on the boat.

I'm new, enthusiastic, and excited about being onboard, so I'm grouped with the Dig-its and pitied. The senior JO's promise that it'll be beaten out of me eventually, but they allow me to work hard to get qualified because it'll improve their lives. I move all my things onboard as we near departure and stuff everything I can into very small lockers in a "9-man," the 5-foot by 10-foot space I share with eight other people. I get very lucky; my rack has an extra "puka" at the head. Puka is a Hawaiian term for storage pouch that's commonly used on submarines. It's strange that now I have no car, no hotel room, no space of my own in my life except for my rack on the submarine. I feel disconnected and excited at the same time.

October 21, 2002

Finally, the day comes after a frenzy of last-minute scaffolding removal and the cannibalization of 50 sail bolts from the ship across the pier so we can put on all the hull plates. The bolts are just another example of how many things get lost while a ship is in overhaul. I hear the words "Station the maneuvering watch" on the 1MC (ship's announcement system). Men rush to their stations with quiet intensity, and I sit in the wardroom with nothing to do. I'm not on the watchbill and have no choice but to stay out of the way. The maneuvering watch has all the positions of a normal underway submarine, with additional navigation and propulsion control personnel to aid in piloting close to land.

I watch and listen to announcements for an hour until it's time to leave. There's no movement, and we all sit still, waiting. We are 30 minutes late when the CO gets on the 1MC.

"Good morning; this is the Captain. We're ready to get underway for Guam, but we've found a problem with some quality-assurance paperwork that's keeping us at the pier while the squadron sorts it out. We're going to stand down the maneuvering watch but maintain our readiness so we can leave in a few hours," says the Captain with an angry, impatient tone.

I ask the first officer to walk into the room what's going on and learn that the pad-eyes that bolt a rope ladder to the sail have not been properly weight tested. I ask the obvious question of how much we use the

16

ladder, and I learn that it is rarely used, if ever. But the pad-eyes are a level of equipment called "SUBSAFE QA" parts (Note 4), so the squadron won't let us leave without the proper paperwork. QA paperwork seems to have the power of God, which I don't understand, but everyone is running around frantically with nothing to do. I sit in the wardroom and listen to complaints, as many people are bored, but the QA Officer, who is also the Weapons Officer, is busy beyond belief. The whole ship is waiting on him and a few petty officers to do a weight test and generate a piece of paper to document it.

After three hours, the weight test is done and the squadron QA officer gives the OK for the ship to leave. The maneuvering watch is manned, and the lines are thrown overboard. I hear the deep, throaty groan of the whistle from inside the hull, celebrating aloud our freedom from the pier. Finally, the USS San Francisco is on its way.

Chapter 2: Qualification

I wake up shivering, and at first, I can't remember where I am. I feel around in the darkness and find the switch that turns on the small fluorescent light only inches away from my face. The cold, worn beige paint on the rack above me fills my vision, and I try to pull my sleeping bag around me to trap more warm air. The walls are soft, with only a thin metal covering over the insulation. The bed is so small that, if I turn on my side, my shoulder touches the ceiling. Graffiti commentary is scratched into the wall above me, and white noise comes from a fan blowing cold air into the small room. I try to pull the cheap blue curtain with plastic fasteners to prevent the rush of freezing air from coming in. I look around the rack and notice the small laundry bag clipped onto the wall and the Velcro on the ceiling above me. I'll have to get some Velcro for my alarm clock. I've stuffed the things that would not fit under the bed next to my feet, and I adjust my position, trying to stretch out and keep the warm air in at the same time.

One thing I learned from my student cruise on Commander Ginda's submarine was that the blankets issued are completely inadequate, and if you want to be warm, you have to bring flannel sheets and a warm sleeping bag. I know this is technically not allowed, but in a 9-man, there's a massive ventilation duct that blows cold air down on the close-packed beds in the space. I'm told by another officer that this was originally a computer room, later converted to berthing. It is 0320 on my first night and I can't sleep. Now that we're under water, the wave action has dropped down to nothing, but I still feel disoriented. The vibration of the ship is new to me, and the hum of the fans breaks into my dreams. The men around me snore loudly, and I think I can identify four people asleep.

After a few minutes staring at the metal above me, I roll out of my bottom rack and throw on my poopie suit, the informal term for our jumpsuits, which is hanging a few feet away near a piece of emergency breathing gear. It's dark because berthing is always kept dark and quiet so people can sleep at all hours of the day. I continue to shiver as I pull on my clothes and fumble around in the tightly packed lockers for my qualification binder. I drop my flashlight, which clatters around before I catch it. This is followed by several curses.

"Shut the fuck up man; I'm trying to sleep."

I turn off my light and feel my way out of the space in the dark, tripping and nearly falling before I get to the door latch. I emerge into the passageway right next to a ladder going down, just in time to see the ENG and the Chief with the bushy mustache who talked to me on the pier. I now know that he's the senior nuclear Machinist Mate onboard. They both brush past me, talking intensely, ignoring me like a bug on the wall. I hear somebody say, "... we're making way too much noise, and I can't explain it."

I try to hear more, but they're already gone toward the crew's mess. I shrug it off because I still don't understand most of what's going on. The eight hours since leaving Virginia have been filled with alarms and 1MC announcements that are fast-paced and hard to pick up. The only thing I did catch was the klaxon and "Dive-Dive" that went off just as I was trying to go to sleep a few hours earlier. I walk to the wardroom, which is empty, and sit down to look at my Qualification book, which people call a "Qual Card" (Note 6).

I stare down at the endless blank pages with more and more despair. There're more topics and practical factors than I can possibly imagine, but I must get started. I have my notebook with a red monkey sticker on the front, and I grab a manual from the wardroom book locker and start studying. The manuals have hard plastic cases and metal bindings. The pages are worn smooth and dirty at the fringes, like well-used paperbacks. I find a mechanical system that doesn't sound too imposing and take notes on the chapter. After an hour, I think I have refreshed my memory and read enough to understand the basics. I know from being a prototype student that you can't spend too long on each topic or you'll take way too long to qualify. I'll learn more from being on watch with enough knowledge to keep me safe than being able to recite the whole book perfectly.

I take a deep breath and walk back to maneuvering, where qualified people are always on watch, twenty-four hours a day. Lieutenant Junior Grade Sprocket is the engineering plant watch officer, or EOOW, and he looks bored at 0430, doing paperwork at the supervisor's desk.

"Request permission to enter maneuvering," I say after fumbling with the heavy sliding door for ten seconds. The EOOW looks at me with grin and replies, "State reason." There's a sneer in his voice, and I can't help but think he is toying with me.

"Umm ... Request permission to enter and speak to EOOW." I try to be as formal as I can.

"Enter and speak," he replies. I come over the threshold into the control area for the engine room. I'm trying to figure out what to say that will raise my chances of getting my card signed. I catch the stares of the other maneuvering watchstanders as I approach the desk. I grit my teeth and say, "Martin, do you have time for a checkout?"

"What on?" he replies.

"Turbines." It's the only thing I've studied.

"I'm not really the best person to give you that checkout. Why don't you go talk to the upper-level watch? Petty Officer Bilbo knows a lot about that. He might help you out if you ask nicely, but don't go to him if you aren't ready."

I nod and turn to leave. As I walk toward the door, the first class petty officer in the starboard chair turns and says, "Have a nice night ... ALEX."

I'm shocked, not only because I didn't know that people knew my first name but also because it's highly inappropriate for a petty officer to call an officer by his first name. I've never met this EM1, but he looks at me, as if daring me to respond. I don't know what to do or what he means by this, so I walk out of maneuvering to the sound of snickers behind me. I'm disturbed because I've read many case studies about proper formality, yet this first class calls me by my first name before I've even met him. I stand in the area aft of maneuvering for a minute, trying to figure out what he meant but shake it off and go to find MM2 Bilbo. I'll talk to the EM1 later.

Bilbo is a short but incredibly muscular man with islander features and coffee-colored skin. He looks at me with amusement as I introduce myself but agrees to talk to me. He asks me a few basic questions, which I apparently answer to his satisfaction, and then gets into deep theory. I begin to falter and use an approach that worked for me in the nuclear power prototype training environment. I explain that I don't know the answer, but if I were a logical person designing a system, I'd do it this way. He chuckles, amused at my attempt, but agrees that I have the right instincts about turbine theory. As we speak, we're walking around the ER; he carries his logs and performs the background activities of the watch. He starts pointing out things I need to know about and listing facts I should look up and where I might find them. He turns to me at 0510 and says, "OK, I'm getting relieved soon; come back on the evening watch and we'll talk some more." He works on a three-section six-hour watch rotation underway, so he'll be sleeping during the day.

"Well, thanks a lot and nice to meet you," I reply and wander further into the ER. The only thing I find that I understand is a treadmill stuffed between some machinery and ventilation piping. I think about working out and how I'll fit that into my schedule. I've had problems keeping my weight down before, and one look at the breakfast as I walk back through the crew's mess convinces me that I'll need to work out.

I'm feeling satisfied with my progress and read the plan of the day to ensure that I have no commitments for the morning. Finally, exhaustion is catching up with me enough that I can sleep through anything. As I undress to get in the rack, I hear a 1MC announcement:

"Good morning, San Francisco; this is the Captain. I want to start by saying Bravo Zulu to all the hard work getting us underway. You've accomplished a lot in the past few weeks. We're having some problems back aft, and after talking to squadron, we're going to go back into port to have an expert look at the problem. This will get us fixed up and ready to get on the road to Guam. We'll be stationing the maneuvering watch in a few hours, and all crewmembers need to do their best to support getting us back to port so we can get on our way. Carry on." The Captain has odd mannerisms and strange word choice, but I understand what he's saying.

I wonder, lying in my rack, if it has something to do with what the ENG and Chief Mechanic were talking about earlier. I'm too tired to care.

I sleep through many announcements, hearing them in a dream-like haze but then falling back into my warm unconsciousness … "Prepare to surface" … "Surface, surface" … "The Officer of the Deck has shifted his watch to the bridge." I finally hear one that seems only minutes later, and I'm still exhausted: "Station the maneuvering watch." I know I'm not allowed to stay in the rack; everyone on the ship must be awake and alert. All the lights go on in berthing, and a gruff voice shouts, "Out of the rack, maneuvering watch…"

I join a grumbling group of people who trip over each other as four people try to dress in a standing space only two feet square. I realize that only two people can dress at once, followed by the next two. I walk to the crew's mess since I'm unassigned and no other officers seem to be free. I sit quietly studying for a few minutes and then decide to go back to the ER and walk around to keep myself awake. As I tour around, reading and trying to remember locations of equipment, I see the EM1 who was in maneuvering on the midwatch. I see now that his name is Fortiner, a solid man with dark hair and an imposing forehead. I ask if he has a minute to talk.

"Sure, Alex … no problem."

"Petty Officer Fortiner, I know I'm new onboard and not qualified, but it's still inappropriate to call me by my first name." I look directly in his eyes to let him know I'm serious. I'm trying to be polite yet firm. He looks at me for a minute and then says, "No problem, sir; I apologize. Won't happen again." Then he turns and walks away. I go over the conversation in my mind, looking for some hint that he was joking, but his reply was totally deadpan and serious. I shrug it off and hope it doesn't happen again, since talking to one first class petty officer was enough to give me serious butterflies on my first day.

The ship returns to port, reversing the eight-hour trip of the day before. I realize I'm not the only one who's tired, since many people had the midwatch and nobody got time to adjust to the underway routine. I walk around control to try to see what's going on as we navigate, but I'm shooed away like a bug everywhere I try to stand. So many people are moving in so many directions that I can't stand still without being in someone's way.

I sit in the wardroom with my head in a book until the sea starts rocking the ship very hard and I can't concentrate. It doesn't seem like a nice day at all. I walk back into the crew's mess in time to see the COB and Lieutenant Junior Grade Sprocket dressed in foul-weather gear. They're talking intensely about going topside for a small boat transfer. I'm eager to learn, and there are plenty of spare life jackets, so I ask, "Can I come topside with you?" I rapidly infer that this isn't a good question based on the looks in their eyes. Sprocket and the COB share a look and then walk away without answering. I hear Sprocket mutter, "Absolutely not" under his breath as he walks to the forward escape trunk. I watch as he slaps the shoulder of a fierce bull of a man, a first class petty officer who's grimy, holding a safety line and a wrench in his hand.

"OK, Broomfield, you ready to go?" Sprocket's manner has immediately shifted from hostile to cheerful, as if he's gearing up for a challenge. Broomfield just smiles, turns his hat backwards, and crawls halfway up the escape trunk. A sailor wearing headphones that look like they're from World War II shouts over my shoulder, "COB, from the Captain, open the forward escape trunk upper hatch and send the small boat handling party topside." The COB repeats the order, not missing a word, and nods to Broomfield, who's perched on the ladder above him. Broomfield disappears, and after a few seconds, a gush of water drenches everyone standing below the hatch. The splash that hits me is freezing, yet the COB and Sprocket charge up the hatch and two more crewmembers come from behind me and follow them up.

Minutes later, a civilian with a large beard comes down the hatch and walks back toward the ER. I guess that he's probably the expert who's here to diagnose our mechanical problem, and I follow him to the very end of the ship, a space called "shaft alley." He's joined in a minute by another civilian technician, and they both look around but mostly listen. The ENG, Machinist Mate Chief, and many others are watching them, waiting for the conclusion. One of the civilians closes his eyes and rests his forehead on the piece of machinery vibrating in front of him. He stays there for minutes, his hands spread wide as we speed up and keep charging

20

toward Norfolk. He looks like he's channeling or praying over the large piece of metal. After an interminable period, he turns to the ENG and says, "You guys have big problems."

Hours later, I'm sitting in the wardroom back at the same pier we'd left the day before. We're getting underway again in the morning, and all my worldly possessions are in storage or on the submarine, so my plan is to sit and read, then go to sleep. The other officers were gone hours before, and it's quiet. Mike Vasquez and Henry Hoover come in and grab me from my book, inviting me to dinner, since they're walking to the Navy Exchange.

"Come on, man; you can't study forever." Henry is an easy guy to like, and I grab some money and change into civilian clothes, happy to be included. As we walk topside and across the brow, I see a barge coming to the stern of the ship, with divers getting dressed. Mike jokes about how much horsepower it takes to get a bunch of divers working on a submarine on a Friday night on short notice. We meet Mark Sheklund on the pier, and he comments that a quick screw cleaning is obviously exactly what we need; he'd heard the divers talking and, apparently, we have the dirtiest, most sea growth-covered screw they've ever seen.

They'll clean through the night and have us ready to go by morning, and I think someone must really want us to get on the road to Guam. When I tell Mark this, he just smiles and says, "Welcome to the Guam Train."

Underway, a few days later

"Where the hell is Juan?" shouts the XO as he storms into the wardroom. We've been underway for two days, and I'm still not quite sure about who's who, but I haven't seen Juan since our brief introduction weeks before. Juan Emilio is wide shouldered Mexican with long (for the Navy) black hair and a mustache. I get a faintly cowboy impression when I meet him from his heavily muscled hands and arms, but he seems bitter and annoyed every moment on the ship.

"Sir, I think he's in the rack," Henry says. He's sitting next to me in the wardroom, and we're both looking for a way to stay out of the way of whatever warpath the XO has in mind.

"The rack ... how long has he been in the rack, two days?" the XO replies incredulously.

"Is that even possible?" I whisper to Henry. The XO's eyes snap at me.

"I don't know, sir," I say with my best blank and innocent stare. The XO shakes his head and laughs as he leaves the room. He moves very quickly, with an intensity that makes you want to get out of his way. I've learned in the last few days that, if you sit around in his presence, you're making yourself a target for unpleasant tasking. I figure out quickly why all the other officers find reasons to leave the room when he's around. No matter how pleasant the conversation, there's always a job at the end of it.

I turn to Henry and ask what's going on with Juan. He explains that Juan has just returned from a qualification ride on another ship. When ships are in overhaul, there are a number of practical qualifications that officers still have to get before being qualified. The Navy accomplishes this by a system of "rides," in which an officer is loaned to another operational submarine. This officer learns as fast as he can, does odd jobs, and stands watch in return for the chance to go underway and complete the experience he needs for qualification. The interesting side effect of this process is that the junior officer gets to see another command team and meet another crew, and he might get along with this group much better than those of his original submarine.

Henry explains that, when Juan went away, he did a great job, qualified fast, and got along great with his host submarine. He did so well that the CO of the other submarine felt confident enough in him to present him with his 'gold dolphin' pin completing the submarine qualification process. Rides are typically used only to complete practical factors, and then your original CO will give you your dolphins, but other situations are not unheard of.

When Juan returned with his dolphins, Commander Lovpock apparently didn't like it and wouldn't immediately transfer Juan's qualification to the San Francisco. Instead, he has to jump through a number of administrative hoops before letting him stand watch, and Lovpock doesn't seem to be in a hurry to get any of it done. Since Juan is now underway but unable to stand watch, he is in the rack. This is the only way to have privacy.

As Henry finishes his explanation, Juan comes into the room, smiling mischievously. Henry starts laughing and asks if the XO found him. Juan nods and describes the rather one-sided conversation. Apparently, the best way to get any underway time over is to sleep through it. Henry explains that, in any three-month underway, if you spend one-third in the rack, it becomes a two-month underway.

"Yep, you gotta sleep until you're hungry, then eat until you're tired." Juan adds his philosophy, slapping the table as an exclamation point. "I just got up because it's chicken patty Tuesday."

I smile because I'm beginning to find out how much submarine life is based on routines. The comforting part about being underway is that you can forget all the distractions of land and just focus on the day-to-day simplicity of the ship's routine.

When we're underway, life starts with a three-section watch rotation. Most of the crew stands watch for six hours, does divisional work and collateral duties for six hours, and then sleeps for whatever time is possible. The senior people on the ship have a normal day and night routine, but most everybody else has no connection with night and day. Monday through Friday during the normal daylight hours, each department has training. One day is usually devoted to the Engineering Department and the safe operation of the reactor. The scheduling is tough because there are not many places on the boat that can fit a large number of people at the same time. Even the crew's mess can only fit about a third of the crew at a time. Another day is devoted to navigation and weapons training. Once a week, the ship runs drills that involve everyone practicing responses to fires, flooding, and all the other bad things that can happen. That leaves a day and a half for all the other training and meetings required to operate the reactor, train for all submarine missions, and enhance the careers of the crew.

On Saturday, the whole crew gets up to clean the boat during "field day." This deep cleaning lasts for three to four hours and is followed by a favorite tradition – burger day. Hamburgers and fries are cooked large and greasy, and, since the whole crew is awake anyway, everyone wants one. Catholic and Protestant religious services are held on Sunday morning. Most people take advantage of the weekend to sleep and catch up on personal affairs, indulging in the Saturday pizza night and Sunday dinner of steak and shrimp. The popularity of these meals is rivaled only by the Tuesday lunch of fried chicken patties.

Though I've been on the submarine for only a few days, I see how it can be hard to exercise with all this good food. The ship drives steadily and the crew settles into a comfortable routine as we head south. I begin to adapt to the schedule, but I also discover a new problem – I'm not getting any signatures. It's not for lack of trying; I walk around the ER at all hours of the day studying and asking people for checkouts, but the answers get more and more repetitive.

"Sorry, sir, I don't have time right now."

"Sir, I'm not the best person to give that checkout."

"Come back and see me next watch; maybe then."

I'm beginning to feel like I'm getting stonewalled, and I don't know why. EM1 Fortiner has been nothing but polite, but I don't think he'd be willing to help me out. I begin to get pressure from the NAV, since I work for him as Assistant Operations Officer, to move forward on my quals. I talk to other officers indirectly, but none of them seems to have the same problem.

Just when I'm beginning to get really worried, Mike Harven finds me and asks me to talk with him in the Engineer's stateroom. (There are three officer staterooms for the department heads and older junior officers. The ENG's stateroom is the furthest forward, followed by the WEPS, then the NAV. Most ships have WEPS nearest to the wardroom and NAV in the middle, but sometime during the re-colonization of the ship after overhaul, ours were reversed.)

22

"So, how are things going?" he begins.

"OK, I guess," I reply.

"All right, I'm going to get right to it, and I hope this is something you care about. A person I trust has told me that you have pissed off a lot of people back aft. I don't know what you did, but they think you have a superior attitude and act like you're better than them. That's not the kind of impression you need to give on a boat because it will kill you as an officer before you even start. You need those guys back there; they know more than you and they keep this plant going. If they're against you, then no matter how good you are, you're going to fail.

"There are two kinds of watchstanders: class A and class B. Class A is the type who respect you, like you, and support you. In a casualty, if there's something you don't do, they'll remind you, and in the end, you look good. They'll back you up and keep you out of trouble. They'll protect you from your mistakes if they can, and if it's really important, they'll cover up for you when you need it. They can make or break your life back there, and you have to spend a great deal of time with them.

"Class B watchstanders will do the absolute minimum to keep their job, take immediate actions, and then do nothing. They'll respond to direct orders, but they won't back you up, they won't make any recommendations, and they'll let you fail. No matter how much you learn, you can't replace all their experience. They'll make sure any mistake you make is noticed. It's your choice what type of officer you want to be, but let me tell you right now, with what I'm hearing, you're setting yourself up for a beating. Do you understand what I'm trying to say?" He finishes as Juan comes into the stateroom and closes the door, listening.

"Yeah, I think so." My mind is reeling, trying to figure out what I've done. The doubt in my mind is overwhelming, and the pit of my stomach sinks to my feet.

"Dude, it's your choice, but you have to fix it now. Trust me, this is not the kind of officer you want to be. I know you're a smart guy, but you just seem to lack a little common sense. Listen to the guys back aft; they can help you." Mike puts his hand on my shoulder and leaves the room as I sit back and try to figure out what to do.

This is a big problem. People skills are not my strong suit. I'm not one of those people who automatically knows what other people are thinking and the right thing to say. I have a lot of education, but my street smarts are still trying to catch up. I've heard this before from my friends and parents, but I realize I'm making the same mistakes. Gunnery Sergeant Sauer in college taught me that "no person, no matter what they do or who they are, is less valuable than you. You can learn something from everyone." I thought I'd taken the lesson to heart, but I guess I've missed something. The seed of self-doubt is sickening, and I respond by avoiding the ER altogether for a few days. I can't continue like this for too long, but I have no idea how to go about fixing the problem. Things are looking darkest as I stand in the forward computer space a few days later, and a first-class mechanic named Spinella comes up to get something from the printer.

MM1 Spinella is a dark-haired, compact Italian who would fit in perfectly as a mafia enforcer. I'm checking my email and reading the message traffic, and I notice that Spinella's orders for his next duty station have come in. He looks over my shoulder and says, "Sir, could you do me a favor and print those out for me; the yeoman shack has been blowing me off for a few days." I didn't know that officers and chiefs are the only people who automatically get forwarded message traffic. We're standing right next to the printer, so I print off a few copies in about five seconds.

"No problem," I reply.

I ask where he's from and we get to talking about hometowns and hobbies, just "shooting the shit" as submariners call general non-productive storytelling. After a few minutes, he tells me that I'm a lot nicer than he was led to believe. This is my chance.

"Spinella, could you tell me what's going on back aft? Something happened, and I pissed somebody off, but I don't understand why. Could you help me understand this and figure out how to fix it? I'm not an arrogant guy. I know when I've screwed up and have something to learn, but this stuff doesn't come easy to me. I don't even know where to start." I try to make my plea sound reasonable and non-desperate. But I have a feeling that the worry in my voice is pretty obvious because I want so much to succeed.

Spinella looks at me carefully for a minute and appears to be considering my question. He finally shakes his head and smiles in reply.

"OK, sir, I'm gonna help you out because you were nice and printed my orders for me. The Engineering Department Manual says that you maintain formality at all times in all Engineering spaces, which includes first names. When you came into maneuvering, you called Lieutenant Junior Grade Sprocket 'Martin,' and Fortiner was trying to tell you that you're not supposed to do that. When you came and had your little talk with him, he told all the first- and second-class nukes that you think you're better than us. You needed to be taught a lesson about who has the power in the ER, so it got passed around to stop all your checkouts until you learned the real power of an officer without blue-shirts." I guess that "blue-shirt" refers to the blue utilities enlisted men wear, as opposed to the khakis of officers and chiefs.

"Oh, God," I say with shock. Hearing it explained, it makes perfect sense, though I think Fortiner could have picked a better way to correct me, but maybe that's just his personality. I continue: "So how do I fix this?"

"Well, Fortiner has been onboard for a long time, and he's pretty bitter and judgmental. You want to go talk to EM1 Robinson. He's probably one of the most influential guys in the ER, and if he's behind you, then his influence can beat what Fortiner said. So you go to Robbie, tell him what happened, and ask him to help you out. You know, make a joke, and tell him to call you Alex. You have to let him know that it doesn't bother you, and then you can start rebuilding bridges."

He smiles and is gone in a flash, leaving me to thank my lucky stars that someone explained all this to me. It's 0300, so I don't get hasty. I get some sleep and formulate my conversation, and I'm more nervous about talking to EM1 Robinson than I was interviewing with a four-star Admiral. I find him in the ER middle level near the electrical muster area and work center. Mike Robinson is 6'0" tall, in his late twenties, extremely fit, and bald. He has a permanent smile that inspires you to want to talk to him. His left forearm is covered with extensive tribal tattoos that run all the way up into his sleeve. He's just "cool." I walk up and introduce myself, asking if he has a minute to talk.

"Sure, sir, what can I do for you?"

"Petty Officer Robinson, I want to tell you a story about a stupid young officer. So this officer is trying to make a good impression on his first boat but ends up talking to a petty officer about doing something that he himself did the day before. This is completely hypocritical because how can an officer hold anyone to a different standard than he holds himself? Now, after a while, he figures out what he has done, but by now, everybody thinks he's some stuck-up guy who thinks he's better than everyone else. All that really happened is he was just stupid about the rules and didn't know how to respond when a senior petty officer tried to help him out. Does that story sound familiar?"

Robinson looks at me for a minute. He seems to be searching in my eyes for something or measuring me up. Finally, he says, "I may have heard something about a story like that." I take a deep breath and thank him.

"Petty Officer Robinson, thanks for your time, and I hope you could pass along my apologies to everyone else ... and you can call me Alex." There's nothing I can do now; hopefully, this will be good enough.

"No problem, sir, and the name is Robbie for short." He shakes my hand, and I begin to walk away.

"Oh, and sir..." I stop and turn back. "You can get a checkout from me anytime," he says, smiling.

"Thanks." I breathe a sigh of relief as I walk back to the wardroom, which is empty. I sit on the blue vinyl bench right by the door and lean back to lie down. It works awkwardly, with my shoulders jammed between the wall and the table. I realize with amusement that I have tension shakes. I laugh and put my hand over my eyes, shielding them from the harsh fluorescent lights among the piping that never go out; they just keep pounding away into my consciousness.

We pick up observers in Florida as I restart my qualification progress. Robbie's influence has allowed me to move forward and talk to all the guys in the ER. I make an effort to get to know people and ask them about their lives before asking for any checkout. I spend an hour sitting with a guy who has just received a "Dear John" letter from the love of his life. She's breaking up with him because he's going away to Guam. He's very angry with her, but I get the feeling that this is not a unique situation.

The senior observers get onboard after a rough trip on the surface and come below decks. I'm excited to see Commander Mark Ginda among them. He is now the deputy commander of submarine squadron fifteen, our new immediate superior in command. I've spent the last few weeks telling the wardroom stories of how cool Ginda is because he was the CO of the USS Pasadena during my college cruise. It's very strange that he's here now and I'm a commissioned Ensign, since I have kept him apprised of my career progress by email for the last three years. I'm looking forward to seeing him.

Mark Ginda has eyes like a hawk. He keeps his head shaved, with only a stubble of grey hair around the edges. His stomach has grown a little on his medium frame since I last saw him, but he's still in good shape. The smooth synthetic khaki uniform crackles as he checks walls and tags on everything, even before he gets down to the middle level. I'm watching him, standing in the passageway squeezed into a corner to stay out of the rush of people as we head back out to sea and prepare to submerge. The expression on his face is one of suspicion and focus, and he walks right past me without noticing. He's sitting on the far wall of the wardroom when I come in, talking to Mike Harven, who's in charge of all damage control equipment.

"... I'm pretty sure that those fire extinguishers have to be inspected every three months, and I saw three that were out of periodicity between the forward escape trunk and here. So I want you to check on that and bring me your inspection records," Ginda says. Mike has a "deer in the headlights" look in reply and gives the only proper military response: "Yes, sir, I will get right on that." Then he leaves the room as quickly as possible. I'm left to wonder whether I'm facing some kind of foul-mood storm from a man I remember being light and cheerful.

"Ensign Fleming. How are you?" Commander Ginda's tone changes slightly as he talks to me, but there's still nothing of the warmth I felt from him the last time we met.

"I'm well, sir; it's good to see you," I reply with hesitant familiarity.

"How are quals going? Are you done with EOOW yet?" Commander Ginda begins to look at a portfolio he's carrying and talking at the same time.

"No, sir, I'm finished with BCLU but still working on EOOW. It's been a long time since Helmsman on the Pasadena." I'm grasping for straws now, trying to find something of the man I knew in 1999.

"That's true, but I knew you would stay in... well, keep charging." He looks up with a face that tells me our conversation is over. I make my goodbyes as he starts to tell another officer about another problem he's found. The other officers around figure out that they need to leave the room as soon as possible or risk being in the gun sights. I'm confused and a little hurt. Commander Ginda had convinced me to join the submarine service with his openness and personal charisma. The person I've just talked to is totally different, like a ghost version of the other man. I wonder what command did to him, and I try to imagine anything I could have done to cause it. Maybe now that he's a representative of my Captain's boss, he can't be seen as giving favoritism without insulting and undercutting my current CO. I also do not yet see the tension between Commander Lovpock and Commander Ginda that becomes obvious in the five days of his ride.

The officers devolve into a chaos of panic as we try to keep ahead of Ginda's attack. When we drop him off in Key West, he leaves a trail of comments and deficiencies that will take us a month to fix. He is absolutely right in all his comments, but he has a way of presenting them that makes you feel like you're on trial. I'm ridiculed for having even suggested that he's a nice guy. My credibility with the wardroom drops, and the only thing that keeps me afloat is my new speed at qualification. We spend the next few weeks cruising around doing sound testing, turning equipment on and off all the time, and I don't really follow what's going on.

I find that it's easy to get so involved with studying that you don't know where you are or what's going on outside the ship unless someone gets on the 1MC and tells you about it. I only know that they turn off the air conditioners for hours at a time, and I sweat more than I can possibly imagine. If a 9-man is cold normally, when the air conditioning is off, the whole boat becomes 90 degrees and humid. I have to lie in my boxers above my blankets even to have a hope of sleep. The DOC starts to do heat stress monitoring in the hottest parts of the ER, and I earn a new nickname.

My first time on the treadmill to try to fight off the incredible volume of starchy food, I get a lead paint chip in my eye and hit my head on the piping as the ship rolls. I stop running and go forward, passing Bilbo with blood trickling down my head and one hand over my eye. The DOC, a Corpsman Chief, gets the paint out of my eye, but Bilbo spreads the story around and I'm nicknamed "Biff" after the movie character from *Back to the Future* and because of my tendency to run into things. Mike and Juan are very happy with the name Biff and take it to heart as I try to qualify and make myself useful.

We have a brief moment of happiness as we surface for a swim call near the Bahamas. It's my first swim call on a submarine, and the whole crew takes childlike pleasure in going topside and sliding off the front of the ship. The ship floats slowly as the group of very pale men floats around in the water. I feel like I'm being teased by getting a faraway view of a tropical island paradise. It's the first truly joyful moment I've had in weeks of studying, and if I can see the sun and the ocean once in a while, then all this pain will be worth it. I look at the ocean, mesmerized by the waves, and remember why I got into submarines in the first place. The Guam Train calls us faster as we dive again and make best speed for the Panama Canal.

Transiting the Panama Canal isn't what it used to be. As we get closer to the canal, I begin to hear stories about the 1999 crossing, when the ship had a steel beach picnic topside with barbecues and sunbathing. They yelled back and forth with women on the shore and generally had a very good time. I get the feeling this is going to be very different. Since the attacks on the World Trade Center, things have changed for all Navy ships. The XO briefs us on some of the precautions as we eat dinner one evening.

The wardroom is set for dinner with a clean and ironed blue tablecloth that has the ship's name embroidered on the edges. I'm standing at the far end of the table since I'm still junior. The officers eat off heavy porcelain plates and real glasses; the crew doesn't. The pitchers on the table hold water and red juice from concentrate. We all stand behind our chairs, waiting for the Captain, until the mess steward comes into the room to say the magic words: "XO, sir, the Captain will not be joining you tonight." People are outwardly indifferent, but inside, I'm relieved. The conversation is always strange when he's around because he insists on telling us about his plans to breed llamas on a farm in Pennsylvania after leaving the Navy. We sit down and the mess steward brings the soup first, served in formal order around the table. The table manners of Naval officers are at a higher level than anything I've seen in my life. After the soup bowls are cleared, the meal is served family style and passed around the table. Sometimes the conversation is lively, but today, the XO does most of the talking. There are baskets and baskets of warm bread on the table, and dessert is always abundant. All the officers are interested in the canal details as we finish coffee.

We will encounter a security and protective detachment of infantry personnel that has many more weapons than we do. These people will be the only ones allowed on deck for the transit. The rest of us will be stuck below decks, and the only people who see anything will be those on the bridge and the people who get to look through the periscope. At least two coast guard vessels will follow us, and a number of army soldiers will be on shore as we pass. The Panamanian Air Force is kindly providing us with air support around our position. The XO tells us all to get some sleep because we are surfacing the ship at 0300.

"Ensign Fleming, 0230, first wake-up, sir," the messenger whispers into my rack, seemingly moments after I'd crawled into bed. The voice is just outside my curtain, but it feels closer. I jump hearing a sound so close to me, hitting my head on the top of the rack and swearing loudly. I mumble an unintelligible reply, and the messenger has the good sense to go away before I take out my pain on him.

On days like today, a special round of wake-ups is done when an evolution is commencing early, and I'm on the watchbill to be the Contact Coordinator under instruction with a Lieutenant named Micah Stevens as my teacher. I throw on my poopie suit and hurry up to control as the 1MC rings out "Prepare to surface." I walk into a dark control room, since the ship is already at periscope depth in the black of night. I make my way back in the dark to the curtains pulled tight around the periscopes to protect the scope operator's night vision from interfering light. In the dark, I find the midwatch OOD doing rounds on the scope, and I ask him if he needs a relief, since I've recently completed my basic periscope operator qualification and I'm eager to be useful.

He's pleasantly surprised to have me there, since it means he can drive the surfacing evolution without having to be on the periscope. Officers are trained to do everything in control while looking out the periscope and not actually making eye contact with anyone, but it's just easier sometimes to be able to speak directly to the watchstanders. I relieve on the scope for the first time, and I'm stunned by how black it is. I can barely see the horizon because there is so little light. I begin to make slow sweeps around and around. I change magnification every time I circle in the dark, trying to avoid boredom. The thrill of operating the periscope wanes quickly and I begin to notice the small things. My eye socket becomes sore as I push it against the eyepiece, and the rubber becomes slick with my sweat. Reaching eye level means I have to bend over slightly, and my lower back begins to ache as I go around and around. There is power assistance to turn the scope, but I still have to pull hard to beat the resistance. My feet get caught on unfamiliar objects as I turn in the pitch black. I begin to hum and sing to myself to stay interested, and I alternate between walking backwards and walking forwards. I understand why they call it "dancing with the one-eyed lady."

I hear the fast-paced surfacing routine going on around me as men pile into control and bring equipment to be ready to hand gear up to the bridge, the area on top of the sail. The bridge is where the OOD drives on the surface and will be fully constructed for our transit through the canal. My first sunrise through the periscope is clear and bright as first the dim light and then light blue begin to spread like ink from the horizon. The lights on land fade away, and I see hundreds of merchant vessels anchored, waiting to go through the canal.

I suddenly smell someone very clean with fresh cologne close to me, and I turn to see Micah Stevens. He asks me if he can take a look around, and I comment that he smells very nice, and he smiles in reply, saying that he always likes to shower and put on fresh cologne when he is contact coordinating. Micah is a Naval Academy alum who received a master's degree from MIT and nearly completed his doctorate before joining the submarine service. Micah initially strikes me as a very hyper, scatterbrained person who is constantly falling asleep in meetings. But as I get to know him better, I realize how incredibly intelligent he is, and he's growing into a friend and confidant.

We're a high-value unit and proceed quickly straight into the entrance channel as the sun comes up. The XO is in control and seems very tense, yelling every few minutes. Micah begins teaching me the finer points of searching and ranging, and I hear equipment being moved up to the bridge. Finally, the call comes down: "Attention, Helm, Control Room Supervisor, Quartermaster, the Engineer has the deck and the Conn." The Engineer's microphone is filled with the sound of wind as he speaks. Then the Chief of the Watch gets on the 1MC.

"The Officer of the Deck has shifted his watch to the bridge." Now the ENG is responsible for safety of ship and the contact coordinator gives reports and recommendations. There is a call down from the bridge because I'm a new periscope operator, and the ENG speaks to me through incredible background noise.

"Fleming, you're new at this, so I'm going to tell you about the running bet I have with contact coordinators. If I see a contact with my two eyes before you spot it with your two million dollar periscope, you owe me a beer. Got it?"

I laugh as I reply. "Yes, sir."

Panama is much flatter than I imagined, with rolling jungles extending as far as the eyes can see, and there's a bustling city right at the entrance channel. The CO stays on the bridge as we are escorted to the first set of locks. Maneuvering a two billion dollar nuclear ship around large concrete walls makes everyone nervous, and the OOD is driving on the bridge with the CO right behind him. The XO and CO have a two-way radio to talk directly, and any mistake is leapt on immediately. The locks close and the ship floods up to a higher level, not without some very tense propulsion orders as we leave the lock. We enter a lake that takes us through a well-marked channel, and we are driving much closer to large merchants than many officers have ever seen. Most submarines like to stay comfortably miles away from large merchant shipping, but in this case, there's no choice, as we're packed like a sardine into the channel.

The jungle becomes flat and monotonous as we wind further into Panama. I head below decks to get lunch and watch the periscope picture on flat-screen monitors throughout the ship. One of the best morale ideas ever, this provides a way for the whole crew to see and critique what is seen through the periscope. This is even funnier as we go through the second set of locks, lifting us up to the final level of the Pacific Ocean. Near this lock is a building and viewing stand where hundreds of people watch us go by. The crew is very excited when the periscope operator focuses closely on some well-endowed women in the stands. I realize how easy it is to excite a bunch of young men who have not seen a woman in three weeks. The COB allows five-minute rotations of people on deck to look at the jungle, but that doesn't satisfy me. I have nothing to do, so I sit in the escape trunk, holding onto a ladder and staring past pipes and metal to see the sky. Even as it grows dark, I stay in the trunk, getting rained on in the twilight. I finally see the bottom of the Bridge of the Americas as it passes overhead, and in an instant, it is gone. I'm soaked in my poopie suit as I climb back down into the crew's mess. Just as fast as that, we're out of the canal and we are late.

We have to catch up to our schedule or we won't be able to dive because we won't "own the water" to submerge. We have to drive as fast as safely possible on the surface at night, very close to a large fishing fleet. This is a tricky exercise, and the Captain calls on the most experienced junior officer onboard, a Lieutenant named Jason Pittman. Jason, or P-Diddy, as he called, is a music major turned nuclear officer who has an instinctive grasp of ship-driving and contact coordination. Micah Stevens is on the bridge, and Jason is below decks telling Micah where to go as we dodge as fast as we can through a constantly changing trawler field. We make it with twenty minutes to spare and dive the ship just in time to catch our water, which has already started to move away at our scheduled speed. Changing from the Atlantic to Pacific Fleet has put us through a number of administrative challenges; the most significant is integrating the navigational planning of two staffs in Hawaii and Virginia, who do not interact as much as they should.

We fall back into the routine of submerged operations and drive as fast as we can for San Diego because the Commander of the Pacific Submarine Force (COMSUBPAC) already has a list of things for us to do. The whole crew has been awake since 0300, and it is now 2200 at night. Everyone walks around the ship like the living dead, with eye sockets that almost match the blue of their poopie suits. Even the CO had not left the bridge once in the trip through, and the crewmembers who can collapse into their racks.

The messenger wakes me a few hours later, and I refuse to believe my eyes. The clock says 0130, and I'm still so tired I can barely move.

"Sir, from the officer of the deck, report to control."

This is the first time any OOD has ever asked for me, so I hurry to throw on my poopie suit and walk breathlessly into the control room to find Martin Sprocket in charge on the midwatch. He says he needs my help listening to something they've detected in the water. The ship is underwater going as fast as it can, and apparently, we've received some kind of underwater communication. My adrenaline is pumping as I go to sonar, and I'm handed a set of headphones that plug into a complicated-looking piece of gear I don't know anything about. I listen intently and hear a voice slowly speaking Russian. Senior Chief Miller, the sonar chief, and Broomfield, the sonar supervisor, look at me intently as I listen to the voice again and translate for the OOD. I'm shocked because the thought that a Russian submarine is around the Panama Canal is groundbreaking.

I turn to Martin, shocked, and tell him that it's definitely Russian. He explains that they've had intermittent contact with an Akula class submarine, and since I'd been a Russian major, the CO wanted me to translate the underwater communications. I walk stunned down to the wardroom, where I find Jason, who lectures me on proper security because I can't tell anyone about the Russians. It's a very big deal for an Akula to be this far away from Russia, and it's probably here just to follow us. I check my email and find a message from COMSUBPAC reporting an out-of-area Russian submarine in our zone, and I'm thrilled by the possibility of tangling with a real live Russian. I have visions of myself as Jack Ryan in an undersea adventure worthy of a Tom Clancy novel; this is the reason I'd joined the submarine force in the first place.

The XO talks to me the next day in training about my Russian skills, and everyone seems to be very positive about my newfound usefulness. I walk around feeling very good about myself, stunned by this whole thing for a few days, until I realize that even the most junior people onboard seem to be winking about the Russians near the Panama Canal. It hits me in one massive stroke after two days of walking around oblivious... It was a joke, the Russian tape, the message, the security concerns, the officers being in on it. Everyone on the entire ship is in on the trick that Fleming is hearing Russians in the water. It may be probably the most elaborate practical joke I could ever imagine. I don't let on that I was fooled, and I just laugh and play along when someone mentions the Russians in the water.

I ask a young nuclear sailor named Gokart why people on subs go to such lengths to make fun of each other. He explains to me that it's all part of the "Finite Happiness Theory" of life on a submarine. There's only so much happiness on a submarine at any time, and it's not enough for everybody. The only way to get this happiness is to take it from someone else, in the form of prodding or practical jokes, or just plain yelling at them. You hold on to this happiness for a little while, until someone takes it from you. This is the only way to be happy on a fast-attack. He explains that my Russians in the water joke took happiness from me but gave it to the rest of the crew, and all I have to do is find some ways to get it back.

As we drive for weeks past Mexico, toward a large and complicated fleet exercise, I begin to plot ways to get some happiness back. Study, Training, sleep, study, training, sleep – the ship's routine marches onward, toward a destination that no one onboard quite understands.

Chapter 3: Problems

"This crew is stuck in the shipyard mentality" (Note 7), the XO shouts as he leaves the wardroom, where I'm sitting against the wall taking notes on a manual chapter. I've been watching the previous meeting with the ENG and a few chiefs about a material problem, doing my usual fly-on-the-wall act. The ENG is left alone and shakes his head with pain as he turns to me:

"He's right, but there's nothing we can do about it." He seems convinced of this, but the way I was introduced to him makes me wonder about his credibility. I nod and agree with him just to end the conversation quickly. I've seen enough in the last month to understand that no one knows what they're doing.

While I'm hard at work on engineering study, there're some other, shorter qualifications that I can get to raise my marginal value. As the new guy, I'm the wardroom whipping boy anyway, but qualifying as Battery-Charging Lineup Officer and Rig for Dive Officer means that I'm awakened at 0230 instead of a more senior officer who has watch and a division and is trying to get a few hours "down." I complete my Battery-Charging Lineup qualification in a few weeks, much to the happiness of my peers, but Rig for Dive takes a little longer.

"Rig for Dive" is actually a condition of the ship, and it means that all the holes that let the ocean into the "people space" are blocked. Other portions ensure that the ship is lined up to surface immediately in an emergency and that we can properly control our planes and external surfaces, but mostly it's about keeping the water out. This is a conundrum because many times a day, we have to do things that either bring water into the ship or push various substances out. After we complete the pumping of things like sanitary tanks (SANS), we have to shut the hull isolation valves and check them shut. These valves occupy a special status called "Rig for Dive," so they must first be checked by a qualified petty officer and then checked by an officer before they can be certified as "rigged." This happens twenty-four hours a day whenever the evolutions can be done, which is why there's a need for a qualified officer to be awakened at 0230 in the morning. The manipulation of any Rig for Dive component requires the Captain's specific permission, and the completion of the rig must be reported back to him.

An officer qualifying Rig for Dive has to do detailed walk-throughs of every space on the ship and learns all Rig for Dive components, how they work, and how to check them. Then there is a series of knowledge checkouts on how to Rig for Dive, the paperwork involved, and what to do for minor discrepancies. I'm completing these checkouts under the supervision of the Ship's Diving Officer, currently Micah Stevens. He is responsible for the Rig for Dive and the compensation of the ship to maintain stability while underwater. It takes me a month to get through all the different spaces, and then Micah interviews me to ensure I'm ready to be qualified.

He sits across from me at the wardroom table, and as the interview ends, he looks into my eyes, pushes the books and papers aside, and speaks slowly.

"Alex, Rig for Dive is all about your word. YOU are the officer saying that the ship is safe, and your signature is the final certification. Now, I don't think you know the whole ship perfectly, and I'll start by assigning you rigs in the engine room (ER) until you get comfortable. You will rig sanitary valves a lot and the Trash Disposal Unit. After you get comfortable with these, you'll start doing more.

"The biggest, most important thing is: If you have a doubt … ASK one of us. Do not sign something off unless you are absolutely sure, and don't be so proud that you can't ask somebody if you're not sure. As an officer, it's OK if you don't know things. You're not expected to know everything; what's bad is if you try to act like you know something when you don't. The Chiefs and petty officers will know this instantly, and it will define you as a leader. So, are you ready to do this?"

"Yes," I reply with a thrill of responsibility.

Micah signs my qualification book and sends me up to the CO for my interview. The interview goes well, and I only get a few look-ups (follow-up research items). I continue to wonder about Commander Lovpock and his temperament, since he continues to strike me as odd. I return after finding out the information in my lookups, and he signs my book, saying, "That should make the other officers happy, another Rig for Dive Officer."

"Yes, sir," I reply, which is the only thing to say when you have no idea what to say and you're talking to a senior officer. I take the Qualified Watchstanders List back to control with a smile on my face. I've taken some of the load off the other junior officers. I'm finally somewhat useful.

It takes me a few days to discover exactly why the other officers wanted me to get this qualification. Since I'm not standing watch and I'm not a division officer, the Chief of the Watch knows I'm the first choice for any battery charge or Rig for Dive evolution no matter what time of day. I study at odd hours, but it seems like every time I get in my rack, a few seconds after I turn the lights off, a messenger wakes me to rig something or check a lineup. This occurs at all hours of the night and day, and I rapidly find out how tiring it can be when you only get a few hours of sleep at a time.

I'm loosely assigned to a watchsection for qualification, but mostly this involves checking in with the EOOW at the beginning of the watch and then working with the enlisted watchstanders on practical factors or knowledge checks for six hours. I don't limit myself to this watchsection so I don't tire out the people who are being nice to me. I get into a schedule of checking with the watchstanders in the first hour of every watch to see if they'll have time for me and then going back later if they do. I'm determined to be qualified in Engineering Officer of the Watch (EOOW) and Engineering Duty Officer (EDO) before we get to Guam. It's OK to be a non-qual at sea, but once we get to port, everyone wants as much time off the boat as possible.

Officer training sessions are more frequent and intense as we prepare for a full-scale exercise in the San Diego Operations Areas. This will be with a carrier battle group, but we get to do the one thing that's most fun for submarines: we get to be on the opposing force. So, within the rules of the game, we're the enemy trying to outsmart the friendly or "Blue" force submarines and "kill" the aircraft carrier. I learn more and more about the incredible safety precautions the Navy takes when it has more than one submarine in a certain area, but it all washes over me so fast that I don't feel confident in any of it. I secretly hope that I'll have a lot of help when we get into the actual exercise.

The weeks go by in a whirlwind of routine. The ship's operation is based on routines, schedules, and procedures that are kept religiously. The guys occupy themselves with movies, books, video games, and an ever-intensifying series of pranks and practical jokes. Smart young men will do almost anything to keep their minds occupied when standing watch in a boring engine room that pretty much takes care of itself. People on watch are not allowed any materials not engineering related, so I discover that they resort to talking. They tell stories of wives, girlfriends, children, sexual escapades, drinking, politics, religion, philosophy, boat gossip, and anything else that comes up. Robbie (EM1 Robinson), standing watch in Maneuvering, is the best storyteller on the ship and has some of the funniest experiences of all. The Maneuvering area watchstanders, including the some officers, also spend hours playing the "movie game," in which someone starts with a movie, the next person gives the name of an actor in that movie, then the next person must come up with a different movie with that actor in it, and so on. This game can last for hours, with sidebar discussions about particularly bad movies or any movies that contain nudity.

The rule of law and formality would tell you that an officer participating in such a game or allowing it to go on is violating his duties as a watch officer. The other side of the argument is that, if you spend six hours with four guys in a very small room and don't allow any conversation at all, it becomes very hard to stay awake and engaged. I witness several different styles of officer leadership as I learn, but the ones I admire most are those who allow conversation and banter when nothing is going on but set clear limits when any evolutions occur. I think this is how I want to be when I stand watch, though I'm almost scared when I witness a watch officer get into a wrestling match with an off-watch enlisted man as people observe. This officer is one of the smartest guys, and I admire him the most. Despite these things that the ENG and CO wouldn't like, the guys love him and break their necks to help him out and execute his orders.

I'm overwhelmed with questions and decisions about my leadership style as we finally surface near San Diego and head inbound. It's before dawn and I'm the contact coordinator under-instruction with the WEPS.

31

He's a cheerful guy who tells me I'm doing well and lets me spend a majority of the time doing the job, only correcting me occasionally. I'm close to completing this qualification, and this watch is supposed to prove to the XO that I'm ready to stand the watch. I look out the periscope and it's easy to see the border between Tijuana and San Diego since the lighting becomes sparse and dim on almost an exact line at the border. We get closer to land and I begin to see how hard it is to pick out small surface contacts at night with heavy backlighting from land. I find a few large merchants by watching for backlighting and seeing when those lights are obscured by something in the foreground. That technique doesn't work for small ships in the foreground, and a few minutes later, the CO calls down, "Contact Coordinator, Captain, report the sailboat 500 yards off the starboard bow." The tone is immediate and angry.

I acknowledge the order as I whip the scope around to find the boat, emerging from the darkness right in front of us. It passes harmlessly across the bow at about 300 yards, just before I'm body-checked off the scope by the XO, who then turns to the WEPS and yells at him to have better control of his under-instruction. WEPS answers the angry senior officer with the only possible response, "Yes, sir," but then turns to me and says, "Don't worry, Alex. These lighting conditions are tough; I wouldn't have seen that guy either."

The knot in my chest begins to unwind, and slowly I gather my confidence as the sun begins to rise and I get my first glimpse of the Hotel Del Coronado in many years. Its distinctive cupolas are easy to spot and used by every ship and submarine to navigate around Point Loma. I feel relieved as we near the maneuvering watch, and then a thrill of rumor runs through the crew; something is broken. We're going to have to dock in San Diego rather than just doing a quick turnaround in the harbor. It will only be a quick overnight, but it means that we get a Thursday night on land after almost six weeks underway. There's only one thought in every man's mind: "Party time!"

The officers are sprawled about the wardroom in a tired daze, some sitting and some just lying on the couches listening to the gossip. The idea of one night of visibly energizes everyone. Just as the excitement and conversation reach a fever pitch, the XO gets on the 1MC.

"Gentlemen, this is the XO. You may have heard that we're going to have to spend the night in port tonight, and we're scheduling a 0800 underway tomorrow so we can get out and support the carrier battle group. I know everyone wants to go out and have fun, but I'm restricting the crew to the Point Loma Naval Base, and there will be a midnight curfew for all hands. In addition, no alcohol consumption will be allowed for any crewmember at all. This is to support our underway tomorrow. The COB will be coordinating housing assignments, but some people will have to sleep onboard for the night. Any man found consuming alcohol will have to answer to me and the punishment will be creative and painful. Carry on."

The officers in the wardroom are as livid as the crew. I walk the passageways and hear mutters and anger in almost every voice. This feeling dominates the maneuvering watch as we drive around Point Loma and dock at the Naval Submarine Base, located across the bay from Coronado right inside the entrance to San Diego Harbor.

I stay out of the way as we moor and secure lines. After the initial rush of people and equipment going topside, I grab my cell phone and head up to see San Diego again. The first thing I notice is the wind. As I clear the hatch, a cool and crisp breeze runs across the harbor, carrying the smell of trees. I close my eyes and stand on top of the ship, trying to feel the wind on every part of my body. The stale smell of the boat is still on my clothes, but I open my eyes to see Coronado laid out before me, and I forget all that. I slowly walk across the metal walkway and take my first step on dry land in almost seven weeks. My legs feel unsteady, like they were used to the movement of the ship and now the asphalt doesn't give enough. I wander away from the ship, not moving in any particular direction, just trying to absorb as much of the moment as possible, as if I could save this feeling in a jar in my rack.

The smell of eucalyptus trees permeates everything. The skyline of the city is visible across the bay and I look at the very small collection of buildings that makes up the submarine base. My mother's voice on my cell phone nearly makes me tear up with its familiarity. That part of my life already seems so far away; I feel like

I've lived ten years since we last spoke. I can't tell my parents much about our schedule, but we make plans to have Thanksgiving in San Diego since they're only a few hours away in Phoenix, Arizona. I wish I could stay on the pier and call every single person in the memory of my phone, but I see Mike angrily motioning me toward the ship.

The talk on the boat through the afternoon, as we work to fix the material problems, is how to get around the cruel injustice of the XO's order. There's a liquor store on base, but it's the only one, and if any of the officers is seen buying alcohol, everyone will know about it. The only way to get off base without a car is to take the bus, but the loading point for that bus is right next to the liquor store, so any person getting on it will be seen as well. The road off base winds two miles through the hills before you even get to the residential neighborhood on Rosecrans Boulevard, and then it's a mile farther to any bars or restaurants. The men express an incredible amount of hate and discontent, but any discussion with the XO is immediately met with angry rebuttals. I talk to some of the other officers, and they tell me that I can do whatever I want, but "don't get caught and don't let any enlisted man see you." I contemplate that for a while, until the Supply Officer tells me that he won't be able to get me a BOQ room because I'm the most junior officer, so I'll have to sleep on the boat. I shrug with acceptance; there's always more studying to be done anyway.

The night starts uneventfully, though I end up sneaking away with a few Chiefs, one of whom has a girlfriend bring a six-pack of beer to the base. We sit down by the ocean in a remote picnic area that hasn't been used in years. The paint peeling off the tables provides an interesting distraction as we sip our two beers apiece, hiding them whenever anyone passes. I feel like I'm in high school, but I'm grateful that the Chiefs would take pity on the lone Ensign and invite me along. We don't get loud or rowdy. We finish our beers by 2100, and then I head back to the ship. When I get back, one of the junior officers grabs me and invites me to dinner. I follow without hesitation, since it's apparent they came back to the boat just to look for me. We walk and sneak the two miles to the gate in the dark, where an officer from another submarine picks us up in a car, Mission Impossible style. We get dinner and margaritas at a Mexican restaurant a few miles away, and then we walk back. I'm cautioned not to speak a word of our outing to anyone.

Everyone shows up the next morning sober, rested, and angry. The muster brings news of more delays, as the crew finds out that our problems will not let us get underway until 1600. Now that the underway has shifted, the questions come.

"Why couldn't we have gone out last night? We have plenty of time to be hung over this morning!" The XO stands his ground, and the feeling passes as we prepare for a bigger role in the exercise than we'd previously thought. Another scheduled submarine participant has been moved to another mission, so we must perform their role as well. Our mission is to support the battle group training, and to do this, we must be in regular communication with the exercise coordinators. But for a submarine, this is easier said than done because it requires us to be near the surface all the time (Note 8).

I'm standing three-section (3 people rotating six hour shifts in an 18-hour cycle) Junior Officer of the Watch (JOOW) now, and my qualifications are slowing down as I realize how the eighteen-hour day can mess with your body clock. The JOOW is the most junior officer in the control room and the job varies based on competence and experience level. My time is mostly spent working with fire control computers since I have more recent training than anyone else. I'm also in charge of message drafting and routing.

Participating in exercises means we have to send updates and messages constantly to all our various bosses detailing our efforts and intentions. We also have to send detailed position reports to allow the exercise managers to see what's going on so they can decide who's winning or losing the scenario. The format for these messages comes from three or four different sources that sometimes conflict with each other, and the JOOW is responsible for drafting the messages as we go, formatting them correctly, and ensuring they get through the radio room on time. Since the battle group commander's only interaction with us is usually our messages, if they arrive even an hour late, everyone starts to get extremely nervous. If this happens, the boss makes our communications requirements more strenuous, thus limiting us more. It's in our best interests to be on time with all messages to keep the Admirals happy.

So six hours of my eighteen-hour day are spent standing in a dark corner of control typing on an old laptop. I share a chair with another watchstander, and when I have to stand, my head hits the ceiling. It's the side of the ship sloping downward, and the only way to look at the computer screen is to push my head against the overhead or bend over slightly. When we're at periscope depth, the ship rocks back and forth, and it's hard to avoid hitting my head. Both positions get old quickly. JOOW duty quickly becomes very tedious, permanently stationed in front of a laptop typing.

The OOD and his primary assistant, the Junior Officer of the Deck (JOOD), are the officers conducting the tactical positioning and maneuvering of the ship, relegating the less interesting jobs to me. I take pride in my work and try to do it well as I also try to watch the two officers above me and how they drive the ship. My OOD is the Navigator and my JOOD is Mike Harven. I learn quickly why they're the best team on the ship. The NAV has incredible experience planning and executing exercises and knows all the tricks, combined with his brute force intelligence. Harven has an instinct and flair for ship driving that lets him effectively position the ship without even thinking about it. The two of them together are an honor to watch, and I learn a lot, even as the messages and reports make me and the other JOOWs want to stab our eyes out. Mike Vasquez sets our account password as "Stupidfuckingreports," and it sticks.

After the first two eighteen-hour cycles, I begin to redefine my understanding of the word "tired." My body is getting used to the rotation, but I feel a constant, underlying exhaustion that won't go away. I try to get a few more hours of sleep and give up some studying, but that only makes it worse, so I settle into three and a half hours of sleep every eighteen hours. The exercise lasts for a week, and we handle ourselves competently, though every other day, some major flap occurs over the inexperience of the watchstanders. The officers begin asserting themselves more and more to get the job done right because we don't have the time to conduct all the training we need to do.

By the end of the week, I'm doing the job of a fire control technician petty officer, spending most of my time tracking contacts on the computer, with the actual technician right behind me so I can train him as I go. I get some positive recognition for this, as the other officers begin to ask me for advice on operating the fire control computers, and I try to cement my place as the computer whiz by studying and learning tricks in my off-watch time. My qualification binder is getting dusty, but I still study whenever I can. I'm so tired that I get into bed to read and rarely make it through one page before nodding off.

The exercise ends with us shooting exercise weapons in a controlled evolution, aiming for one of the carrier escort ships, but it seems that we "accidentally" hit the carrier. The exercise managers analyze our shot and grudgingly agree that we probably would have destroyed at least one of the escorts and probably the carrier if our shots had been real. The Captain is exhilarated because this is the kind of thing that gives him bragging rights over surface captains. We have one more hurdle before we can take a weekend off for Thanksgiving: Basic Submarine Assessment (BSA).

BSA evaluates our ability to fight the basic casualties that a submarine may encounter: fire, flooding, lube oil ruptures, and a few other big drills. The coordination and speed of our responses will determine how well we can recover the ship before we move on to tactical mission training. Our BSA is to be given by a group of chiefs from Submarine Squadron 15 in Guam, and the senior member is Commander Ginda, the Squadron Deputy. We head in after the exercise to pick up the assessment team, and as we near the port, a tug comes alongside to take people off and bring people on. The tugs spin us around in San Diego Harbor, and we hear the announcement: "Commander, United States Navy, Arriving."

I'm sitting in the wardroom, and every head in the room drops. Every officer holds his breath and waits for the pain to start. Micah Stevens comes to me as we are outbound and tells me that, because of some other tasking, I'm going to have to rig the Forward Compartment Upper Level (FCUL) for dive. I'm thrilled that I can help out, though he warns me to go slow and ask questions if I have them. My first checker is a first class petty officer named Sweden, a slight, thin man who is brisk but competent. He hands the lineup to me and I go about finding all the valves. I move very slowly since I've only done this space a few times, and more than once, I have to ask a crewmember about the location of a component.

I get to control and check valves carefully as I move around the space. To check a valve "OPEN," you have to turn it in the shut direction to verify that it moves. If there's no motion, you know it's shut. One of the things I'd been warned about in my qualification is not to jam valves all the way open on their "backseat" when I re-open the valve since the metal tends to stick and it's not good for the valve. I get to one of the valves right above the Chief of the Watch on the ship's control panel that controls water input to the depth gauges. It's a large valve that takes about 10-15 turns to fully open or shut. Its rig position is OPEN, so I turn the valve in the shut direction for five turns, it moves, and then I turn it back in the open direction until it hits its backseat. Then, remembering the admonishment about jamming valves, I take it a few turns back in the shut direction. I'm satisfied and move on to the next valve.

I'm exhausted from the exercise, so I go to my rack as soon as the maneuvering watch is secured even though we're still on the surface. I'm awakened at 0045, a few minutes after the diving alarm, by Micah Stevens standing in the 9-man. I'm confused and groggy as the conversation starts.

"Alex, did you rig the depth gauges in control for dive?"

"Yes," I reply as the pit of my stomach drops at his tone.

"Alex, are you absolutely sure you checked all the valves?"

"Yeah, I went slowly. I even asked the guys in control when I wasn't sure." I'm waking up fast, confused and worried.

"Are you sure there were no material problems, or you were not confused about anything?" Micah appears defeated and grasping for straws.

"I don't think so..." Doubt is beginning to enter my voice.

"OK, Alex, I need you to get up and get dressed. When we dove one of the gauges didn't work, and when the Chief of the Watch checked the valve, it was partially shut." He leaves before I can ask anything else, and I dress quickly and find myself shivering, but not because of the cold. I have failed, screwed up, done something clearly wrong. I've spent my whole life as a geek, getting good grades and succeeding in everything I tried. But now I've put my mind to something, done my best, and screwed it up. I'm so scared that I can barely sit still when I go to the wardroom and Micah explains what happened.

When the ship was diving, the control party with the CO and Commander Ginda right behind them had noticed that one of the depth gauges was not tracking with all the others. The Chief of the Watch quickly reached up, opened the valve above him, and got a few turns in the open direction, after which the needle popped and the gauge began to track. Commander Ginda immediately jumped on the CO, telling him that this valve was rigged for dive and out of position, compromising the ship's safety. Commander Ginda watched closely as the COW looked in the book and found out that I had rigged the space, and he then asked how we could be sure the space was rigged safely. The CO immediately ordered Micah Stevens to investigate and get another set of people to rig the Forward Compartment Upper Level. As Micah explains this to me, I see a very tired MM2 Joseph Ashley (nickname Cooter) walk by on his way to rig the Forward Compartment Upper Level. This process takes an hour and it's being taken out of his sleep time.

I feel ashamed and scared as I walk with Micah up to the command passageway and stand outside the stateroom in the dark as Micah talks to the Captain. I'm not even called in, and Micah emerges after ten minutes with terse words: "Alex, I have to disqualify you for Rig for Dive. To re-qualify, you're going to have to walk through every single ship rig with me, and it's going to be painful."

I'm on the verge of tears as I go back to the wardroom. Disqualified – I'm such a disgrace. I sit down and Mike Harven comes in to talk to me. They assure me not to worry, that the best of us make mistakes and I just have to keep working and bounce back. I'm so tired and frustrated that I'm barely listening to them; I've put the ship in danger with my incompetence. Mike pats me on the back after a while and orders me to the rack. I undress slowly and roll into my bed for a frustrated sleep. I hope that I'll wake up in a few hours to find that this is all a bad dream.

I wake up the next day, and the crew already knows that Ensign Fleming messed up Rig for Dive his first time out. It's clear I'm being treated with distaste, and the CO and XO haven't spoken a word to me, though the CO seems disgusted with me every time he sees me. He and Commander Ginda don't seem to be getting along. Commander Ginda is constantly correcting the CO while the officers and crew can overhear, and it seems they have some serious differences of opinion.

Despite my disqualification, I'm still in training, so I spend the BSA learning how the ship responds to casualties and practicing as a phone talker. Phone talkers position themselves throughout the ship to communicate vital information that helps the crew coordinate its response to a problem. The XO is always the man in charge of the scene of a casualty, and the CO is always in control. The XO, by tradition, has a junior officer right next to him as a phone talker to pass his orders and reports to Damage Control central. I'm in training to be the XO's phone talker, and once I get in the right mindset, it's incredibly fun to rush to the scene of a fire or flooding and help fix the ship. The adrenaline rush, even if it's just a drill, makes it a good time and I feel like I'm learning more and more ways to make myself useful.

My conversations with Commander Ginda are brief and business-like, and one time he inquires if I've been on the bridge for a maneuvering watch yet. I respond, "No" but think nothing of it as he nods and walks away. In a whirlwind of drills and evolution, we finish the BSA and head back toward San Diego, and I take my usual maneuvering watch place in the wardroom, studying. I hear Jason Pittman go to the bridge and assume the watch for his last drive into port before he transfers to shore duty. The speaker in the wardroom squawks: "Attention Helm, Control Room supervisor, Quartermaster. Lieutenant Pittman has the DECK ... and the CONN." His tone is official bordering on comedy, and the officers in the wardroom howl with laughter. A few minutes go by and the messenger rushes into the room with a quick knock.

"Ensign Fleming, sir, the OOD would like you to report to the bridge." The young man turns away as I nod in puzzlement. I quickly grab from the stowage location a body harness, which must be worn by anyone going to the bridge, but I've never put one on before and I fumble with it as the other officers watch. Finally, Juan takes pity on me and mutters that I'm doing it wrong as he helps me fix it. He shows me once how it's done and then pats me on the shoulder as I head up to control. The harness is tight and bites into my legs as I walk; I'll have to make it looser next time.

"Chief of the Watch, Request for Ensign Fleming to go to the bridge as ordered," I say loudly and formally. The Chief repeats back and sends my request to the OOD. The reply comes down.

"Control, Bridge, send him up." Then the Chief turns to me.

"Ensign Fleming, lay to the bridge, sir." I repeat his order and crawl up the small ladder to the top of the sail. The bridge trunk is damp, and I struggle not to slip on the ladder. Cords run everywhere up to the bridge, and I have to suck my stomach in to get past obstacles. I squeeze up and around people who seem to be jammed everywhere in the sail. I get up and see Jason Pittman, who greets me with a smile and tells me to clip in and come on up. I see the CO, who is clearly not pleased to have me, and then Commander Ginda, who says, "Mr. Fleming, I wanted to bring you up here so you could watch and we could screw around with you a bit." He says it with a smile and I understand that my presence on the bridge is probably not what the Captain wanted.

I stand up on the sail after clipping in my safety line and I'm thrilled by the wind and the ocean as we approach San Diego Bay. There's some talk, but mostly I watch Jason drive. The sun is rising and the Coronado beaches are rising in front of us. I immediately know that, if I can do this, be in charge of driving a submarine on the surface, it will all be worth it. I push aside the shame of being disqualified, and I swear that I will do whatever it takes to get back up on the bridge.

Jason efficiently drives the ship into port, carefully turning the ship around and controlling the discussions with the pilot and tugs. I stay quiet, learning and absorbing as much as I can. The evolution goes slowly, and as we near the pier, I begin to make out a crowd of people waiting for us. One man is in working khakis and has a sea bag, and he is tall but slender. He has a square jaw, and his nose is crooked from a boxing injury. He looks up at me on the bridge and waves; I smile and reply. I turn to the CO and say, "Sir, that's Lieutenant Priests, the new Engineer," pointing him out. Commander Lovpock looks at him, nods, and then focuses his attention back on the line handling. Once we are moored, I remain on the sail after the others go down, once again enthusiastic about submarines. I remember Matt Priests's words from five months earlier to "not take anything personally," but the disqualification still feels personal. This job is my whole life; how can my failures not be personal if this is how I spend every day of my life? I try to shake off the feeling as I go below decks to change. My parents are in town at a hotel waiting for me, and maybe getting away from the 711 for a few days will help me bounce back from my feelings.

I talk to the ENG, and he says he doesn't need me for anything; another officer is EOOW under-instruction for the shutdown, so I decide to bolt and take the bus downtown to meet my parents. I can think of nothing but getting off the ship for a while. I change into civilian clothes, pack a bag, and begin to walk quickly toward the forward escape trunk, passing by the wardroom where the XO and CO sit talking. I hear the XO's yell with a feeling of dread.

"Mr. Fleming, Get back in here." I stop and sigh. I didn't get away.

I knock and enter the wardroom in my civilian clothes and stand at attention as the CO and XO look at me.

"So, Mr. Fleming, where do you think you're going so early?" the XO inquires with an amused smile. I take a nervous breath and reply.

"Sir, the ENG doesn't need me, so I thought I would go downtown and meet my parents. They're here for Thanksgiving." The look on both their faces is very negative. "Uhhh ... or maybe not."

"When will we see you again?" The XO still looks negative but also too tired to deal with me.

"Sir, I'm scheduled to be Mr. Harven's under-instruction as EDO on Friday. So I will here Friday morning for turnover." I'm grasping at anything I can say to get out of here. The CO and XO share a cryptic glance.

"OK, Mr. Fleming, get out of here, but you need to talk to the CO sometime about Rig for Dive." This is the first time the XO has ever spoken of my disqualification.

"Aye, sir," I reply as quickly as possible and get out of the room and up the escape trunk before someone can change his mind. The bus ride to the Old City Trolley station, followed by the San Diego Trolley ride, fills me with joy to be in the sunlight and out of the place that has caused me so much pain. I decide not to tell my parents how I'm really doing and just enjoy Thanksgiving.

Friday morning, the day after Thanksgiving, 2002

Mike Harven puts down the phone in maneuvering and looks at me; I've been following him around earning his job all morning. He tells me I'm secured as under-instruction, I've done a good job, and I have to report to the Captain's stateroom. The Captain is waiting on me. I'm pretty sure I know what it's about.

I hurry to the command passageway and knock on the CO's door. He invites me in and tells me to shut the door. I stand at attention as he begins to read from notes in his flip-book.

"Mr. Fleming, you have failed in one of your primary duties as a watch officer by not adequately executing the Rig for Dive. This is an essential procedure for ship safety, and the fact that you cannot be trusted with it makes me wonder how I can ever trust you to do anything else. How can I leave you alone with a nuclear reactor if I cannot trust you to check a valve?

"Your failure also came while senior inspectors were onboard, and this reduces the reputation of the ship and calls into question our ability to safely operate for our superiors. These failures reflect not only on you but on me and the whole crew.

"Mr. Fleming, your lack of attention to detail put lives in danger, and I have instructed Lieutenant Stevens on your Rig for Dive upgrade, but you should know I will be watching you. You have a long way to go before you earn my trust as an officer. Is that clear?"

"Yes, sir," I reply. I manage to keep a straight face and remain at attention for the whole speech. There's nothing I can say in reply, and I'm not asked my opinion.

"Dismissed."

Commander Lovpock's curt reply sends me from the stateroom as quickly as I can reasonably walk. I don't go back to the ER; I can't stand to face anyone right now. I change into civilian clothes and leave the ship. Perhaps if I ignore the problem for a few more days, it'll get better and I can start rebuilding.

This is all common knowledge for the whole crew. There is very little secrecy about my failures on a submarine with thin walls where the gossip mill never rests. One hundred twenty guys underwater don't have much else to talk about, so the whole crew knows that I've been counseled by the CO and I'm on a very short leash.

Things always seem to be breaking, and we're a day late leaving San Diego the following week. The Commodore of our Squadron is coming to ride the ship from Hawaii to Guam, and he's ordered that we'll be in Guam before Christmas. It's a major priority for crew and family morale, as well as for the senior Navy leadership, to say that we only got to Guam three months late. We drive hard as fast as we can, and I return to my manual studying, trying to get past my failure and get qualified.

News and sports results underway come in the form of a page-long summary that glosses over the top stories with very little elaboration, followed by a much longer summary of the sports scores. I'm always frustrated by how much more effort is put into the sports than the news since I'm used to being up on world affairs as a student. I feel disconnected from the world, and seeing my parents for a few days has only made the feeling worse. We're a day out of Hawaii when a chill runs through the boat.

A super-typhoon is developing in the Western Pacific. It is named Pongsonwa, and its winds are already above 100 miles per hour and growing. This is just a different name for a category 4 hurricane in the Atlantic. Forecasters are predicting the strongest typhoon in 20 years, happening right in the middle of the Pacific typhoon season.

The storm is on a direct course for Guam.

Chapter 4: Federal Disaster Area

Underway, a few days out of Hawaii

The mood on the ship is grim as the typhoon approaches Guam. There are some conflicting reports, but the course holds true and people begin to worry about family more than work. The Commodore, Captain Mulloy, and his Command Master Chief are onboard observing us. Our first encounter with our new boss seems to be going well, though driving straight as fast as we can is not much of a strain. Mike Vasquez and I are studying hard as I race him to finish Basic Engineering qualifications. The other junior officers are not hostile, but they do find ways to make me remember that I'm causing them to lose sleep.

I'm sitting at a cramped desk with my knees jammed against one wall in the Engineer's stateroom taking a four-hour exam during the evening watch, and right next to me is Mike. We've been working for two hours alone, as exams for officers are very much an on-your-honor system. Suddenly, I smell the rank and very potent smell of human feces. I sniff and turn to Mike.

"Dude, did you do that?"

"No way, man. That is foul," he replies.

I try to ignore it, but the smell is too bad. I stand up and look through the doorway into the wardroom passageway, looking for the culprit. I see no one standing around, and I walk aft to the wardroom, looking for the source of the ever more potent shit smell. I hear some muffled shouts and the pound of feet as I walk through the wardroom to the pantry and look into the galley and trash compactor room.

It's hard to comprehend what I'm seeing, but a flow of raw sewage, the color and consistency of Yoo-hoo, is flowing out of the galley, over a pile of laundry bags, and into the trash room. I look through the hatch and see that the same flow of brown is coming out of the crew's mess and running down middle level passageway. I'm standing behind a two-inch lip on the floor, so I back away and stare as the Galley Chief hustles into the trash space (his hands, feet, and arms soaked in shit) and begins to stuff clean laundry bags into the hole between the galley and TDU room, trying to slow the flow of feces.

I can't understand how sewage could possibly be coming out of the galley and food preparation areas, but I step back as I realize that one of the many laundry bags being used to stem the flow belongs to the Squadron Master Chief, and another belongs to the Commodore. I step back into the wardroom, laughing at the insanity of the whole situation, and I see Captain Mulloy behind me. His expression that is studiously neutral as he takes in the scene and then walks back forward. I come around to the middle level passageway and attempt to help crewmembers throw down a line of towels on the floor, funneling the flow of brown to where it has already gone. The flood has come to the outside of a 9-man and begun to waterfall down the ladder to the lower level and the machinery room.

The next hour dissolves into mayhem as people try to contain the unending river of shit. The pressure source is removed quickly, but the flow has already contaminated the galley, crew's mess, trash space, lower level head, laundry room, and a good portion of the middle level passageway. Nobody can move anywhere as the Chiefs try to begin cleanup. The smell is unbearable; it's like sticking your head in a toilet for hours on end. There's a line to puke in the head. I finish my exam and then go into the wardroom to find out what happened.

It turns out that a junior mechanic had been aligning valves to blow sanitary tanks (SANS) overboard. There are two ways to get rid of SANS on a submarine, pumping and blowing. Pumping involves using a very large and loud pump to suck the tanks and pump them overboard. Blowing involves securing all the heads on the ship and filling the tanks with high-pressure air to push the feces overboard. Blowing is preferred because it goes much faster and creates much less noise, if done correctly. This junior mechanic left a valve out of position that cross-connects two sanitary tanks. When pressure was applied to the larger tank, the feces chose the path of least resistance, which happened to be away from the ocean, through the cross-connect into another much smaller tank. This tank overfilled and pushed the overflow up a pipe to a garbage grinder conveniently located in the middle of the food preparation area. The feces overflowed out of the grinder with enough pressure to overcome the ocean depth, causing it to spray spectacularly over the very small space and flow outward. By the time the OOD found out about the casualty and secured the pressure source, we had sprayed almost 700 gallons of raw sewage into the food preparation and service areas.

The officers sitting in the wardroom listening to the story from the off-going OOD are howling with laughter. The scene strikes me because we are stuck in this horrible situation. Even ventilating with the outside air has not helped the smell, and yet this group of friends thinks it's the funniest thing in the world. Many people swear that, no matter what happens, they will never eat galley food again.

The off-going EOOW is walking up from the ER and a new petty officer named Sobeski is handing out shoe covers to anyone who has to walk through the crew's mess. He turns to Henry and says, "Being called sanitary tanks, the contents don't appear that sanitary." Sobeski smiles and Henry shakes his head as he walks away pondering the strangeness of some of the people onboard.

The petty officer who made the mistake has been given a new name: "Shit-mate," a play on the polite "Shipmate." He kneels in the middle of the galley, sponging feces into a bucket as other crewmembers look on, some helping, some just enjoying his pain. I understand better than ever: In the Navy, when you make a mistake, you will fix it, no matter the cost.

No meals are served for thirty-six hours as the cleanup proceeds. Officers and guests are delivered some of the clothes that have been washed, but they still reek of shit and Mike Harven barely touches his laundry before shoving it in the trash. The Commodore and Squadron Master Chief say very little to us, though there are whispers of some strongly worded conversations in the command passageway. Hunger builds as everyone breaks into private food and soda stores to get through the day. The pacts to never eat again begin to fade as hunger sets in.

Finally, after almost forty-eight hours, the announcement is made that the galley is clean, and the ship's Corpsman has completed bacteria samples on all food service surfaces. We laugh at this idea since the floor still squishes and runs in the crew's mess and the carpet in the wardroom has brown stains that won't wash off. Micah tells anyone going to the first meal that they're insane, and he seems determined to never eat another meal on the submarine. I look around the galley. The smell is gone, and I decide to take my chances since we're still four days away from Guam. I guess this is what the XO means by having an inexperienced crew. The pain endured by the mechanics because of one man's failure is lesson enough to last for a very long time. Everything that happens is done scrupulously and reviewed without mercy, as everyone tries to avoid being the next screw-up. Then there's the critique.

I'm learning that critiques are how the submarine force formally assesses a specific problem, finds the root causes, and decides on the punitive and corrective actions. The running of critiques varies based on the senior leadership, but right now, the XO is the prime motivating force behind the critiques because his personality is a lot more forceful than the Engineer's. The critique happens in the wardroom and all the people involved in a mistake gather, along with their chain of command and all the books and documentation of the procedure. Junior officers are assigned to gather all the data for the critique and put it in the wardroom. Once all personnel and material are present, the senior leadership is invited and the initial problem statement is made. In this case, I hear the first words before someone closes the door: "SANS were blown into the galley when attempting to blow SAN 1 overboard."

Then the critique proceeds in a trial format. Each person involved is questioned about the evolution, preparation, training, equipment, attention to detail, use of procedures, and level of supervision. I'm sitting in the stateroom right next to the wardroom, and I can hear the whole proceeding through the wall. Uncomfortable questions are asked about intentional versus unintentional failures. Once the CO, XO, and ENG ask their questions, the junior people leave the wardroom. The remaining senior personnel decide on the short-term and long-term corrective actions, and they also decide who gets punished. The main punishments can include removal from watchstanding, disqualification, and formal charges for the Captain's mast.

Disqualification means you have to do a whole qualification over again. Removal from watchstanding is a less intense punishment, and usually the upgrade procedures are a slap on the hand. "Shit-mate" is disqualified from all his watches and has to start his career progression on the submarine all over again.

The distraction of blowing shit everywhere fades quickly. We begin receiving news reports that Pongsonwa is arriving on Guam with maximum sustained winds of 145 miles per hour. It's the strongest typhoon to hit Guam directly in 20 years. The short summaries describe the loss of power and water to the whole island. As the storm passes over the island, hundreds of homes are destroyed and power lines are knocked down. The destruction causes a fire in the fuel storage tanks near the harbor, and the smoke covers half the island. The squadron sends word that all the families are accounted for, but there has been extensive damage to Navy family housing.

The men onboard are very worried about wives, children, and our destination. We receive word that Guam has been declared a federal disaster area, and the fire burning in the fuel storage facilities has spread to other tanks. The reports make it sound like half the island is on fire. We get closer and closer, but even the Commodore tones down the optimism of his rhetoric about the great reception we're going to get. We have been underway for ten weeks, and we have a long list of repairs that need to be done, but when we reach Guam, there may be no resources for us.

Despite the concern, life marches on as the routines of the ship are kept. I'm ready to qualify EOOW, and the final hurdle is a qualification board. I'm very worried; the Captain's words from my counseling session still ring in my ears. The final qualifying officer is the CO, and the board will be the CO, XO, ENG, and the Engineering Department Master Chief (EDMC). It takes place in the wardroom with a whiteboard, dry erase markers, and me alone on one side of the table, standing. The questions come quickly and intensely. I'm put in hypothetical situations with casualties to the nuclear reactor and asked to describe my actions and those I would direct. Any weaknesses are explored with more questions as the board members try to find the limits of my knowledge. Each initial question comes with several follow-ups from each board member, until they've heard enough. We go through each major problem the plant could have, including the nightmare scenario in which all cooling to the reactor is rapidly lost. The other officers have prepared me for this, so I'm ready with answers, but the board members keep pushing until they find something I don't know.

I know the board isn't really about knowledge; it's about whether the Captain trusts me to make the right decision in the engine room. I'm not so sure about this, and Matt Priests has warned me that I could have all the knowledge in the world, but if the CO doesn't trust me, he won't qualify me. This thought remains in the back of my mind as the board continues and I get a list of things I don't know. After two hours of questioning, I'm exhausted and just want the experience to be over, and I'm asked to step out of the room while the board members consider my fate.

I stand in the passageway in limbo for ten minutes, noticing small things. Metal is missing on one small corner of the wardroom door and a safe handle in the passageway is loose. A small link of chain hangs off the end of a locked locker in front of me and a bulb in the fluorescent light on the ceiling above me is out. The time becomes unbearable, and then I hear my name shouted. I walk in and the Captain informs me that I have "sufficient knowledge to be safe," and he has seen fit to pass me with lookups. He instructs me to see Lieutenant Priests with my lookups, and when I'm ready, to come see him. I quickly find out all my missing information from the manuals in the wardroom, and then I go talk to Lieutenant Priests. Matt is still in turnover and will soon be taking over as the Engineer. We sit down in one of the staterooms and he tells me to close the door.

"Alex, I wanted to talk to you before you go see the Captain," he says. "You did a good job in your board, and I think you know enough to be safe back there. This is a very important time for you, especially since you've had problems with rig for dive. You're going to get qualified, go back aft, and take the watch. Then the standard you set is entirely up to you. The second and third class petty officers who've helped you through your qualification process, been your buddies, given you checkouts, are now going to be working for you. You have much less experience than they do, but when you go back there and take the watch, YOU are the officer, and YOU are in charge, whether they like it or not. They'll try to joke and be informal with you because they've seen you as a novice since you got on the boat, but you have to set high standards and maintain them. It's a lot easier to set high standards and relax them than to start with low standards and let the guys walk all over you. These are little things: phone communications, entering maneuvering, repeat backs, addressing each other correctly, not having comfortable discussions in the ER. You have to set the standard, even though they aren't going to like it. You're the officer, and this is your chance to establish what kind of watch officer you're going to be. Do you understand?"

"Yes, sir," I reply. I understand what he's saying in theory, but I'm not quite sure how I'm going to execute it. I walk up to the Captain's stateroom, and he asks me a few questions before signing my qualification card and putting me in the qualified watchstanders list. He explains that he doesn't fully trust me, but he doesn't want to hurt my career progression by holding back my qualification. I'm on probation, and I have to prove myself ready to lead.

I nod and reply in the affirmative, and then he turns to me and says, "Congratulations. Go back aft and relieve the watch, right now." I'm shocked but excited; I didn't expect it to come so fast. There are about four hours left in the watch and I'm taking charge for the first time. The officer on watch in maneuvering is very pleasantly surprised. Now that I'm on the watchbill, more sleep and free time will be available for everybody. I shiver with fear and excitement as I finish my turnover process and speak the simple but powerful words for the first time: "I'm ready to relieve you."

"I'm ready to be relieved," Mike Harven replies.

"I relieve you," I say with excitement.

"I stand relieved. Attention in Maneuvering, Ensign Fleming is the Engineering Officer of the Watch." Mike smiles and signs the logs over to me.

"Reactor Operator, aye."

"Electrical Operator, aye."

"Throttleman, aye." Each maneuvering watchstander must acknowledge my relief. I sit at the desk as Mike leaves and realize the EM1 Robinson is the electrical operator. I don't know it, but he's been assigned to this section as a senior petty officer for the sole purpose of keeping an eye on me and making sure I don't do anything stupid. The desk is tall, so I can see everything in the room. There are patterns of scratches in the plastic, apparently made by bored officers on watch.

It takes me ten minutes to realize how boring it gets in the ER when nothing is going on. The guys begin talking about movies to keep each other awake, and I listen without joining. Robinson gives me recommendations for each request that comes in, explaining what's going on for each evolution. I decide I'm happy with having a relaxed environment, especially since every time I remind someone about formality or tell them to stop talking, they give me an evil look and make it ten times harder for me with the next order that comes in. I realize what "malicious compliance" means as one watchstander takes every little order I say to the maximum interpretation until I realize that they're pushing me.

I decide to sit quietly and try to observe the common standard so I can fit in. I've been on watch for two hours and I'm beginning to feel very sleepy when an alarm suddenly sounds. It's a reactor scram, a real one. The adrenalin starts pumping as I get on the microphone and make the announcements to recover. I realize what's happening as the Engineer comes into Maneuvering a moment later and tells me that the scram was a drill for training and that I need to recover the plant as quickly as possible. I get my procedures and listen to Robinson's recommendations, and the ENG never says a word. I realize this is all part of a test to see whether I can handle myself in the ER. Mike Harven and Matt Priests are standing nearby whispering in my ear if I look unsure. I get everything restored, and the ENG gives me a brisk "Good job" as he leaves.

Mike Harven waits until Priests and the ENG are gone and says, "Good job, man, you just got your cherry popped. You're not a real EOOW until you've handled a scram on your own." He smiles and pats me on the back. The enlisted guys tell me that I did a good job and didn't "fail open," which means to stop talking and stand there like a deer in the headlights. The only comment I get is to remember to think before I talk on the microphone. I'm relieved at 2330 by Henry, who has the midwatch, and I go forward to report my relief to the Captain with the off-going OOD. Relief reports are summaries of the watch that the officers give to the Captain describing the events of the watch. The EOOW also gives a relief report to the ENG with more specific details about the plant and operations. My reports go quickly and painlessly, which almost surprises me. I walk to the officer's head and look in the mirror. My hair has grown longer and I haven't shaved in three days. There are large purple circles under my eyes, but I'm a watch officer, no longer dead weight on the ship.

December 18, 2002, 0430 hours

"Surface, surface, surface." The announcement on the 1MC wakes me up. I roll out of the rack shivering and throw on my poopie suit, thinking about the news summary from the previous evening. The island of Guam has lost power and water to 70% of homes and businesses, though utilities on the base have been partially restored. The fire that burned for four days in the fuel storage tanks finally burned out, but there has been extensive damage and fuel rationing is in place for all residents. Squadron reports that all the families are safe and back in their homes, but power is still intermittent. The federal government has promised aid, and it could be months of work since most of the island's power and phone lines are above ground, though this seems counterintuitive in a place with strong storms every year.

I'm not on the watchbill for the morning, so I eat breakfast quickly and go to control to take a look out the periscope. The island is silhouetted with the sunrise behind it, and it's much flatter than I imagined. It looks bleak and destroyed, as if every green thing has been blown away. The Contact Coordinator pushes me off the scope as a ship appears, and I decide to find another place to hide while people prepare for the maneuvering watch. I go into radio, a very small, cold room. I've spent very little time in there, and I find the Chief working intensely. He is a small man of very few words who shrugs when I ask to come in and talk to him. I realize as I sit down that he's listening to the radio. When I ask about it, he says that it's an FM station from Guam, and they're talking about us.

I laugh and tell him I didn't know he could tune in commercial stations. He gives me an amused look and says, "Sir, it's a radio room." I laugh and realize the stupidity of my question. We sit there for a few hours, listening to a show called "Malefunkshun Boys." Apparently a catch phrase on Guam is "It's not broke; it's just malefunkshun." I realize how much our arrival means to the people of Guam, especially after a devastating typhoon right before Christmas (Note 9).

I sit in the wardroom watching the periscope feed on our widescreen TV as we come into the harbor. The south side has a huge rocky cliff called Orote Point that towers 200 feet over the sea. The north side has a low rock wall built on coral reefs, and I see three large merchant ships at anchor in the outer harbor. Smoke still billows from large fuel tanks at the far end of the commercial side. I know that the Navy base is on the south side of the harbor.

I'm dressed in my summer whites to go topside and man the rails. We are arriving at a new homeport, and even with the destroyed condition of the island, we're expecting a ceremony. The line of men in whites goes topside and we stand as we pass through the breakwater into Guam Harbor for the first time. Another ship is docked at a fueling pier just inside Orote Point.

We slow and turn around a large coral reef toward the entrance to the inner harbor in the southeast corner. One side features the dilapidated and rusted buildings of the Guam Shipyard, which none of us can believe is still working. There are several hulks of old ships and a large blue floating dry-dock, and now we all understand what people mean by "Big Blue." Opposite the Guam Shipyard and main Navy base, which the islanders call "Big Navy," we see a large surface ship docked on a small peninsula with a few shacks and a large parking lot. The peninsula is called Polaris Point, and it will be our home. The ship is the USS Frank Cable (AS-40), one of the two operating submarine tenders in the U.S. Navy. On an island with no naval repair organization, the Frank Cable will be our source of parts and labor support.

The ship brings tugs alongside and we swing around to come next to the Cable and tie up on her starboard side. Cable is moored with her stern pointing at the pier at a ninety-degree angle, allowing submarines to moor on both sides of her. We draw closer and closer as I realize exactly how small a submarine is next to a hundred-foot high ship. We gently push up against the small rubber separators as a loud and excited bunch of wives and children watch us from the pier. In the destruction of the island around us, a small tent has been erected with music playing. It seems a very weak attempt at a welcome ceremony, but the guys are mostly happy to see families on the pier. Some of the submarine wives are very good at dressing up scantily when their husbands and boyfriends return. We tie up and secure lines, and then a small ladder is lowered from a hatch in the side of the Frank Cable, touching down aft of the sail. The senior officers and off-watch crew hurry off the ship for the ceremony and the topside phone talker turns to me.

"Sir, from the Engineer, report to Maneuvering for the shutdown." I hurry below in my whites to take the watch and get the plant shut down so we can all leave and get our lives in order. The hard part about being a nuke is that the forward people get to rush off the ship as soon as we touch the pier, but the Engineering Department's job is not finished until the reactor is shut down with shore power installed. The men are impatient, and even the Engineer seems distracted as I go through the procedures of my first qualified shutdown.

It goes OK, and I only make one minor mistake that is easy to recover from, but the ENG yells loudly. It's confusing because he'd been standing next to me when I'd given the incorrect order but said nothing. The yelling ends quickly and I think everyone's mind is elsewhere. The reactor is safe and power is coming from the Cable as I am relieved and head forward. My entire life is stuffed into small lockers in a 9-man and the ship is a ghost town in the forward compartment. Everyone has left already to find their lives. I pull out a small bag with my car shipment paperwork and get the instructions I have been given for temporary housing on the base. I pack my messenger bag with enough clothes for two days and dress in shorts, Tevas, and a t-shirt.

I walk up the wobbly stairway to the Cable and immediately become lost. This ship is huge, with thousands of people onboard, and I have to ask my way three times to get to land. The walls are simple, like those of any Navy ship, except that I encounter large boxes labeled "Condoms" every few yards. The stories I've heard about the Frank Cable being a "love boat" may be true. I smile and shake my head with silent laughter as I walk down the brow and set foot on the island of Guam for the first time, at 1500, in the blazing sun and scorching humidity. I look around at the desolate landscape with low hills, but I see no green. All the trees have been blown bare. I begin to sweat immediately, and I wonder how I'm going to get to my car.

Polaris Point looks like it might have had a lot of buildings at one point, but now it gives me the impression of being a junkyard. I see uneven cement lots, parking labels in multiple colors and styles for the Cable, a few rusty shacks that appear to be falling apart, empty vending machines, and Dumpsters. I walk through the parking lot, looking at the harbor and cars around me, since apparently there's a shuttle to the office where our cars are being stored. The grass and jungle are fighting a winning battle against the parking lot, and the brush is growing over what used to be much more extensive paving. As I walk, I see Sobeski, a reactor technician, pull up and drop off an electrician at the boat. He waves at me and I ask him for a ride to the auto shipping office. He tells me to get in, and I have my first experience of what "shipmate" really means.

We drive away from the Frank Cable parking lot and I see the rest of the harbor on our left. Rusted pylons and piers are everywhere, and we make a slow turn to see a beach area with shacks that could once have been a family recreation area but is now just abandoned. The jungle and low trees have been stripped bare like a shaved dog. The bleak branches left are all swept in one direction, like a great hand has pushed them down. We drive past a security gate and fence line that separates Polaris Point from the main road, since Polaris Point is not part of the main Navy base. Outside the gate stand a number of very shabby-looking cars and what looks like a junkyard of burned-out cars. I guess these cars are in such poor condition that they can't be allowed to drive on base; they're also referred to as Guam Bombs because of their low cost. We reach the main road, called Marine Drive, and see a full-sized model of a Polaris Missile sitting at the intersection and jungle in both directions.

Outside the base, all the buildings look shabby, in a way that reminds me of Mexico. A Taco Bell and a Pizza Hut stand right outside the main gate, reminding me that I'm still in America, and then we show our IDs to cross into the sprawling Naval Station Guam. The Navy owns and protects the entire peninsula on the south side of the harbor, and the acreage is vast. I see signs for a Mobile Construction Battalion, Security Squadron, the ever-present McDonalds, and an old power plant.

He drops me off at a massive warehouse, and I see my blue Ford Bronco sitting in a parking lot, looking like a gift from God. I thank him and finish my paperwork as quickly as possible. I get in my car, which appears to work, and face my most immediate problem: I have no gas. Shipping cars in the military means the automobile must have less than a quarter-tank of gas. It appears that they have driven my car when loading and unloading it, so now I'm on empty. The people giving me the vehicle advise me not to drive off base until I get a Guam registration, but I've heard stories about the Guam police and decide that I'll take my chances since the one gas station on base is not working.

I'm driving around lost, looking for gas, on an island that has just had a fire in its fuel reserves. I pick a random direction as I leave the base and find myself driving through villages worthy of northern Mexico with gas station signs that all read "NO GAS" or "OUT of GAS." I've been driving for five miles when I start to worry. I finally find a station that's working and wait in line for 20 minutes. I pull up to find out that I can only buy $20 worth of gas, but that's enough for now. I ask the clerk how to get to the main part of the island, and he smiles and points north, back toward the base. I guess I was wrong, but I had a fifty-fifty shot coming out the main gate anyway.

I head north and find that Marine Drive becomes a scenic route north of Polaris Point. A spectacular ocean view emerges on one side, with beautiful hills and wave breaks. Beaches and coral reefs are close enough to throw rocks at, a stark contrast to the destruction on the eastern side of the road. Every single light pole and telephone pole is on the ground. Electrical wiring runs along the ground down the length of the street, sometimes caught on trees and blocking side streets. I pass a coal power plant on the northern side of the harbor that has ENRON stenciled in huge letters, and these letters are apparently in the process of being painted over. All the windows on every building are boarded up. I weave through a few more sharp turns and suddenly I'm in a town, which the signs call Agana.

I see the same type of destruction, except now the buildings are bigger. There's an ACE Hardware, a white-columned District Court building, a cathedral, and a group of touristy-looking huts labeled Chamorro Village. I pass through the main part of Agana and find myself sandwiched between the ocean and a steep cliff ledge on my right. I've looked at maps of the island before, so I know that one area has lots of hotels and clubs, and that's where my instincts are taking me. I come out from under the cliff line and enter a more populated area, but with a different type of business. I see signs for Ichiban Massage, Memories Massage, Venus Massage in decrepit shacks with few windows, and I guess that these may be more than just massage parlors. I've heard stories about this, but seeing the signs right on the street is something else entirely. I continue driving, now lost, just letting my instincts take me. I decide to turn left at a light where I see a mall, apparently called Guam Premium Outlets. I drive on until I reach a cliff overlooking the ocean, and then I'm in Tumon Bay.

The first hotel is the Hilton, and the others line up along a picturesque beach, one after another. The generators are humming since the power is still out, and most windows are still boarded. I'm on an empty four-lane street, dodging trees and fallen lampposts as I enter the really expensive section of Tumon, called Pleasure Island, according to signs that still hang in tatters. I see a curved white building at the northern end of Tumon, and that's where the road ends. It's nearing sunset, and the ocean begins to light up with the most incredible color I've ever seen. The sky is cloudless as I park at the Hotel Nikko and walk to the grass overlooking Tumon Bay. It's so harsh but so beautiful that I sit down and fight tears. I name the emotion: joy.

45

I'm so happy to see a sunset and feel the wind after three months on a submarine that I can't speak. I've never been so happy in my life. The submarine has held only study and pain so far, and this sunset, which needs a poet to do it justice, is the most happiness I've felt since leaving Virginia. Here I am, 7,000 miles away from home, and I'm alone. I think that, if I can just see sunsets like these, I might be able to get through this.

The second night in Guam, all the officers head out to Tumon to get a feel for the nightlife. I'm sharing a small temporary house on base with two officers, and we still have no power or water. We begin drinking beer at 1500 and head down to Tumon just after 2100. There is only one really popular bar, called Mac and Marti's, but it's still closed after the typhoon. We keep driving down the strip until we see lights on, still dodging fallen light poles. The lights are from a place called Club USA that sits in a decrepit and run-down building across from the Outback Steakhouse. It advertises "exotic dancers nightly" in neon lights and seems to be the first business to reopen after the typhoon. A very drunk group of officers stumbles into their first Guam strip club.

Club USA is a small, rectangular room packed to capacity since it's the only club open. We sit down at a table and are soon surrounded by girls who want to sit with us and the Mama-sans trying to get us to buy the girls drinks. The beer is moderately cheap, and we're all feeling very good. Whenever one of us particularly likes the girl onstage, we take our supply of one-dollar bills and sit by the stage to get a better look. The old ENG is feeling particularly good after thirty-six months of the hardest job in the world, and his hooting and hollering fills the club. He's heading home to Virginia tomorrow to his family. Vasquez, Juan, Mike Harven, Henry, and his wife Alli are all out with us tonight.

Mike and Juan get louder and more amusing by the minute, and I see how they earned their "white guy and the Mexican" title for their escapades in Virginia. We are distracted as an extraordinary woman takes the stage. She's six feet tall with dark skin and golden brown hair. She keeps her long-limbed and muscled body under tight control as she hangs upside down on the pole in gravity-defying positions. She is very well endowed and draws many new men to fill the empty seats by the stage. Her dancing is incredible, but then she walks naked over the stage and comes to our table, pointing at the old ENG. She wants him on stage to help her.

He looks around happy and wide-eyed, and I see Juan and Mike exchange a mischievous grin behind his back. The old ENG is dragged up on stage and his hands put on the ceiling as his back is turned to the crowd. The dancer, whose name, we learn, is Alicia, slinks around the stage waiting on the cheers. The old ENG attempts to resist, but the naked Amazon woman convinces him to comply.

The audience erupts into pandemonium as she enthusiastically whips him. I hear the passes of the leather, and the old ENG seems to be in extraordinary pain after ten licks. When it's finally over, the old ENG limps back down and drinks more alcohol to chase the last of the pain away. I think he's going to feel serious pain in the morning. We stay at the club drinking with the girls until 0330, leaving and collapsing on the beach since we can't find our car keys.

This kind of night will apparently become normal on the island.

I pass my qualification board for EDO a few days later. No one spends much time on the boat, since the XO wants us to get our lives in order. The house I'm staying in still has no power or water, so it's not really useful, and I speed up my search for a better apartment. I'm showering and shaving on the boat. The CO and XO do make time to qualify me because, now that we're in port, the more people who are qualified, the more people can take leave on Christmas stand-down.

Stand-down is a time when you only come to work if you have duty, usually once every three days. The leadership of the boat tends to come in every few days to deal with issues that can't wait, but most of the junior guys get to enjoy a few uninterrupted days off the boat. My first duty days occur during a stand-down and I'm excited to be helping the watchbill and taking responsibility.

Duty days in the Engineering department start one hour before turnover. As the oncoming duty officer, I show up to work around 0530 to dress and head back to the ER. I tour with the off-going duty officer, and as we inspect the spaces, we talk about what's going on and any verbal directives from the ENG. Then we get to Maneuvering and I look through all the paperwork we maintain to ensure reactor safety. Once I'm satisfied with the paperwork, I review the logs of all the engineering watchstanders and look through the status of indications in Maneuvering. Turnover is at 0630 in the crew's mess, and the entire group of oncoming watchstanders is briefed on the condition of the ship and any important evolutions. Once this is complete, the Engineering section goes to the area aft of Maneuvering, where I brief them on specific plans for the day in the ER. Questions are asked and the section leader reads the watchbill. The Engineering Duty Petty Officer (EDPO) and the section leader do most of the talking as they give out cleaning assignments and other personnel tasking.

The day officially starts with an announcement: "Oncoming Engineering duty section has permission to conduct watch relief." Then I say the magic words in Maneuvering and take charge of the ER for twenty-four hours. Generally, every day has about three to four hours of actual evolutions to get done, but this is made longer by the problems we find in Guam.

Thirty minutes into my first duty day, we lose shore power. The island power supply fluctuates enough that it puts us on our own power. The reactor is shut down, so there's no easy replacement to fix the problem. We have a diesel generator as backup power to keep the reactor safe, and we quickly become accustomed to using it. There is a loss of shore power every day, sometimes twice a day. Sometimes it's only a brownout or severe frequency isolation, which normal people only notice as a flicker of the lights, but when you're dealing with nuclear equipment, it makes you very nervous. I'm talking to the new Engineer, Matt Priests, one morning when we lose shore power again. He just laughs at me as I take the proper actions with a look of extreme frustration.

The more we find out, the more we think that Guam and Polaris Point are not ready to support home-ported submarines. The staff of Naval Base Guam doesn't know how to deal with us, and the supplies we get are not delivered urgently enough for the submarine world. We're sidestepping procedures left and right to get what we need in a homeport that is technically "forward deployed." All the books are written for ships passing through, and having the CoCC (City of Corpus Christi) and us here is a new problem that hasn't been adequately considered. We're confused because it's not a surprise that we're here, but apparently people just said, "We'll figure it out when they get here." The losses of shore power are only the most obvious symptom of the problem.

Standing watch also gives me the chance to establish my standards, or realize how hard it is to change a standard once set. My relaxed attitude from the underway has already been promulgated as my "style" as an officer. Anytime I try to push performance beyond the level of formality that I've established, I encounter extreme resistance. My desire for the guys to "like" me is overriding my dedication to nuclear power. Both the CO and ENG have warned me about this attitude, but I think I can handle it and maintain standards, as I've seen other officers do.

The guys are frustrated on a different level because the crew housing is not what we were led to expect. The COB and EDMC spend a great deal of time trying to get the base to provide furniture to the empty houses that single guys were expecting to move into and have life set up. There are no beds, desks, dressers, tables. The rooms are bare and empty, and for the moment, they have no power or water. I understand why everyone is drinking and going to clubs every night. Christmas is approaching, and we're far from home on a destroyed island that's not getting any better.

I spend my first Christmas Eve on the ship, as the most junior qualified EDO. Duty schedules are very prejudiced toward married and senior officers during the holiday season. No matter how much sleep I get in a duty day, I'm always exhausted at the end. There are calls for me in the engine room throughout the night, and I can't stay in bed for more than a few hours. I drive away from the boat on Christmas morning and keep going around the island. I have one contact on the island who has invited me to a party, Joey Lopez, a businessman and chamber of commerce leader. I'd met him and his family the previous year, and when I called them after the typhoon, they invited me to a party so I wouldn't have to spend Christmas alone. I was thankful and thrilled to accept.

A winding road takes me over the hills above the base and I find myself dodging fallen light poles on Cross Island Road. The view is spectacular as I climb over a ridge and see both sides of the island at the same time. I stop to admire the raw beauty with the sapphire ocean extending to the horizon in both directions and a humid wind whipping across the hills. I cruise downhill onto the eastern side of the island and turn into a golf course community called Windward Hills. The house of Mark and Vicki Fish is the nicest one I've seen on the island, with full generator backup and a huge water tank. Mark works for a bank of some kind and is only the second person I meet from the Guam Chamber of Commerce. The party is incredible, and I feel intense happiness from being included with only a phone call from my parents 8,000 miles away on this Christmas morning.

My thoughts return to what I'm going to do on this island with no apparent choirs, clubs, or any of my other standard activities. I'm already drinking more than I ever have in my life before, but I know that this isn't a healthy habit. As I wander around the party, I begin a conversation with a young couple who seem to sympathize with me. The woman introduces herself as Challenger Deep and her husband is Bamboo-boo. I'm skeptical, but they tell me to show up at the Pacific Daily News building in Agana on Saturday and wear clothes I don't mind getting really dirty.

I ask them what these "Hash House Harriers" are about, and she just smiles and replies, "You'll see … it's a drinking club with a running problem."

Chapter 5: Examinations

Searching for apartments after a typhoon is a very troublesome concept, especially when the Navy Housing office is not trying to help you out. The Navy on Guam will not approve any lease agreement without an inspection by a "qualified" worker, and part of that inspection involves verifying that the power and water work. The problem is that we've been on Guam for three weeks and there is still no power and water off the base, so the housing office won't let anyone move into apartments and we're stuck in temporary housing with no furniture.

For once, the whole ship is thankful for the XO's temper. The Navy has many leadership styles, but the intermittent yelling type is one that gets the most publicity, and this is the XO's style. The stories of these problems start to filter up and he goes to the housing office with his particular brand of passion. The housing office begins approving leases the next day, since apparently somebody has decided that the San Francisco should not be waiting for the Guam Power Authority and Guam Waterworks. I've been seeing apartments every day with a realtor, and most of them are so roach- and mosquito-infested that I can't believe they're rental properties at all. I finally decide to go for the most expensive possible apartment, and I'm taken to Oka Towers.

Oka is a fourteen-story building on a razor coral cliff overlooking Agana Bay and Tumon. The apartment is a penthouse with decks on three sides that overlook the entire island and a beautiful surf zone. The 1,700-square foot, one-bedroom layout is more space than I wanted, but the decks hook me. I stand on the balcony looking at the waves as they crash against the rocks. I can see the southern part of the island in the distance, and I decide that this view is worth whatever rent I have to pay. There's minor water damage from the typhoon, but the metal protective shutters work, and I have enough furniture to hide the stains.

My Navy inspector comes to look over the place, and I convince him that a large building with penthouse apartments probably has power and water normally. He reluctantly signs the form and I'm relieved enough that I move out of temporary housing immediately. I'm sleeping on a couch with no air conditioning and carrying a garbage can of water from the basement for every toilet flush, but at least the apartment is mine. The three months with everything in my life stuffed in a locker in a 9-man has given me a new motivation to live alone in a place where I can see a lot of sky.

The entryway to my new place opens onto a marble floor, where there is a storage room and a 16 by 16-foot deck that will hold my barbeque. I christen this the "party deck." My bedroom and kitchen are on the left as you walk down the hallway, and the small deck and windows in the bedroom face east. I have a perfect view of Tumon, the northern end of the island, and the Guam International Airport. The hallway continues and opens into a 1,000-square foot room that has massive windows and a large deck that faces the surf zone of Agana Bay, from which I can see the entire southern end of the island and the harbor. I'm home, even without furniture. I move my things in a few weeks later.

I'm in that warm, fuzzy half-awake zone right before consciousness. I roll over in the brand-new clean sheets of my queen-sized bed, satisfyingly cozy. This is the first night with all my furniture in my new apartment, and I'm still enjoying the fact that one air conditioner is powered by the building's emergency generator. My dreams begin to fade away as I feel the warmth of a bright sunrise through my windows... wait a minute ... sunrise. It's light outside. My eyes snap open and I jerk upright in bed.

"Oh, FUCK!" I glance at the clock and see that it's 0645. I have to be at work at 0715; I'm going to be late! I leap out of bed and begin to run around the room gathering clothes and shaving as fast as I can. I still marvel at my apartment and the view that greets me.

I shave as fast as I can and cut myself four times. I try to stem the bleeding as I throw on my clothes and run with my bag out the door into the parking lot. It takes me ten minutes to get to work very early in the morning, but the later it gets, the more traffic there is on Marine Drive. This is the great joy of driving on Guam because the speed limit is 35 mph for the whole island except on Marine Drive during morning rush hour, when everybody goes 60 mph and drives like they're in midtown Manhattan. These crazy drivers are separated by rusted-out trucks going 25 mph with groups of large Chamorran men sitting in the truck bed.

I get to the Polaris Point turn by 0700 and scream around the corner onto the single-lane road, where I slam to a stop behind a line of seventy cars. This is what happens when the Frank Cable comes to work, and if you hit it, you're pretty much screwed. I twist and yell at my steering wheel, and I get through the gate at 0710. I run down to the boat and change in a 9-man, still out of breath, before running to officer call in the wardroom. I'm two minutes late, and the XO is in a really bad mood this morning. My traffic excuse is not taken well and I have to endure screams for a few seconds until the anger shifts to another target. There's not a lot of time to spare for late Ensigns since we're a few weeks away from a major engineering inspection.

The Navy has certification procedures for every portion of a submarine and its crew. These tests are organized roughly in the same way as the ship. The Tactical Readiness Evaluation (TRE) involves the weapons, sonar, tactics, and navigation of the ship. The Engineering Department must face an examination by a different team of only officers who were Engineers and one very senior post-command officer. Though the emphasis on tactical proficiency is on the rise again, engineering inspections have long been the most feared exam for an operational submarine. The results of these inspections can make or break the careers of the CO, XO, and ENG.

The ship has a very detailed Microsoft Access file that tracks the monitoring and assessment of day-to-day evolutions. This file is so huge that it's the focus of every officer's life to get monitors and corrective actions into the Access file. The plan of the day every day has a list of outstanding monitors, and the XO secures liberty frequently if they're not done. "Securing liberty" means that you can't go home on a certain day until you talk to the XO. During the intense preparations for the engineering inspection, the XO feels that people aren't making enough progress, so during this officer call, he decrees that all officers and chiefs will check out with him before going home from work every day. The men emit roans of sadness and barks of anger.

Officer call at 0715 is followed by Officer/LPO call in the crew's mess at 0730. The XO runs this meeting, since he apparently thinks the COB is not mean enough, and tells the Chiefs the same things that the officers have just heard. The chiefs are smart and experienced enough not to make a sound. People who spend long enough in the Navy are used to dealing with different kinds of leaders, and the Chiefs tell us that fighting the personality of an XO is like shouting at the rain. I run around the ship all morning spending hours in training and then doing administrative tasks for the ENG. I don't have a division yet, so I'm an easy target for "copy-bitch" type work. I do my best and get grudging thanks for each job done. I still don't have my dolphins, but I qualified EDO quickly, so the other officers allow me some slack on not being qualified Rig for Dive.

I don't allow myself any slack, since I feel that I've shamed myself and need to make up for my mistakes. In the afternoon, I take advantage of Micah Stevens to do another compartment walk-through of rig for dive. These walk-throughs are not fun at all, but Micah has explained what he's doing, and the idea is to make it such a painful learning experience that I'll never screw up again. Mental pain is a very good way to get a college-educated officer's attention, and the chain of command has decreed that I will feel some pain in return for my embarrassment of the ship in San Diego. The memory of that event is fading in everyone's memory but mine.

At the end of this Friday afternoon, all the officers and chiefs onboard line up outside the XO's stateroom before they leave for the weekend. I have duty on Sunday, so I want to enjoy my day off, but the line is slow moving as jobs are handed out before people can leave. I'm junior enough that the XO has nothing for me, so I change into shorts and get off the boat as fast as I can before someone thinks of something else for me. I race home, feeling the warm ocean breeze out my car window. I'm learning to appreciate every moment of freedom off the ship because we've already had two more typhoon scares that brought us within hours of leaving.

I spend Friday night unpacking boxes, slowly shaping my new apartment and drinking vodka and orange juice on my balcony overlooking the ocean. I'm excited because Saturday at 1600 is the Hash House Harriers' run.

A large group of dirty cars descend on the *Pacific Daily News* building at 4 o'clock, and a group of people gather who look like they've just emerged from a mud-soaked Salvation Army store. The clothes and shoes are caked with the coarse red dirt that covers the island, and they trade stories about parties and bars from the previous evening. I can tell it's a tight-knit bunch of young people who spend most of their time together. I pay five dollars to an attractive half-Asian woman who introduces herself as Wednesday.

The clock ticks to four and yelling begins.

"Where's the fuckin' map?"

"Why are we waaaaaiting?"

A short, muscular man called Lucille runs up to a signpost and puts up a hand-drawn map to a water tower south of the base. The whole group jumps in their cars and drives like maniacs to the beginning of the run, called the "box." The only way I keep up is by following the cars with foot stickers on their bumpers. People park wherever they can and put on long socks and cotton gloves. One person loans me a pair of gloves and promises that I'll need them. Lucille grabs a bag of flour and welcomes everyone to his run before dashing off into the jungle. Even though this is my second run, I come to the front to watch as a tall, blond man calls for FNGs ("If you don't know what an FNG is – you are one") and begins his speech:

"Welcome to the HASH. My name is Tampon and I'm the Tyrant. We are here for one purpose and one purpose alone – to get to the beer. That crazy guy who just ran off is the hare, and he's going to lay a trail for us to get to the beer, but he is also going to try and trick us. He's going to put down marks to get us off trail so he doesn't get caught, and if you look at the ground here, you'll see the kind of marks we have. The first is a single dollop of flour, and this is called an ON-ON. If you see this mark, it means you're on the trail and you shout ONON, or blow two blasts of the whistle or two blasts of the horn."

The speech is punctuated by a horrid, broken horn blow by a large and colorfully dressed woman standing behind Tampon.

"The next mark you may see is this cross of flour, which is called a CHECK. This means that the trail could go in any direction and we have to find where the path to the beer goes. When you get to this mark, you yell CHECKING, or one blast of the whistle or one blow of the horn."

The woman, whom I learn is called Pink Torpedo II, blows her horn again.

"Now, there are a number of things that can happen off a check; the first is that there could be three single ONONs followed by nothing. This is a false trail and you should return to the CHECK. The second is that the trail could go on for a while and then come to these three marks perpendicular to the trail. This is called an ON-BACK, and it means that the wily hare has fooled you and you need to go back to the last CHECK and go a different way. If you get to this mark, you yell ONBACK or ON-BACK or OH SHIT! The last mark is an arrow in the direction of trail, and if you get to this, you follow the arrow and call ON ARROW or ON ARROW or …. ON ARROW.

"Now, at the end of this run, we're going to have something called religion, in which we're going to ask all of you to tell us your name and where you are from and then tell us a joke, sing us a song, or show us a body part. If you're not wearing a Hash shirt when you get to religion, you'll have to turn it inside out in front of the whole group.

"One last thing: if during the course of this run you decide that you think we're all crazy people and you want to go home, please tell someone so that we're not out all night looking for you. We've had FNGs home warm in their beds while we wandered around in the jungle until two in the morning to find them. So, there are …One, two, three…. nine of you today. Hopefully, you will all be here at the end, and welcome to the HASH." Tampon finishes his speech with a flourish and the run begins.

It's a mad scramble through deep jungle and across streams onto a bare ridge line. I immediately see the purpose of the gloves since sometimes the only thing to hold on to is a long, sharp grass, logically named "sword grass." We run in the blazing sunlight up a steep, knife-like ridge above Agat until we reach the top of a hill. I look back from the shouts of "ON-ON" to see the sun going down on the ocean. I can see the southern portion of the island, and the green of the jungle hills is magnificent in the afternoon light. The island's beauty fills me as I put one foot in front of the other on the trail. I forget about the submarine, Lovpock, Rig for Dive, quals, and all the other problems in my life. The run takes us through a grove of palm trees called Hidden Valley and back down a different ridge to a field with a fire and four large coolers of beer called ON-HOME. I grab a cold Miller Light and sit in the grass; I'm sweaty, muddy, and exhausted. This is the group that will keep me sane on this island. The sun goes down and there is much more debauchery before the night is over. The hashers have a bond that I envy, and I want to become one of them.

My hangover on duty the next day does not dampen my joy, and the sword grass cuts that cover my arms and legs remind me that there are sane people on this island. I can make it as long as I get to see them once a week.

We get underway on Tuesday. This trip is dedicated to improving our performance on drills and continuing administrative preparations for the approaching engineering inspection.

I discover something interesting the first few days. The sword grass cuts on my legs become inflamed and infected almost immediately. I ask the other officers why, and they explain that the ship operates under water with only 18-20 percent oxygen in the atmosphere. The reasoning behind this is that it slows the progress of fire, the true nightmare of any submariner. I'm amused to hear stories of Captains who want to motivate their crews in difficult times by raising oxygen levels one percent. It's just another illustration of how the Captain is God in our little microcosm of society. The side effect for me is that my cuts become infected easily and heal very slowly. The same applies to any cut or scratch, and the scars form on my arms and legs quickly. I have already established a reputation of being clumsy by running into valves and ventilation piping on the treadmill. The only nickname that is more prevalent than Flembot is Biff for my tendency to run into things.

The random copy work continues as records are assembled for the engineering inspection team. The wardroom is cleared out since the team will convene there for the two days they're onboard. No other inspection team can ever demand the total use of the wardroom, kicking out all officers except the Captain. This gives them a special status above any other inspection team. We perform a BSP to pick up the team, which involves driving into Apra Harbor and turning around. We then bring a tug alongside and load the three Lieutenant Commander post-Engineers and the Senior Board member, a post-command Captain.

The Commodore also comes aboard since he'll be observing. This came about because of the career importance of these inspections to Captains. There apparently have been occasions where Senior Board Members and ship Captains got into disagreements about comments and evaluations. This is a sensitive situation because so much is riding on it. The presence of the Commodore provides someone to serve as a mediator between the two officers if any disagreements arise. I think this is the real reason, as opposed to the stated Commodore concern of "observing operations of one of his units." I thank fate that I'm not chosen to be one of the direct participants, and my only involvement is running documents, serving as a recorder and clipboard holder, and giving watch relief to officers who have divisions. The mechanics of the inspection proceed, the officers eating their meals standing up in the staterooms and catching a few hours of sleep whenever they can between administrative tasks for the board.

We have begun to realize something else in the course of the workup and inspection. This boat is not in good material condition. Things are failing left and right. Small pieces of equipment have clearly not been maintained through the shipyard. Coupled with the mistakes of an inexperienced crew, this means that every underway is delayed, and every time we get to sea, the time is cut short by some failure that forces us back to port. Even the inspection comes to an end six hours early because of a material problem, but the team has seen enough. They seem to have found the same problems that we already know about. The inexperienced personnel and poor cleanliness and preservation are specifically noted in the report, which labels us as safe but below fleet standards.

This means different things to different people. The Navy understands that we're fresh out of overhaul, and they expect us to take time to restore operating proficiency. The squadron thinks their first inspection with the ship has failed, and they decide to give us increased monitoring no matter what the board requires. The inspection team gives us many areas to work on to improve; the full report is eighty pages long and includes pretty much every area of engineering on the ship. The ENG doesn't have to worry about this inspection reflecting on him personally since he's only been onboard a month.

The CO and the XO have both been around longer than six months, and this performance hurts both of them. It means that the CO is not effectively managing or improving the ship after overhaul, and it reflects directly on his "competence for command" in the minds of his superiors. The XO takes a specific hit for his massive monitor database. The Senior Board member says that the database is ineffective and actually hurts the honest assessment of what is happening on the ship. The junior officers laugh as we hear this because it confirms that the board is actually in touch with reality, and they see that we were putting in whatever bullshit was needed to get our names off the plan of the day and go on liberty in the afternoons.

The CO seems to take out this failure on the XO personally. We are remotely aware that they don't get along, but the Captain begins to talk down to the XO in public in a way that makes us think the CO places the blame for the inspection on the XO. The poisoning of their relationship only gets worse as we return to port and get back into the daily routine. Despite the inspection, the show must go on and we have a schedule to keep.

The master plan for the use of all submarines in the Pacific is maintained by the Commander, Submarine Forces Pacific Fleet in Hawaii, and it is used to plan missions and usage years in advance. We are already behind by months, but we are still scheduled to support the Seventh Fleet in November 2003 as a mission-capable asset. Every inspection is pushing toward that date, and the squadron is responsible for getting us ready to meet that obligation. The pressure for the Guam experiment to succeed is larger than ever since now the force needs mission days gained to justify the money spent.

This complicated by the fact that we still don't "work" for C7F (Commander, Seventh Fleet) in Japan, even though he is closest to us geographically and has more experience with Guam. Our operational commander is still in Pearl Harbor, eight hours and a day away. This obtuse and illogical relationship poses a number of logistical problems that make the schedule even harder to meet.

We're never allowed to forget for one minute that we are on a schedule and we have to deploy in less than a year.

I'm slowly working toward Rig for Dive requalification, but I also have to find something to enjoy at work. I look around for an area that I can lead and excel in, and I find an interesting opportunity. One of the jobs of the Guam-based units is to provide Mining Warfare support for the Pacific Fleet. Unfortunately, none of the officers onboard has any practical experience with mining. A few of us are sent over to the Corpus Christi to learn the system with the squadron fire control chief. I decide that this is going to be my specialty, and I dedicate myself to learning all things related to mining.

Once I have read all the manuals and instructions, I play with the computer system that controls mines until I'm a master of it. I then locate all the reports from the last ten years on mine warfare and read them. This gives me a passion at work and something that I do better than anyone else in the wardroom. Matt Priests encourages me to have a specialty, and it's nice to be respected in discussions, even if it's only during Mine Warfare training. The approval is like a drug, and I begin to think that things are on the rise.

The drinking, strippers, and hashing continue. The officers and crew of San Francisco go out every night. We are rapidly established as big spenders with every exotic dancer, karaoke bar owner, and club manager on the island. There's only one place on Guam to regularly find most of the white women on the island: Saturday night is Country Music Night at Gameworks. The crewmembers are fixtures there, and the island is so small that we can't go out without officers and enlisted men mixing. This is technically against the rules, but on a strange island with no family and a busy schedule, it's hard to find friends. The credit card bills go up and up as the Mama-sans start to prey on us. The spiral of unhealthy living catches me along with a lot of the single officers and crew.

Onboard the ship, we continue frantic repairs and training. We have several short underways to support training of the other submarine. Not a single underway happens on time because of various failures and material problems. We begin to use an expression in the wardroom about "the football," referring to the officer whose division has the underway-limiting component. Since the CO is making periods at sea more and more uncomfortable, we also have "the good news bunny" when something breaks that will keep us in port. When any officer finds a problem that will convince the Commodore that we should not get underway, he makes the bunny ears symbol.

We also have a new officer arrive onboard, Adam Johnson. Adam has been expected for months, and Matt Priests has told us his story in advance. Adam is young, but he's spent the last three years teaching in Nuclear Power School. Once he got tired of teaching all the officers and enlisted personnel who man nuclear reactors, he decided to go through as a student and come to the fleet. He's incredibly smart and has some of the best grades anyone has ever seen. We desperately need him.

Other problems are developing on the boat with enlisted leadership, specifically in the mechanical division (M-Div). The move to Guam forced a number of early and later personnel transfers. The short-term situation was held together by the momentum of the Guam Train, but now that we're here, the Captain and XO are realizing that the divisions don't have enough depth of experience. Just like many officers don't want to go to Guam, the enlisted people in the training pipelines don't want to come here, either. The detailers send us only new recruits and people at the bottom of classes. There are only two sea-returnee first class petty officers on the ship, and these men are usually the backbone of any crew.

M-Div has lost its Chief to kidney stones. Several first class petty officers have been doing his job in the interim, and the new Chief is having trouble finding his feet in a difficult job. The long absences of leadership force Micah Stevens, the division officer, to step in and become much more involved than an officer should be in the day-to-day operations of the mechanics. They love him because he's smart, enthusiastic, and realistic. But he can't replace the operational experience and technical background of a Chief Petty Officer. The new Chief needs Micah's support because, if there's any sign of weakness, the guys in the division will respond ruthlessly. Nuclear enlisted men are very similar to schoolyard bullies; if you show a weakness, it'll be exploited. The loss of many leading petty officers in M-Div has cemented the problems and left the division flailing.

Small ships have no secrets, so all these problems are common knowledge to the officers, chiefs, and any crew who are watching and listening carefully enough. The ENG is working hard coming off a hard inspection, but he can only do so much. We push on with the operational schedule, and I get re-qualified in rig for dive. The interview with the CO is actually shorter than my first one, and all he says is, "Mr. Fleming, everybody makes mistakes, but if you repeat them, then you are stupid. Don't screw up again."

Every bone of resolve in my body tells me that I'll do right this time. I've never failed at anything until now, and I will kill to avoid doing it twice. Even so, Micah doesn't assign me the same compartment to rig, instead giving me a simple space to get my confidence back.

We're preparing for a trip to Hawaii when news of another typhoon comes. All ships and submarines in Guam are ordered to prepare to sortie and leave port to avoid damage in the storm. We're put on alert that the ship will get underway and submerge for safety. Everyone puts their houses in order and comes to the boat. I frantically pull my typhoon shutters for the first time and pray that they work. The families are being left alone to ride out the storm with only the small squadron to help them out. We're starting up the ER when we encounter a problem that delays our underway for four hours. The storm is already less than two days away and the Commodore is screaming for us to get underway. Finally, almost seven hours late, we throw the lines over in a torrential downpour. I watch through the periscope camera, and I can barely see the other side of the harbor, let alone the ocean. Mike Harven is on the bridge driving with Mark Sheklund under-instruction and the Captain sitting behind them.

The tricky part about driving in and out of Guam Harbor is the crosscurrents at the mouth of the outer harbor. Glass Breakwater on the northern side and Orote Point on the southern side jut out from the island so that the harbor entrance is the westernmost point of the island. A coral reef traces around the edge of the whole island, but it drops off quickly so that you're in 1,000 fathoms (6,000 feet) of water when you get a mile offshore. This means that strong and deep ocean currents come right up to the harbor entrance and typically run about 1.5 to 2.0 knots (nautical miles per hour). This seems very small, but when you're trying to keep a massive nuclear submarine off a coral reef in a space only 1,000 yards wide, even one knot can be a big problem.

The way you fight this when entering the harbor is by crabbing (pointing the bow off your line of advance) away from your track to compensate for the crosscurrent and stay on a line to enter the harbor. You also drive the ship with at least 10-12 knots of speed to give you sufficient forward motion to overcome the current. Exiting the harbor presents the exact opposite problem since the currents are close to neutral in the outer harbor but the ship must speed up above 10 knots before exiting the breakwater. Once you have speed on, you have to watch the drift as soon as you clear the breakwater and begin to compensate. If the ship doesn't steer to compensate, the current pushes you onto the large coral reef around Orote Point. Grounding a ship in the Navy is the fastest way to end the career of any Captain, and hitting another ship is a close second.

The approaching typhoon only makes the situation worse since now we have a 2.0 knot cross current and ten-foot waves outside the harbor entrance. The sail of the ship only comes 25 feet above the water line, so it doesn't take a very big wave to send water over our heads. I'm on watch as Control Room Supervisor for the maneuvering watch, which is mostly about directing traffic to and from the bridge and getting yelled at by the XO for random failings of the watch section. We clear the breakwater going thirteen knots; my gut wrenches to the side and I feel the pull of my seat belt as we begin to take thirty-degree rolls. Everyone holds on to the nearest object, and I have the advantage of being belted into a chair. This is going to be impossible weather to rig the bridge, and gallons of water begin to thunder down into the control room as waves wash over the sail. We begin to turn into the waves to head for our dive point.

Suddenly the ship rolls sickeningly to starboard and a massive gush of water comes down into the control room. We hear a garbled yell over the announcing system.

"Man Overboard, Starboard Side!" The yell comes from a frantic Mark Sheklund. The XO begins yelling and screaming immediately as the ship continues to move. We're stopping and turning in an attempt to avoid chewing up the man in the propeller. The XO makes a mayday call on the bridge-to-bridge radio to alert Coast Guard units. Chiefs and crew flood into the control room and begin pulling ladders and gear from behind the ship's control panel, a tight space with many valves that contains ladders and other emergency equipment. I pull out of the procedure because I have much more help than I need and it's clear that the more experienced people in the room are there to take charge. We hear a follow-up report, this time from the Captain.

"There is NO man overboard, I repeat, there is NO man overboard. Lieutenant Harven has been washed out of the sail and is STANDING on the starboard fairwater plane. Lieutenant Sheklund has the deck and the Conn." Everyone in control is silent as they listen to this, and we start to get engine orders to keep the ship moving or we'll be a sitting duck in the waves. All the people on the bridge wear full body harnesses and are clipped into hard points on the top of the sail. Mike Harven's harness has done its job and he's hanging in his harness over the side of the sail. His feet can barely touch the planes, and he's lost his glasses and is mostly trying to get a hold of something that he can use to pull himself back up.

"Captain, XO, Lieutenant Sheklund is not qualified." This communication is ignored as we try pulling a large ladder out from behind the ship's control panel. A stored canvas bag is yanked out and the ladder pushed upward when we get the word that the Captain and Mark have pulled Mike back up into the sail. He is unhurt with the exception of losing his glasses. Other personnel are sent down from the bridge as Mike secures and rigs the bridge for dive as quickly as possible. Every minute we have people on the bridge raises the chances that something else will happen. Twenty minutes later, the OOD is down, and Mike Harven comes into the control room soaked to the bone and says with a flourish, "Chief of the Watch, last man down, hatch secured." There is a smile in his voice gets a round of applause as he walks down to change. There is only one problem – he's lost his last good pair of prescription eyeglasses.

Six hours later, I'm asleep in my rack when Micah Stevens comes to find me again. I'm immediately worried as he asks me if I rigged the Forward Compartment Upper Level for dive. My stomach drops into my toes and the fear begins again as I recall the scene from the hours before.

"Alex, you need to rig Forward Compartment Upper Level for dive. I know it's your first time since getting re-qualified, but Mark has to relieve Henry so he can work on this material problem and get us underway. Go slow and you'll do fine," Micah says quickly. I try weakly to protest, but I stop since this is a perfect opportunity to prove myself.

Ship's Control Panel and Ballast Control Panel valves are a large portion of the Forward Compartment Upper Level rig. The hard part about this space, and the reason it's usually assigned to junior officers, is that getting behind those panels is a pain in the ass. You have to crawl over a large reel of wire and a number of bags of emergency gear to get to the valves. Checking each one requires you to crawl in and lay your body on the reel while pushing over into a small cavity. The twenty valves are small and infrequently operated, and reaching some of the far ones is near impossible. I have the added problem of being six feet tall and now weighing about 205 pounds thanks to the good food, beer, and lack of regular exercise.

I do the valves from easiest to hardest and end up stuck upside down on the other side of the reel. I'm too embarrassed to call for help, and I flail my arms and legs to find some purchase to pull myself up. I finally drag myself upright and check that I've initialed all the valves in this space.

I move on very slowly, ensuring that everything is done carefully and by the book. I will not screw up this time.

This whole sequence flashes through my mind as Micah tells me to report to control. I find MM2 Ashley and his Chief standing and talking to the DOOW. They explain that, when they were venting the depth detection system, the movement of the gauges told them a cross-connect valve was open where it shouldn't be. Ashley checked and found that one of the normally shut Rig for Dive valves was cracked open.

He shows me the valve behind the SCP and I notice that it's much less crowded without the ladders that were pulled to rescue Mike. He motions me closer as he points to the valve and then whispers, "Sir, I'm sorry about this; I tried to handle it and keep it between us, but the whole room saw both depth gauges pop." I nod and pat him on the shoulder, humbled by his loyalty and kindness to me. I've made the same mistake twice, and the depression I feel is almost palpable. The Captain calls me into his stateroom with Micah Stevens.

"Mr. Fleming, did you check those depth control valves?"

"Yes, sir," I reply.

"You're sure?" The Captain is almost as angry as I am defeated.

"Yes, sir. I spent almost thirty minutes behind the SCP." I'm desperate to think of anything that could explain the valve being out of position.

"I don't believe you, Mr. Fleming. I believe you are lazy and lack attention to detail. Why can't you check a simple valve?" He pauses for effect. "Your word has no weight for me. I'm disqualifying you Rig for Dive again, and you are only one little mistake away from being disqualified EOOW and every other engineering watch." I can say nothing in response. I'm told to leave the stateroom as Micah takes his turn for the poor execution of my retraining.

I stand in the command passageway and realize that it's possible that the valve was moved when the ladders were being yanked out from behind the SCP. I pace back and forth and nearly leap on Micah as he leaves the CO's stateroom. I tell this to Micah as he walks me back to the wardroom, but he just shakes his head.

"Alex, it doesn't matter. Lovpock has made up his mind about you, and nothing you say is going to change it." I want to scream with anger at myself. The next few days bring suspicious looks from the officers and chiefs. It's clear that I've been labeled "untrustworthy" and the mental persecution from the other officers starts afresh when they get woken up to rig things for dive.

I'm finally taking a division as the Reactor Controls Assistant, and I focus on learning about my men and their passions. Chief Harbin, my chief, sits me down and explains how it works for a junior division officer. He's here to run the division and protect me while I learn to drive the ship. I should come to him with any questions and ask everything that comes to mind. I ask how I can best help him, and he puts me in charge of the maintenance monitoring program. This allows me to pour myself into an administrative project and execute the day-to-day lifestyle of an officer in the ER. I'm not hungry much anymore. I rarely come to meals to avoid sitting with the CO and XO, and I spend a lot of time studying and doing divisional paperwork. I do interviews with each member of RC-Div to find out who they are and where they're from. The shocking part is that most of them are older than I.

Time goes by and things break. We go back to port and then out to sea for three- to four-day spurts. There's plenty to do, but we just can't keep working long enough to get a rhythm. My new leading petty officer, Brian Powers, comes onboard, and I like him immediately. I realize after a while that Chief Harbin is protecting me, and I get to ride on the momentum of his confidence and expertise during a number of vital repairs.

We finally have to leave for Hawaii to do a tactical exercise and certification that can only be done there. A few days of note occur before we go, as a tall man named Rick Bonner reports onboard as the new XO. He's an incredibly experienced navigation and weapons operator who seems to yell much less than Kevin Jorges. The junior officers are reluctant to form opinions because it only takes a few weeks on 711 to bring out someone's true colors under stress. Our goodbye party for Kevin Jorges involves a great deal of alcohol and sea stories in Juan's apartment. We make a t-shirt for his departure that reads "Junior Officer Protection Agency: I survived Super typhoon Jorges. USS San Francisco, Guam."

The men say goodbye to their families as we get ready to depart. I've been intermittently dating a nurse named Lisa, and I say goodbye to her, sad since she's the only good thing in my life. I close the typhoon shutters on my apartment again; the heavy metal is rusted enough to make it hard to move. It doesn't feel like home yet because I only spend time there in the dark drinking beer on the balcony. Just before we leave, another officer named Craig Litty checks onboard. Craig is a small man and a prior enlisted Corpsman, the Navy equivalent of an Emergency Medical Technician. He stands five feet four inches tall and wears his hair in a Marine Corps style, high and tight. He's cheerful and upbeat and immediately makes a name for himself by helping the crew with their officer application packages.

The underway to Hawaii is late, and we each go home and come to work not knowing whether we're actually going to leave that day. I eventually just leave the typhoon shutters closed and live in a pitch-dark apartment since it's too much work to open them every day. Several days of hard steaming give us plenty of time to continue tactical training and for me to work on qualification, though the Captain shows no sign of changing his attitude toward me. The new XO discovers my affinity for mining and allows me to become a key player in that area, but this does little to change the Captain's viewpoint. One day out of Hawaii, a major piece of equipment breaks, and we pull into port, delaying our certification. The assessment comes back that this problem will take a month to fix, and now we're stuck. We're rapidly getting the reputation of a ship that's always broken.

The month in Hawaii passes in a whirlwind of classes, trainers, hangovers, and frantic repairs. The squadron and Captain are frustrated by the ship's condition, and we've already had to put off our November mission to the following year. The men on the ship are separated from their families and left to live the single life on an island that has much more to do than Guam. Regular destinations are Barnes and Noble, Wal-Mart, Best Buy, and other stores that we don't have on Guam. The officers are put in a brand-new set of barracks that has barely any furniture or sheets. I room with Craig and admire his health and exercise routine, while I focus on the partying aspect of being in Honolulu.

The frustration of the crew at the ship's condition is showing in a series of DUIs, drunk and disorderly arrests, car accidents, and other events. I'm still the whipping boy of the wardroom as Matt Priests ratchets up the pressure on me. He demands constant improvement, and I focus on the parts of my job that I'm doing well: qualifications, mining, monitored maintenance, and divisional operations. I'm also becoming the resident expert on the tactical computers and chat rooms used to control strike operations. This earns me yet another nickname: "Chat Monkey."

The news that our tactical certification has been delayed cements the feeling that we're a failure and the whole trip to Hawaii is a waste of time. My 23rd birthday passes without great recognition, and the only interesting note of the whole month is when the CO, XO, Mark Sheklund, and I go to a Dining-In party with the officers and chiefs of the Pearl Harbor squadrons. Most of these people are living in paradise on their first choice boat, and having us around is like dealing with an annoying cousin who won't leave. The leader of the proceedings, Master Chief Cramer from Squadron 7, makes fun of us for showing up in the wrong uniform and not bringing any of the Chief's quarters. We certainly did not bring the choker white uniform on a trip that was only supposed to be three weeks long.

We leave Pearl Harbor late, repaired and without any further progress toward mission. The pressure is building as we race across the Pacific with our tail between our legs.

We return to Guam after a two-month absence and we're well on our way to a humid Guam summer. It's so bad that breathing becomes labored as soon as the sun comes up. Temperatures during the day average ninety degrees with one hundred percent humidity. Rick Bonner starts a lunchtime soccer game on Polaris Point, and it's clear that he appreciates athletics and having fun as much as doing the painful missions. Our next underway is three weeks away for a Mining Readiness Certification Inspection and then a quick stop back in Guam before a week of CO discretionary underway time. The small repairs are piling up and we have a four-week maintenance availability scheduled to help fix some of the problems.

I'm happy to return to the Hash, and I see more and more of the island with this beer-drinking running club. I take Micah and his wife Natalie out the Hash with Henry and his wife Alli, and I feel horrible when Natalie breaks her ankle a quarter of a mile into the run. When I talk to Lisa, the nurse I'd been dating before we left, she shocks me by telling me she's engaged. My jaw drops, and I ask if it's someone she met after I left. She says yes, and I end the phone conversation quickly in disbelief. I've heard stories about this phenomenon, how submarine crews will come home to find at least ten percent of wives and girlfriends gone after a long underway. I realize how hard it can be to have normal romantic relationships when you leave for weeks and months at a time.

My persecution by the officers leads me to grow closer to the enlisted men I meet in the clubs and bars. The guys are nice to me, and many of them understand the struggle of trying to do well when people have decided you're a dirt bag. I develop a friendship with a group of enlisted men and their non-Navy friends who live in the apartment building next to mine. These are the people I hang out with because, whenever I'm with the officers, the conversation inevitably turns to Rig for Dive and why I can't check a valve shut.

A week after I come home, another submarine called the USS Bremerton shows up carrying a friend of mine from college named Scott. Scott and all the officers are being promoted to Lieutenant Junior Grade and Lieutenant. Scott calls me and asks if they can use my apartment for a wetting down party (Note 10).

The Bremerton wardroom has $2,000 to spend on their party and I offer my apartment since I'm eager for some distraction. I take advantage of the situation to invite a random group of people from the Hash and the boat. The tough part about this is that word gets around about it on the boat and I have to be very careful not to give the impression of fraternization. I don't actually care because the enlisted guys are nice to me when the officers are horrible, but I'm attempting to maintain the pain in my life at an acceptable level. I leave the door open and my key under the mat for Scott and his friends to stock the fridge with beer and food.

I'm stuck on the boat until 1830 writing messages, and I finally drag myself home, exhausted. I find a decent though very male-heavy party in progress. I ask around to figure out who's in charge and ask what's in store for the night. One of the people from the Bremerton explains to me that they've hired a stripper for the evening. I'm reluctant and immediately ask them who, since at this point I know every stripper on the island by name and face. They don't remember the name, but they assure me that she's hot. I shrug and begin to drink more and invite everyone listed in my cell phone to come to the party. My next-door neighbors promise to come up and say hi, and Micah and Natalie come up as well, even though Natalie is on crutches thanks to my stupidity.

The CO and XO of the USS Bremerton show up to party in my apartment. My XO shows up as well, but he looks wary as he sees the enlisted people in my apartment. He shrugs but shoots me a warning look. I'm drunk and talking to the Captain of the Bremerton after shots of vodka. He seems like a really nice guy and nods as I describe my troubles. He doesn't offer any advice but agrees that I have to work hard to fix the situation. Then he asks why my Captain isn't at the party. I almost reply that Commander Lovpock is a dork and doesn't drink, but I catch myself and just give him the Captain's cell number. Every duty officer has the CO's and ENG's cellular numbers memorized.

I laugh with glee as I imagine the embarrassment of the CO when one of his peers calls him from a party at my apartment. I don't stop to think that this might not be good for my image, but I don't care. I've drunk enough vodka that, when the doorbell rings and I see Alicia, I don't think to ask why she's at my door. She grabs my shoulder and whispers, "Alex, they hired me to dance. That's why I brought a security guy." The large islander standing behind her is suitably scary looking.

"Alicia... Do they know what you do?" I've seen her in action, and I don't think the Bremerton wardroom knows what they're getting into.

She looks embarrassed but has a mischievous smile:

"I don't think so," she says.

So, as a highlight of my party, the wardroom of another submarine gets whipped with a leather belt on my living room carpet. This puts things over the edge, and the dancing continues into the early morning. I wake up on my couch, alone, in an absolute disaster area. I'm tired but satisfied with my first good party.

In the aftermath of the party, the XO speaks to the ENG and tells him to send me a message that partying with the enlisted guys isn't the best idea. The ENG give me this warning, but he also tells the Captain while Matt's in a fit of rage about a lost piece of paperwork. The Captain goes ballistic at the news that I have unduly familiar relationships with enlisted men, and the ENG tells me I'm on thin ice, as if I didn't know it already.

The next underway is the Mine Certification, and I'm ramping up for my lead role in the certification. I've re-qualified Rig for Dive after a series of more painful walk-throughs and interviews that are getting beyond desperate. The Captain signs my book quickly, as if he expects me to fail again. I'm assigned to rig topside for dive, the hardest space, and I've never done it before. A submarine qualified officer normally rigs topside, but in this case, we're short of people because of schools and temporary duty. My first checker is a sonar technician who's never rigged topside before, either. The situation is making the hairs on the back of my neck stand up, and Commander Ginda is onboard, never a good sign for my performance.

I go slowly, identifying every component and even forcing crewmembers to reopen bolted plates to allow me to verify caps installed. Some things on the rig sheet are not applicable to our type of ship, and the first checker has put N/A in the blocks indicating where we cannot complete the rig. I look carefully down the rig but don't pick up on the fact that "Aft Escape Trunk Holddown Shackle" is actually installed on our ship. The shackle allows underwater vehicles to attach to the ship in an evacuation scenario. I allow the "N/A" and complete the rig, heading below decks as we clear the harbor.

That night, a fleet representative and Commander Ginda become suspicious of one Rig for Dive sheet that's mislabeled, so they ask for all of them to review. The post-Captain deputy notices my mistake with the holddown shackle immediately and goes to the CO with a demand that topside be placed as an exception to Rig for Dive. I'm clearly not knowledgeable enough to perform the rig, and I'm disqualified quickly and quietly.

When Micah tells me about the problem, I simply drop my head in defeat. I feel no resistance or passion anymore. I've given all I can and failed again; I'm convinced I'm not worthy to be a submarine officer. I now doubt every skill and piece of knowledge I have ever gained.

However, the Mine Certification goes smoothly mostly because of my preparation and performance. I'm thrilled by the opportunity to excel. The Rig for Dive problem doesn't freeze me in my tracks; at this point, the other officers are used to my failures. I keep going one day and one watch at a time, just trying to keep myself qualified EOOW.

We pass the Mine Certification with good marks and return to port. We're now one of the designated mining assets for the Pacific fleet. The small victory pales in light of the long year of failures, but the men are happy for a little while. I'm not happy, sliding further and further into depression. I skip beer and go straight to drinking vodka every night of the week. The moment I walk in the door, there's a drink in my hand until I pass out on the couch. My work suffers equally, and I'm late two days in a row the week before CO discretionary time.

Matt Priests gives me an ultimatum: if I'm ever late again, he's going to fire me from my division officer job and disqualify me every watch, effectively making me start over again. He writes my first official counseling sheet (Note 11).

I try to pass off the "alarm clock power failure" excuse for my tardiness, but Matt sees through that one. The week gets worse and worse as I stay at the boat longer, falling asleep in every training session and meeting because of my hangovers and nightmares. The ENG assigns me to be the Startup EOOW on the Sunday night before the underway, and the brief is at 0200 in the morning. I study hard since I still have some iota of pride to grasp.

On Monday morning, the phone wakes me and I look at the clock; it's 0204.

"Oh, SHIT!" I answer my cell to find Powers on the other end.

"Sir, I think you're supposed to be here right now." I'm swearing and beyond horror that I've overslept the last chance the ENG gave me.

"Powers, let me talk to the ENG." He finds Priests and puts him on the phone.

"Sir, I'm so sorry. I don't know what happened. Oh, FUCK! I cannot believe this. Sir, I know you're angry with me and I have no excuse at all, but … FUCK. I did not mean to do this." The ENG listens, and even though he speaks slowly, I can hear the anger in his voice.

"Alex, I'll deal with you later; right now, Adam has been up all night preparing for the startup and I need you in here as soon as possible." I tell him frantically that I'm on my way, and I throw a few pairs of clean underwear into a bag and run for my car in the humid Guam night. There's a slight wind, but no stars. Thick clouds cover the island, only allowing faint patches of moonlight through. The night fits my mood as I set a new speed record on the empty Marine Drive and park my car on the base at Sierra pier, opposite Polaris Point but closer to the Guam shipyard. The important units get to berth at Polaris Point, but the less favored units are at Sierra, where the crew must walk a quarter mile to get to the ship. I run down the pier, adrenaline still driving my every mood. I arrive, sweaty, embarrassed, and gasping, at the ENG's stateroom.

He seems to be saving his explosion for later. He quickly brings me up to speed for the startup brief. I've studied and prepared, so the briefing at 0300 is not a complete disaster, though the ENG is clearly annoyed with me to the point of exasperation. The watch team heads back to the engine room, and he turns to me and says, "Mr. Fleming, get back there and get this plant operating. If your delay causes the underway to be late even five minutes, then I will make sure you're off this ship for good." I practically run back to the ER and take the watch to complete the startup. I'm on watch for eight hours until the plant is self-sustaining. I am relieved and sleep in my sweaty clothes on top of my blanket for a few hours. I wake up and see Adam Johnson walk into the 9-man. I groggily ask what's going on and he tells me that a squadron monitor has found a leaking oil sight glass that'll prevent us from getting underway. I ask how much the sight glass is leaking, and Adam tells me three drops per hour. I'm puzzled, but I shrug and return to the ER to shut down the reactor and reverse all the work from the morning.

The squadron monitor has convinced the Commodore that this small leak is indicative of a larger problem with attention to detail on our ship and we shouldn't be allowed to get underway. The reactor is shut down and I find myself at 2200 volunteering to write a message for an officer who's already left the ship. I've been working since 0300 with a two-hour nap, and I'm operating on caffeine alone. The Commodore has mandated the message, and both the CO and ENG want to send it just to get the squadron off our backs.

I research and write a message entirely outside of my job and division that takes me until 0100. When it's over and transmitted, the ENG and I collapse into chairs in his stateroom and just sit, staring at the wall. After a few quiet moments, he begins to talk to me, not making eye contact.

"Alex, you fucked up today, big time. I had to convince the Captain even to let you keep standing watch. I appreciate the hard work you did on the startup and shutdown and for staying around to write this message. You helped me out a lot when it wasn't your division, and for that, you get a stay of execution. You're still on thin ice, but I know that you're taking this all too seriously and letting it kill you. I told you a year ago that this is not personal, but you're taking it that way.

"The XO wrote you an award for your mining performance and your excellent tactical computer operation, but the Captain tore it up. He's never going to award a guy who keeps screwing up Rig for Dive. I don't think he's going to ever re-qualify you, and now you are getting close to your twelve months onboard. You need to fix whatever problems you have and recover from this; otherwise, the failures you've experienced so far will only be a preview of the pain to come. Do you understand?"

He's right, and I only nod. I live all my waking hours on this submarine, and I don't understand how I shouldn't take it personally. I'm too tired to argue, and I leave the stateroom. It's too late to go home, and I crawl into my rack without undressing. I fall asleep instantly, but my dreams are bleak and disturbing.

Chapter 6: Hitting Rock Bottom

The Captain's discretionary time at sea is cancelled. The morning after our aborted underway, we have a meeting of all the crew on the pier, called "quarters on the pier." It has to be done on the pier because nowhere on the ship can we fit all the crew within sight of each other. It's a damp and cloudy morning, and the crew waits at attention as the Captain walks up the brow in his odd manner. The XO explains that some material failures have kept us in port, and we're going to take advantage of this to start the repair period early. We're scheduled to have four weeks in port for maintenance, repairs, and a break from the busy five months early in the year. It's easy to tell that the CO is disappointed, but the crew is very happy at the prospect of not going to sea.

After quarters, I'm promoted to Lieutenant Junior Grade in the wardroom. There's no flexibility or individual adjustment for this; it happens automatically for officers who've been commissioned for two years. The Captain gives me my oath of office in the Wardroom with all the officers present, and Juan cuts my Ensign insignia off my collars, to be replaced by the small silver bars. I can't help but think that the CO would not be promoting me if he had the choice. My change of rank means it's time to write me a fitness report.

The Navy has a very careful way of evaluating all levels of personnel performance. Your "reporting senior" at each command evaluates you from the moment you enter the service until the day you depart. First class petty officers and below get their performance recorded on an Evaluation, and Officers and Chiefs get Fitness Reports (Fitreps). Fitreps happen every year, with a counseling session at six months to tell you how you're doing. Fitreps and Evals also happen after promotions, before transfers, and when there's a change of reporting senior for officers. This means that, whenever a new Captain comes onboard, all officers get Fitreps from the outgoing CO and start again.

Fitreps have a number of informational blocks that describe the member being evaluated. Though these blocks seem trivial, they can be a deciding factor in officer promotions much later in career progress. An officer must have a Fitrep or be on leave for every day in the Naval service, and any gaps can be a serious pain in the ass to fill in later. The meat of the Fitrep is in the following sections: command employment/achievements, primary/collateral/watchstanding duties, performance traits, and comments on performance.

The first two sections are lists of jobs and accomplishments, but the last portions are where the form gets interesting. Each person in the military is given a 1.0-5.0 number grade on these performance traits:

1) PROFESSIONAL EXPERTISE – Professional knowledge, proficiency, and qualification.

2) COMMAND CLIMATE/EQUAL OPPORTUNITY – Contributing to growth and development, human worth, and community.

3) MILITARY BEARING/CHARACTER – Appearance, conduct, physical fitness, and adherence to Navy core values.

4) TEAMWORK – Contributions toward team building and team results.

5) MISSION ACCOMPLISHMENT AND INITIATIVE – Taking initiative, planning/prioritizing, and achieving mission.

6) LEADERSHIP – Organizing, motivating, and developing others to accomplish goals.

7) TACTICAL PERFORMANCE – Basic and tactical employment of weapons systems.

People get grades in each area; 1.0 is Below Standards, 2.0 is progressing, 3.0 is Meets Standards, 4.0 is Above Standards, and 5.0 is Greatly Exceeds Standards. The overall point average is always referenced to the individual reporting senior. So when I get a Fitrep as a Lieutenant Junior Grade, my numbers are compared to the summary group average made up of every Lieutenant Junior Grade that Commander Lovpock has ever evaluated.

I sit down in the CO's stateroom for my performance review, feeling sweaty and apprehensive. I've reached the point that I avoid the CO whenever possible, so this is actually the first time I've seen him in days. I'm here to get a Fitrep but also to be presented with my first Letter of Instruction for substandard performance. He shows me my Fitrep first. I've been given ratings of 3.0 in all areas. The comments section is carefully worded to be benign:

Ensign Fleming, a typically effective and improving junior officer, is well on his way toward full qualification as a submarine officer. Specific accomplishments include:

-During the ship's Mine Certification, his operational expertise and thorough understanding of all aspects of offensive mining were key to the ship's strong performance during a simulated wartime scenario.

-As the ship's Diving Supervisor, he improved command scuba dive reporting by improving the quality and comprehensiveness of the command smooth log.

-As Reactor Controls Assistant, he contributed to the continued safe operation of the reactor by making strong recommendations to the Chain of Command when confronted with numerous other Reactor Instrumentation troubleshooting scenarios. Ensign Fleming's mastery of nuclear maintenance and communications associated with reporting reactor plant problems greatly enhanced the ship's ability to discuss technical problems to off-hull support agencies in an effective and timely manner.

Ensign Fleming has a strong work ethic and a desire to learn. As his leadership abilities catch up with his tactical and technical competency, Ensign Fleming will become a key member of my wardroom.

I sit reading and I understand what it means. I'm actually surprised it's not worse, and I understand that the code of Fitreps is what is not said. "Typically effective" means sometimes I'm not effective at all. The phrase "leadership abilities catch up" means that my leadership abilities are far below where they need to be. When the report says I "will become a key member of my wardroom," the Navy understands that, on a ship with fifteen officers, everyone is a key member of the wardroom; if you're not, then something's wrong. The straight 3.0 marks are given to conserve my career in my first evaluation, but I'm sure they don't reflect the Captain's real views.

"Mr. Fleming, this Fitrep is one way of describing your performance and the good things you've done onboard. This Letter of Instruction describes another viewpoint on your efforts, and I think it's closer to the truth. I don't want to ruin your chances for promotion, so I'm going to file this Fitrep. But I want you to read this letter and look at it as your actual evaluation." He hands me the letter after I sign my Fitrep.

11 JUN 03
From: Commanding Officer, USS San Francisco
To: Lieutenant Junior Grade Alexander C. Fleming, USN

Subj: Letter of Instruction

1. Your professional growth and qualification progress as a Submarine Warfare Officer and Engineering Officer of the Watch/Engineering Duty Officer have been substandard. The following deficiencies have been noted in your performance:

- Poor military bearing, as manifested by frequent tardiness for duty, training, and scheduled meetings.
- Lack of sensitivity toward Rig for Dive, the most fundamental procedure to the safe operation of a submarine submerged, as manifested by two Rig for Dive valves being discovered out of position for which you acted as second checker.
- Poor leadership, as demonstrated by informal demeanor toward enlisted personnel both on and off duty, which at times has bordered on fraternization.
- Inadequate supervisory control of your watch team as a watch officer. Frequently, you have asked questions, rather than give orders and firm direction to members of your duty section, thereby creating an environment in which you cannot succeed in discharging your responsibilities.

2. In order to assist you in improving your work as a Submarine Officer and Nuclear Propulsion Plant Supervisor, I direct you to complete the following actions by the dates specified:

a. Show up early or on time for duty, training, and scheduled meetings effective immediately

b. Assemble all Pacific Fleet Tactical Readiness Exam comments regarding Rig for Dive from the examinations administered in the past year. Conduct a 100% audit of our own Rig for Dive program against these deficiencies. Assist the Diving Officer in remedying these deficiencies as discovered. Submit a written report of your findings and recommend corrective actions to the CO via the Chain of Command no later than 10 July 2003.

c. Develop a tickler for administrative requirements and other divisional responsibilities associated with being Reactor Controls Assistant. Submit a comprehensive tickler to the ENG by 21 Jun 2003. Enforce higher standards in the discharge of your responsibilities effective immediately.

d. Desist from informal behavior toward enlisted personnel effective immediately.

e. As an upgrade for your informal watchstanding practices, stand at least eight additional SDO under instruction watches as directed by the Senior Watch Officer during the 3A2 availability. This will upgrade your watchstanding practices by allowing you the opportunity to learn proper watch team control from more senior, fully qualified officers.

3. These requirements constitute the bare minimum necessary to improve your professional performance as a Submarine Warfare Officer onboard USS San Francisco. Furthermore, meeting these requirements will elevate your performance to a level consistent with that of your peers. However, failure to meet these requirements may jeopardize your potential to succeed as a junior officer.

4. Individuals in your chain of command are always ready to assist you or provide additional guidance. Request help from myself, the Executive Officer, the Department Heads, or your fully qualified peers whenever you need it.

5. This letter is non-punitive in nature and is addressed to you as a corrective measure. It does not become part of your official record. You are advised, however, that failure to comply with the requirements outlined above could result in further administrative or disciplinary actions.

P.A. LOVPOCK

The sickening feeling is back in the pit of my stomach, but now it's overcome by the exhaustion I feel. The meeting ends quickly with the same repeated warnings and expressions of disappointment. I spend a few moments rereading the LOI, but then I put it away and leave the ship for the day. I feel like I haven't slept in a year and I smell like a locker room.

The cancelled underway puts us into the first long maintenance availability in Guam, and it's also the longest period in port for six months. Despite the billions of dollars spent on submarines, they are by no means self-sufficient. The crew of a submarine can only support a certain level of repairs and maintenance; anything beyond that requires the support of a higher-level maintenance activity. The problem is that Guam has no intermediate maintenance activity, so we have to deal with a number of possible solutions depending on the problem. The Frank Cable can provide a great deal of support except on the nuclear and large machine work fronts. Guam Shipyard is an independent organization that can do large-scale non-nuclear work, but the quality of their product is low. Any other repairs require a fly-away team to be shipped in with all their equipment from the Pearl Harbor Naval Shipyard, which is hilariously expensive in terms of labor and transportation.

The lack of a maintenance activity means that the Navy look at every way possible to push repairs to a lower level and avoid sending fly-away teams. The squadron is responsible for deciding what jobs we can do ourselves and which jobs we really need help for, and this puts our experienced workers in unique situations. We are discover that the mail and technical publications that update all our records are not yet being forwarded to Guam, or they're coming very slowly. The day before the availability is supposed to start, we receive fourteen inches of documents with technical manuals, updates, changes, and other material instructions. We simultaneously start to get messages asking us why we haven't reported completion of the actions directed in the mail we just got. Between the squadron and the Pacific Fleet, it's clear that the bugs haven't been worked out of this system.

The main work we have to do in the ER is a number of alterations to the plant to meet new standards. Nuclear reactors are by no means static pieces of equipment, and as the Navy finds problems, the engineers design changes to solve the problem and then send instructions to the boats on how to make the changes. We're frustrated because some of these changes have existed for a year, and the ENG from the shipyard didn't get them done in Norfolk. He saved a pile of alterations to be done "at some later time" when he didn't have to worry about it. Our first priority is clearing these off our plate so we can relax for some of the time in port.

I'm standing every third day duty EDO rotation with Vasquez and Hoover. The schedule is pretty intense because you have twenty-four hours on duty, then a workday, then one night at home, another work day, and then you have to get up at 0400 the following day to start duty again. Three section also means that your weekends are demolished at least three weeks of the month by having Friday, Saturday, or Sunday duty. Saturday is by far the worst day to have duty because you never get to sleep late at all. Friday and Sunday are bad but not horrible because you can go out one night and sleep in one morning.

Duty officers in maintenance availability periods live a life of work control problems and solutions. Submarines at sea generally operate as intended with all safety features and redundancies in place. When we go into port, we begin to do work that requires plant manipulation into abnormal conditions where things don't respond the same way. These abnormal conditions mean that duty officers have to take more time doing everything to ensure that safety is maintained and that everybody understands what's going on. These goals are accomplished by a system of danger tags and work authorization forms to control the isolation boundaries and initial conditions for every single job in the plant. When we add high temperature systems, steam, high-pressure fluids, hydraulics, air, radiological control, refrigerant, seawater, and high voltage electricity, I can see how the situation becomes complicated. The consequences for mistakes are not schedule delays but lives and equipment damage.

I'm beginning to see that Matt Priests is right; setting standards and holding them is the only way to succeed as an officer. The relaxed and trusting attitude I had maintained at sea isn't working to keep duty section evolutions going, so I try to ramp up my intensity. I immediately discover it's a lot easier to set high standards and then lower them than it is to set low standards and then raise them. I meet resistance and pressure from both above and below me in the chain of command. The enlisted guys know my situation as well as the officers since there are no secrets on a submarine, and some of them take advantage of my failures to get what they want. I don't want to take these people to the ENG for discipline because I'd be seen as a puppet that doesn't protect his people and whatever small amount of credibility I still have would disappear.

I decide to focus on two things: 1) I will try not to be disqualified. 2) I will try to protect my people from the insanity going on above them between the ENG and squadron. This mission is tough for a person playing catch-up all the time, but I have some help from the Chiefs. Chief Harbin tells me he knows I have a good heart; I just need to listen to my Engineering Duty Petty Officers and they'll try to keep me out of trouble. I seek advice from all the officers on how to move forward and get mixed advice, most of which is impossible from the position in which I find myself. The ENG takes me into his stateroom a few days after my meeting with the Captain to give me a warning.

"Alex, I want you to know that one LOI can go away. But the Captain is concerned about your performance, and you're on very thin ice. I shouldn't even be telling you this, but I want you to understand what's going on. I wrote that LOI, and I've been directed to begin making a detailed record of your performance deficiencies from day to day. The only way to get rid of an officer for good is by having a clear, documented record of repeated failures. You're too expensive to fire straight out, or you'd probably be gone already. When the Captain goes to the Commodore to get you off the ship, he has to have the paperwork to back it up. I've been instructed to create that paperwork.

"Alex, you know this is not personal, right? You need to get your act together or you're going to be off this ship. I'll be watching you closely, and I'm not the only one." I nod soundlessly in reply to Matt, and I'm even more scared than before.

The Captain is taking advantage of this period in port to take his family to Australia, leaving the XO acting while he is gone. I dedicate myself to studying and improving my knowledge. I swear that I won't leave the boat until all my corrective actions are complete. This lasts three days before I'm completely exhausted and burned out since I never sleep well on the submarine. I decide to spend a night at home and then return with a vengeance the following day. The major alteration of the availability will be complete soon, and the ENG is pouring all his attention into getting it done as soon as possible. M-Div is working around the clock with their new Chief and new division officer, Adam Johnson, to complete the upgrade. Tension is high on all fronts.

It's Thursday afternoon and I've been on the boat for four days straight. Even the ENG tells me I need to head home for a while as he goes back to the ER for the retest of the new alteration. I'm too tired even to be happy at the prospect of leaving. I nearly nod off on the road at 1300 in bright sunlight, and I shower and collapse on my bed. I jerk awake at 1800 and rush to put my clothes back on and head to work. I have duty in the morning, and it's a lot harder to be late waking up when you're already on the ship. I stop at the Old Hagatna Grill for a steak on the way to work, marveling at the people relaxing and talking like they enjoy their jobs. The one good part of living on the ship is that I have plenty of money to spare.

I get back to Polaris Point at 1930, and as I park my car in the broken lot that still looks like a junkyard, I see Commander Ginda walking toward the ship. I glance around the parking lot and see a lot of very senior parking places filled for our ship, the squadron, and the tender. This can't be good; the only reason for this many people to gather at work is that something bad has happened. I grab my bag and head down to the ship. As I walk past the topside watch, I ask what's going on, and he replies, "I don't know, sir; something back aft. Everybody is here." I hurry across the brow, nearly slipping off the slick black surface of the ship into the water. I hear yelling and screaming as I come down the ladder into the command passageway. Commander Ginda is on my left and the XO on my right; the XO has just finished saying something with an excited voice, and Commander Ginda turns and yells, "XO, I don't care what you think. RIGHT NOW, YOU DO NOT HAVE THE SITUATION UNDER CONTROL!" I've never heard the squadron deputy this angry in public, and I'm stuck in a t-shirt, shorts, and Tevas between these two angry men. I look aft to see the WEPS, who's on duty, standing in the CO's stateroom wearing a pair of headphones. It appears that the WEPS is manning Damage Control Central alone because no other officers are onboard. The XO looks at me, and I ask where he needs me. He glances at my outfit and apparently decides I don't need to change.

"Go relieve the WEPS in DC Central." He shoulders past me into his stateroom, following Commander Ginda. I turn and walk to the Captain's room. WEPS gives me the headphones, which are monitoring the reporting circuits for the casualty. I begin to take reports as he describes what's happened on a large grease board with a layout of the whole ship. This board has drawings and the current status of everything that is wrong. The summary takes about a minute.

"... And there are no injured personnel. The only assistance is coming from the Frank Cable, who's sending a team of people down to help us out. Do you have any questions?"

"I have no questions. I relieve you," I reply.

"I stand relieved; now I have to go make about a million phone calls." The Duty Officer is not supposed to be held down anywhere to maintain his ability to respond to casualties. I find myself alone, in civilian clothes, manning a set of phones at 2000. I marvel at the strangeness of my job as I take reports. The man in charge of DCC is supposed to keep the status board up to date, back up the guys on the scene with the procedure, and make 1MC announcements to keep the whole ship up to date on the situation. I frantically keep up with everything going on, but it is clear we're in the very early stages of a problem we don't understand. I can hear the ENG yelling and screaming in Maneuvering over the phones, so I try to help him in any way I can.

The clock rolls to 2200 and I'm still the man in charge. Officers flood onboard until we have all the officers, most of the chiefs, and almost the entire engineering department. Finally, Juan comes in uniform to relieve me. I usually get more joking and crap from him, but he's all business tonight. I run down to the 9-man to change into uniform and run into the ENG in the passageway. He looks harried and exhausted and he's wearing someone else's jumpsuit. He stares at me blankly for a moment.

"Alex... I'm glad you're here. I need you to change and relieve Adam back aft. We're going to have a critique right now. Make sure you meet with the man in charge on each level from the Frank Cable before you turn over." He pauses and takes my shoulder.

"Alex, I need you to hold it together back there; this is a highly abnormal condition. Be careful." His eyes drill into me with desperation.

"Aye, sir. I'll hold down the fort," I say. I go back to relieve the watch. Adam looks worse than the ENG when I finally make it to Maneuvering. He gives me the whole story about the failure during the retest of the alteration. The situation is under control, but as the Mechanical Division Officer, he's responsible for the long-term fix. He's looking at a critique with Commander Ginda in the room, the most horrible thing any officer can imagine. His workers did the work and his Chief was supervising when the problem occurred. I conduct a careful review of all documents and status, since this is the most dangerous time in plant operations – when people think things are over.

I relieve Adam and continue finding problems and trying to fix them. Fifty people are wandering around the engine room trying to help and generally making my job harder. A new Chief is on watch with me, and we discover and combat several problems. A few petty officers choose this time, in front of sailors from another command, to mouth off to me. I correct them loudly and harshly since I can't afford to have any questions about who's in charge or what's going on right now. Several problems we find and fix are things that would normally be a very big deal, but the Chief and I decide between us that the best option is to fix them and keep them off the radar. It's hard enough with one critique going on at 0100, and we want to try to protect the ENG from anything else tonight.

Adam comes back at 0300, and I don't have the heart to ask him about the critique as he relieves me. He just nods and thanks me for covering. I head forward and get the ten-second version: we screwed up. The alteration was done improperly, and our suggestions to fix it quickly and move forward have been squashed. The Captain is flying back from Australia early and the XO has to clear every decision through Commander Ginda until the CO is back on the island. The Commodore will pre-approve all maintenance and evolutions that occur throughout the ship. We're in the nuclear equivalent of a lockdown. I digest the news solemnly and crawl into my rack for a few hours' sleep.

The next day, the squadron makes it clear that we're in for a long haul. Outside monitors happen every few hours on every part of the ship. The work inputs to the Commodore must be prepared and put in very early in the morning, and anything that's not on the list is not done. Squadron Fifteen sees us as their wayward boat that needs as much help as possible. Each monitor watch has ten to fifteen comments for which we have to provide root cause, short-term corrective action, and long-term corrective action. Adam Johnson is working to rebuild a demoralized M-Div to complete this repair, but now the work package is under much higher scrutiny. MM1 Bilbo was one of the supervisors at the time of the work, and he's been removed from watchstanding along with all the other mechanics involved. Adam and his Chief now have to work with their less experienced team to correct the problem.

The longer we stay in port, the more problems we have. We have to start planning for a much longer time than four weeks, and the Pacific Fleet schedule changes to push our mission back three more months. Major incidents are followed by days and days of training, discussions, and retellings to ensure that every single person onboard learns the right lessons. The Captain comes back with the frustration you might expect from a man who has just cut short an Australian vacation. Rumors spread that he and the Commodore had a "you're thin ice" speech not long after his return. Despite the pain, that thought makes me smile.

ENG DEP is working every day of the week, and Adam Johnson is taking it worse than the rest of us. Writing nuclear repair packages is never easy, and with the supervision imposed, he's being pushed to do things perfectly. The pressure of monitor watches begins to take its toll as well. Duty days are like walking on pins and needles where one misstep will get you disqualified. Mistakes are made and the duty rotation worsens.

67

I'm standing aft of Maneuvering one morning when the second squadron monitor of the day comes to me and tells me that a watchstander is doing pushups while on watch in Maneuvering. This is inappropriate, and I'm annoyed that the petty officer in question would even think to do something that stupid in this environment. I know he's dating a girl who works at a nightclub and he stays up until 0400 every day. I've never heard about it before a duty day, but apparently the strain of dating a dancer and drinking every night is getting the better of him. I go into Maneuvering.

"Petty Officer Oden, you cannot do stuff like that. You know what's going on around here right now. What are you thinking?" I'm trying to approach him so he doesn't go on the defensive and shut down.

"Sir, I know, but I'm just trying to stay awake," he replies, and he looks sincere enough. I think hard. I'll talk about it with his Chief later to reinforce the message.

"Just don't let it happen again," I say, but unfortunately, the squadron monitor has already taken it further than that. The ENG calls a minute later and tells me to have EM2 Oden relieved from watch and disqualified immediately. I acknowledge, and then he orders me to report to his stateroom. I'm braced at attention a few minutes later.

"Mr. Fleming, I'm disappointed in you. Did you not think this was important? When a squadron monitor tells you about a watchstanding problem like that, you tell me IMMEDIATELY. Got that? You are not enforcing standards back there. Why would Oden do this ON WATCH, IN MANEUVERING if he didn't think he could get away with it? What are you doing back there? Are you trying to fuck me? You're trying to fuck me, aren't you? That's what you're going to do. You are pushing the line, Mr. Fleming, and you are pushing me closer to pulling the trigger on you. DISMISSED!" I have rarely seen Matt Priests angrier, and though I understand everything he says, I don't know how to fix it. I seek advice from Craig Litty and Adam Johnson, both of whom are much better natural leaders than I am. They advise me to protect my guys and try to stay under the radar, but I think it may be too late for that.

I get a rare night off after my next duty day, and I decide to go to the strip clubs with a friend of mine, Alan, a Doctor at the Naval Hospital. Alan's wife likes to get him out of the house a few times a week with the boys to keep him happy, and she encourages us to go to strip clubs as long as she gets to hear all about it. I tell him about what's going on, and he is sympathetic, though he doesn't know what to do about it. We're at Vikings, a popular club with a wheel for handcuffing people as part of the act. It's a good night, and I'm only remotely thinking about the evolution brief I have at 0600 the next morning. It's early, about 2300, and we're about to head home when my phone rings.

"Sir, it's Josh Gokart." Petty Officer Gokart is a member of my division, and all of them have my cell phone number in case of an emergency.

"What's going on, Gokart? Are you all right?" I'm immediately worried and I leave the club so I can hear better.

"Sir, I have a big problem and I need your help. We're at the Dungeon, and Crow is passed out on the floor. He's been drinking Red Bull and vodka for seven hours, and I can't move him. The bartender says I need to get him out of here or he's going to call the cops." The Dungeon is a rave club frequented after-hours by the crew. "Sir, I don't have a car with me. Can you come and help us?"

I think for a moment about my letter and fraternization and what the ENG would say, but I stop that thinking as soon as it starts. This is the right thing to do, and I'm glad Gokart called.

"Gokart, keep the bartender calm. I'll be there in a minute." The Dungeon is only five minutes away, and Alan and I find Crow snoring loudly on a couch. Alan examines him and we do a quick stimulus test to make sure he's asleep and not in a coma. He has good pupillary response and responds to stimulus, so we walk him outside to my car and put him in the back. Gokart and I both know the problem.

Crow has had alcohol incidents before, and if the police get him, he'll be in huge trouble that the Navy might not be able to control. Crow also has duty tomorrow and is supposed to be at my evolution brief. I decide to take him to my place, ten minutes away, put him on the couch, and then get him to the boat in the morning and turn him over to his Chief. Alan and I get him to my apartment and I hand him a large glass of water and an empty trash can. His first sign of recovery is profuse vomiting.

I sit up in bed for an hour, wondering if I'm doing the right thing, but Crow is better off on my couch than in a jail cell. 0400 comes quickly and he walks on his own to my car and sleeps again on the drive to the ship. I get him below decks and get caught up in a rush of activity leading to my brief. I haven't had a chance to talk to the M-Div Chief in private, and I want to brief him before anyone else. Crow is not at the briefing, even with my help. As soon as it ends, I hear the ENG yell, "FLEMING, GET IN MY STATEROOM RIGHT NOW!" This can't be good.

I describe what happened and how I found Crow. Apparently, Crow told his Chief, who went immediately to the ENG. The ENG looks at me hard.

"Alex, you could have been the hero today, but you fucked it up. You did the right thing, except you didn't call me and you didn't tell me the instant you got here today. I have a cell phone for a reason. You are not loyal to me. You are more loyal to Crow than you are to me, and that is screwed up. I trust you even less than I did yesterday, if that's possible. Get the hell out of my stateroom." ENG doesn't yell anymore; he just looks at me like I'm a lost cause.

I sit in the 9-man exploding with frustration since I'm sure I did the right thing. The other officers agree with me, but they all say I should've called the ENG earlier. My level of give-a-shit declines even further as the duty days get more painful. It becomes harder and harder for me to talk to the ENG, and I start looking for senior people to ask for help. The one man I admire but haven't been involved with is the NAV. I decide I have to talk to someone, so I wait until a night he's not on duty and call him at home.

I tell the NAV I'm sorry to bother him, but I'm desperate and I hope he will just listen to me. I'm worried that I'm not going to make it, but the ENG just won't let up on me. I'm angry with the ENG because he accuses me of not being loyal, but who inspires more loyalty: the guy who is making my life hell or the one who follows my orders and helps me out as best he can? How can I be loyal to the ENG when he's inflicting more pain on me than I've ever experienced in my life? I begin to break down and my voice cracks as I beg for help. The NAV listens politely and tells me that we all have bad times as a junior officer and that I will make it. He promises to talk to the ENG about my situation and try to communicate some of my feelings.

I talk to my mother about once a week, and I never tell her specifics about what's going down on the boat, but she promptly announces that she's sending my dad to come visit me. I tell her that I'm not going to be able to take leave and entertain him, but she doesn't care. I'm excited to see my father, but it's unfortunate that I won't be able to spend any time with him. He arrives from Phoenix via Tokyo and I put him up in my room while I sleep on an inflatable bed in the living room. My father is a great listener and he patiently absorbs all my venting. He's smart enough to know that my sanity is hanging by a thread and making any demands or assertions will cause me to shut down. I'm standing three-section duty as we try to put the failed alteration back together, so I give him my car and the keys to my apartment. I see him for a few hours at night before collapsing into bed, and he gives me rides to work at 0430 in the morning.

Things on the boat are getting worse, even as Matt Priests assures me nothing is personal and to let it all roll off my shoulders. I have the same problem as before because I spend all my waking hours at the ship; how can I not take it personally? The other officers support me somewhat, but they are also distancing themselves from someone who's had repeated problems. Craig Litty and Adam Johnson are constantly supportive because they're enduring the same pain that I am. Adam has been at work twelve hours a day since the failure rewriting the packages to get the work done. He keeps fighting with a stamina that amazes everybody, though his attitude and optimism suffer. Important evolutions are often assigned a squadron monitor. I get the Squadron Engineer for the performance of reactor control and instrumentation maintenance when my father has been on the island for four days. Powers and Sobeski are the performers, and I'm confident in their ability to get the job done right.

The maintenance starts well, with good formality and efficiency. The squadron monitor is quietly watching from a few feet away. A few steps in, Powers makes a small misstep and pushes a button one too many times. The mistake is easily correctable by backing up through another button push. Powers turns to me.

"Sir, this is not a problem; the manual allows us to manipulate these screens, even though the specific procedure does not say that. The overall technical manual allows us to do this. I intend to back up one step and then continue." Powers is the leading petty officer for my division and the most experienced worker. Chief Harbin trusts his technical expertise, though the Chief is not onboard the ship right now. I consider the pros and cons for a minute, but in the end, I decide to trust Powers' recommendation.

"I concur," I say to Powers, and he continues the procedure. I hear a rustle and turn to see the Squadron Engineer's back as he hurries away. I immediately begin to worry about where he's going, and so does Powers as he looks over my shoulder. We exchange a questioning look, and he recommends that I brief the EDO just in case. I go to Maneuvering and tell Henry what's going on, and he seems satisfied. But a call comes into the space from the ENG.

"Stop all RC division work and have Mr. Fleming report to the Engineer's stateroom." Henry repeats the order and turns to me. I just nod and head forward, I have a strong feeling that the Squadron Engineer has something to do with it. I find the stateroom empty and stand by in the wardroom passageway. After five minutes of waiting, the ENG comes down the passageway and yells, "Mr. Fleming, you are DISQUALIFIED Engineering Officer of the Watch and Engineering Duty Officer. Get a new qual card." I just nod and accept it I am relieved, and I print out blank qualifications cards in a daze. Chief Harbin comes back to the ship to find his division officer, his leading petty officer, and one of his reactor operators all disqualified. He's furious as I tell him what happened. Apparently, the Squadron Engineer walked directly to the CO and told him I was an ineffective supervisor who provided no input at all. The CO made the decision to disqualify Powers, Sobeski, and me before the ENG even got there and long before Chief Harbin returned to the ship. Chief Harbin listens to my story and tells me that he probably would have done the same thing if the environment had not been so insane. He convinces the ENG and CO to re-qualify Sobeski, who had no say in the decision to deviate from procedure.

I leave the ship that afternoon feeling better than I have in months. I breathe deeply in the sunlight and smile easily for the first time in a long time. My Dad picks me up and we head home as I tell him what happened. I'm so relieved not to be standing duty that I'm almost ecstatic. The next day at work, the ENG explains to me that since I'm now disqualified, I'm delinquent and will participate in delinquent study until I complete my requalification. This means extra study from 1900-2100 every night of the week and 0800-1000 on Saturday. I'm only angry because I get to spend even less time with my father, who has traveled 7,000 miles to see me. Any suggestions of postponing delinquent study are met with one of the ENG's favorite phrases: "Alex, every man WILL do his duty for the republic."

I get home at 2200 that night and get to talk to Dad for half an hour before I fall asleep. The next day, we drive around the island for the one day we get to spend together in his ten days on the island. The talk turns inevitably to work, and he gives me his recommendation. He thinks I should find a mentor on the ship and tell him exactly what's going on and what I'm feeling. I know that this won't be the ENG, but I think about the men I admire the most and who appreciate my work, and the XO is the one who comes to mind. We agree that, if things get worse after my disqualification, I'll go to the XO for help.

A few days later...

21 JUN 03
From: Commanding Officer, USS San Francisco
To: Lieutenant Junior Grade Alexander C. Fleming, USN

Subj: LETTER OF INSTRUCTION

Ref: (a) Letter of Instruction dated 11 Jun 03
(b) Requalification program

1. In reference (a), you were advised that your professional growth as a Submarine Warfare Officer has been substandard. Since being issued reference (a), you have demonstrated continued poor performance as a watch officer and as a supervisor. The following deficiencies have been noted in your performance:

- Poor judgment, as manifested by your local consent for Reactor Controls Division maintenance personnel to deviate from the approved procedures without informing watch section personnel and the chain of command on 18 June 2003.

- Habitual inattentiveness, as manifested by your falling asleep in a majority of meetings and training sessions, regardless of the time of day.

2. As a result of these lapses in judgment and performance and your unresponsiveness to prior counseling, you are disqualified Engineering Officer of the Watch and Engineering Duty Officer.

3. To improve your performance as a Submarine Officer and nuclear propulsion plant supervisor, I direct you to complete the following actions in addition to those specified in reference (a):

- Requalify as Engineering Officer of the Watch and Engineering Duty Officer. A requalification program conforming to the minimum requirements of reference (b) will be proposed by the Engineer and approved by me. Your requalification process must be completed no later than 11 July 2003. The proposed requalification program will be achievable within this timeframe.

- Ensure that you obtain adequate rest before reporting for duty and take appropriate measures to ensure your alertness during scheduled meetings and training sessions.

4. These requirements constitute the bare minimum necessary to improve your professional performance as a Submarine Warfare Officer onboard USS San Francisco. Furthermore, continued failure to meet these minimum requirements will compromise my confidence in your abilities to attain qualifications and assume positions of higher responsibility.

5. Individuals in your chain of command are always ready to assist you or provide additional guidance. Request help from your fully qualified peers, the Department Heads, Executive Officer, or myself whenever you need it.

6. This letter is non-punitive in nature and is addressed to you as a corrective measure. It does not become a part of your official record. You are advised, however, that failure to comply with requirements outlined above could result in further administrative or disciplinary actions.
P.A. LOVPOCK

The meeting with the CO to get this letter takes little time and involves very little conversation. I say nothing as the CO presents my second letter. I know its purpose; he now has a very good paper trail to "pull the trigger" and get me off the boat if I do anything else. He probably even has squadron backup after my disastrous monitor watch. I leave as quickly as possible and add the letter to my budding collection.

The delinquent study continues, with added pressure from the other officers since I've made the watchbill worse for everybody. The ENG makes an Officer Delinquent Study Binder to log my extra hours, which Juan throws across the room as soon as he sees it.

"Officers do not need that shit. You get ordered to do hours, you do them." Juan is disgusted that the ship and wardroom have come to this. I continue my study after my dad leaves, so now I have a life of coming to work at 0600 and leaving at 2100 during the week.

The weekend is my first free weekend in almost a month since I no longer have to stand duty. I'm excited to run the Hash and get my mind off the insanity of the ship. Saturday morning study goes by quickly and I head home to relax and unwind. I take a nice nap and then get my dirty clothes ready for running in the jungle. I drive down to the PDN building and take simple joy in joking with people not in the Navy. The map is posted and I throw my bag into a friend's truck for the trip to the box at the Ordot dump. I check that my car is locked and see my phone ringing just as I close the door. It's an UNKNOWN number, probably just my mother calling to tell me Dad got home. I answer.

"Mr. Fleming, this is the ENG. We've had a problem on the boat with RC division, and I need you to come down here right away to draft a message." My jaw drops and I wave for my friends to go ahead, forgetting about my bag. Anger fills me quickly as I try to think of some legitimate excuse.

"Sir, I ..." He cuts me off.

"Fleming, I don't care what you have going on. You are not standing duty. This is your job. Suck it up and come to the boat right now." There's nothing I can say to that.

"Yes, sir." I'm insane with rage as I get into my car and drive away from the Hash group. I get to the boat in ten minutes and change as fast as I can. I gather all the books and manuals and have Chief Harbin explain the problem. The message writing and referencing takes three hours, and I stay angry. I finally finish and get the message transmitted off the ship. Matt Priests offers me a "thank you" that I don't acknowledge as I walk out the door. It's dark and I've missed the entire Hash run, the only thing that gives me joy on this island.

The clouds look ominous and rain begins to fall as it only can on a tropical island. My full-sized Ford Bronco makes good headway until the rain becomes so heavy that I can't see three car-lengths in front of me. The water thunders down on the metal roof of my car until I can barely hear myself swearing in frustration. The torrential downpour is like nothing I've ever seen, but even the awe does not heal my anger at the Navy. I creep at 30 miles per hour on Marine Drive because I can't see anyone, even with the high beams on. I remember my bag in the back of the Hash truck and yell, taking a detour.

I'm mad at myself, at the boat, at the Captain, at Matt Priests, and at everyone who ever supported me entering the submarine force. I'm most angry with myself for failing so miserably. I climb up a steep hill, heading for the Ordot dump in the center of the island. I pass the access road to the Leo Palace Resort on my way to where I know the Hash cars are parked. I speed up as the rain lightens even as tears of anger fill my eyes.

I'm going 45 mph when my truck hits a bump and I realize that the road has become dirt, really mud. The slide starts to the left, and I overcorrect, causing the car to spin right and slide down the road sideways. The spin happens so fast that I barely understand what's going on until I see the flash of a concrete pole out of my left eye. I have just enough time to register the obstacle before my car slams into it at the driver's side door. The last thing I remember is the surreal sight of the car door crumpling inward and hitting my left leg.

Chapter 7: Strange Luck

The first thing I see when I regain consciousness is graffiti. I'm still in the driver's seat, but the door is crumpled into my side and my head is resting on the concrete pole that the car hit. The rain is still coming down and dripping from the concrete onto my forehead. I taste the copper tang of blood in my mouth and slowly begin to move my limbs to see if anything is wrong. My left leg isn't moving right, and it's jammed against the bent door. I feel shards of glass in the bottom of my feet, and sticky blood is soaking my Tevas. I sit for a while and determine that I can move the rest of my limbs. I'm on a dark, muddy road with no other cars around.

I pull myself across the seat and open the passenger door. The more I move my left foot, the more it hurts. I try to put weight on it, but knives shoot up my leg and I have to hop on one foot around the car to see where I am. I've ruined the driver's side door, the steering column, and the console, but the car appears to be straight otherwise. My front wheels are in a ditch with the rear of the car extending into the center of the road. I get on my cell and call Mike Vasquez, who sounds asleep but agrees to come help me. I'm exhausted and dizzy from my first hop around the vehicle, and it's still raining like crazy. I sit back down in the car and shut my eyes until Mike's truck comes down the road. He attaches his towing gear to my back bumper and I start my car back up, surprised that it'll still run. We get my car out of the ditch and then I drive, very unsteadily, back up to the asphalt. Something is seriously wrong with the steering system and front end, but I get onto the shoulder and turn off the car. I grab my bag and lock what's left of the doors so Mike can take me to the Naval Hospital.

I call the Guam Police as I get into Mike's truck and describe what's happened and where. They ask me if I'm going to the hospital, and I say yes. The dispatcher tells me to call the police when I get back to the car the next day and they'll come out and take the report then. I'm shocked, but this is pretty average for the Guam PD, so I shrug and end the call. Mike laughs and shakes his head when I tell him – typical Guam. We come down the hill into Agana and then climb a steep road onto a coral cliff overlooking the ocean. The sprawling building with mold stains on the walls is the Guam Naval Hospital Complex, one of the largest military medical facilities on this side of the Pacific Ocean.

Guam has two hospitals. The Naval Hospital serves all military personnel and dependents along with veterans and retirees. The Guam Memorial Hospital (GMH) in Tamuning is the only major medical facility available to the general public of Guam, but it's not an accredited facility. GMH is constantly being investigated for fraud, loss of controlled medications, and malpractice. The government of Guam pours money into the facility to no avail, and the quality of doctors and patient care is extremely low.

People on the island will find any way possible to get care at the Naval Hospital, but the only non-military personnel treated are emergency trauma victims. Even the Naval Hospital is on the outer edges of American medical care, with a number of specialties, such as neurosurgery, that have no doctors at all. Only two or three attending physicians are available in most other fields and any serious case must be evacuated to the Tripler Army Medical Center on Oahu on a seven-hour Air Force flight. It's a grueling process that sometimes risks further destabilization of the patient in the air.

I hop on one foot into the ER at 2200 and I'm seen quickly. A young nurse with bright green eyes tells me that the real busy time doesn't start until the bars close at 0200. I'm diagnosed with a bad sprain after the shards of glass are picked out of my foot. The X-ray shows no break, but I'm put in an air splint and given a pair of crutches. I can't walk on it for at least seven days, and I have to come in for a follow-up on Monday. I'm warned that it's going to hurt really badly, which I can see from the swelling that's already doubled the size of my foot. The 1,000 mg Motrin tablets will allow me to sleep, but I can only take one twice a day. Mike takes me home to my apartment and I collapse onto my bed into an exhausted sleep. My life is in shambles, but I'll deal with it in the morning.

I wake up several times during the night, trying to find a position where my foot will stop throbbing. I get up in the morning and discover the joys of being unable to stand up at all. I limp to the bathroom and get in the tub, holding my leg still as I fill the tub with all the hot water I can get. I crouch awkwardly and toss water over my back and face, like I'm trying to make it rain. I don't feel clean at all. After a one-legged breakfast, I get to the couch, exhausted already, and put my leg up. It's time to call the boat. I dial the number and hear Henry's voice.

"Unit Eleven Duty Officer. This is a non-secure line; may I help you, sir or ma'am?" He speaks as fast as he can, our habit on duty.

"Hey, man, it's Fleming," I say, and I explain the car accident, stressing that alcohol was not involved. This is a big deal because we've had a number of alcohol-related incidents lately and the powers that be are very sensitive. Henry is shocked; a car accident is something people like to know about immediately. I tell him my ankle is sprained and I won't be able to come down to the boat for a while.

I still have to come to work on Monday, crutching in uniform. I'm sweating through my khakis before I even get to my car in the apartment parking lot. I'm not allowed on the ship, so I sit on a concrete pylon on the pier, waiting for instructions. The NAV is so furious that I can't stand duty that he doesn't even speak to me as he walks past because there are now only six officers to cover forward and aft. Everyone is standing three section duty rotations. NAV sends up random copying and bitch work for me to do on the pier. His stated intentions are to make me sit on my concrete pylon doing paperwork outside all week long while I can't come onboard. I'm sweating like crazy at noon in the Guam sun, and I ask one of the other officers to bring me a blank leave chit. I have plenty of days since I haven't taken any leave since arriving onboard. My chit is approved in 30 minutes and Craig signs me out. I'm sunburned and in pain as I depart on leave and crutch my way to my crappy rental car. I'm so tired from sweating in uniform on the pier that I collapse onto the couch and take a Motrin three hours early. My foot is huge, purple, and throbbing.

The next four days give me a great deal of time to sit on the couch. I settle into a position that lets me put my foot up high and gives me a view out the window. The most shocking thing I realize is how long it's been since I last saw midday in my apartment. I re-read the entire *Ender's Game* series, the Harry Potter series, all Tom Clancy's books, and everything else in my apartment. I read and I sleep, praying for my foot to heal.

I think a lot about my situation and the Navy. I have a decision to make. My career is at the point where all I have to do is stop working and I'll be kicked off the boat. I don't want to be in the Navy anymore; it has turned from a dream into a nightmare, and there is a way out. I have enough stock and savings that I can cash everything out and end up with about $20,000. I can buy a plane ticket to Australia and then fly there with only a backpack. Then I can destroy all my documents and credit cards when I get to Cairns and disappear into the outback. The cash will get me anywhere in the world as a passenger on a shady merchant ship, I can handle the lack of a passport with bribes, and all I need to do is end up in a non-extradition treaty country with no ID and I'll never be in the Navy again. The only thing I have to accept with this option is that I'll never be able to return to America. I don't know if I'm willing to accept that.

There is another option. I can keep working and slug it out. I want to do well, despite everything that's happened. I can go to work, do my job, pray for luck and execute the orders I'm given the best way I know how. This is the hard way because I'm already in a deep hole, but it's the only way I'll feel honorable. I will not shame myself or my family by running away. I look out at the sky and the ocean and decide that I'm going to finish my time on the San Francisco, no matter the outcome. I'm going to complete my obligation to the Navy in whatever way they'll let me. The resolution gives me strength and makes the pain in my foot slightly more bearable.

My car is totaled. The cost of repairing the steering column on a 1992 Bronco is more than the market value of the car. Though I'm tempted to buy a very nice, expensive SUV, I also want to leave the Navy as soon as possible. My parents convince me that getting a used Nissan Sentra is the way to minimize future cash flow with car payments during grad school. I use my credit card to purchase the used white Sentra with no

74

financing. I turn in my $20-a-day rental and continue my sleeping and reading on the couch. I extend my leave three days as the damage in my foot slowly heals. The skin is so swollen that the place where my ankle bends pushes out in a long blister to relieve the pressure. It's still swollen when I strap my boots back on and limp down to the boat. I could milk the injury a few days longer, but I have duty and I don't want to screw the other officers any more than absolutely required.

Other officers are having a tough time in Guam as well, and this is taking a toll on the families. Micah Stevens' wife has become ill, and he has to leave the boat to take care of her at a hospital back on the mainland. Guam is an overseas station where service members and their families lack advanced medical care. Sick family members cause people to be de-screened from overseas eligibility, and they have to go back to the continental U.S. I visit him in the Naval Hospital one day and we talk about my life since he's my best friend and counselor onboard the ship. As we walk the concrete paths outside the building, he tells me that he has faith in my abilities and I should ignore all my tormentors and continue to try my hardest. I'm sad about him leaving because now Martin Sprocket is the Ship's Diving Officer, and I'm about to need a major checkout from him. I ask Micah to sign off my checkout before he leaves and spare me from having to deal with Martin, who will use the situation to torture me. Micah agrees because he doesn't want to give Sprocket the satisfaction of having power over me again, and he signs my card while I'm on leave.

The nightmare on the boat continues as the punishments are handed out for the first failure with the alteration. The Mechanic Chief and every single person who worked on the job are taken to Captain's Mast and given a reprimand. MM1 Bilbo takes the brunt of the punishment since he was the quality assurance supervisor for the procedure. He is reduced to MM2 and placed on thirty days restriction; his terminal leave is cancelled, as is a trip to Australia. He will spend the rest of his time in the Navy confined to the submarine. More than one person thinks there is a great inequity in the amount of punishment Bilbo receives. Rumors spread that there was drama and disagreement between Bilbo and the CO during the mast that led to the increased punishment. I hear the whole story when Mike calls and tells me to come in and get ready to stand duty.

I have to take my requalification exam, and in my absence, I've been moved to another division. The CO and ENG tell me that I need to work on my leadership skills in the Electrical Division, giving Mike Vasquez responsibility for Reactor Controls Division. The electrical chief is an EMC named Ed Gradwell, who is very stubborn and extremely experienced. The ENG tells me that Chief Gradwell's new job is to fix me as an officer, and I would be wise to listen to everything he says. Our "quick" six-week availability has turned into an extended work period with no end in sight. Every time we try to get the alteration finished, another small problem arises. Each small problem means the work package must be changed and approved by the whole chain of command and people off the ship. The package approval process takes another week for each new iteration, and we've already done the job four times. Adam Johnson faces writing and revising each package, and he has to do this with the most junior members of his division because all the senior people are under punishment and disqualified. Luckily, two junior petty officers named Devon and Sidson step up and fill the void.

The crew is happy to be home, but the ship is making it all so painful with material failures and schedule changes that many would rather be out to sea. I have come to realize that life is simpler at sea. You don't have to deal with wives, girlfriends, finances, paychecks, alcohol, family, or any other things. At sea, you do your job the best you can and then sleep. You can watch movies and interesting things happen, but mostly the routine is steady. Proficiency comes over time, and you get into a rhythm. In-port time doesn't give nearly the satisfaction, but the XO announces that we will be starting drill days every Monday and Friday at 0500. This means the whole crew will have to muster at 0445 and station underway watches to practice being at sea.

These early mornings make everyone resent work even more. All we want is to get fixed and go to sea. The "bastard child" feeling is coming from squadron at incredible volume, and it's clear they have no interest in helping us. They come down to do their monitors and show how conscientious they are, but really they just want to find anything wrong. It doesn't help when the other ship in the squadron, the City of Corpus Christi, goes on its first mission. We begin to refer to the squadron as Anti-Submarine Squadron Fifteen in recognition of the pain they inject in our lives on a daily basis and their apparent incompetence.

I begin to stand duty again, but my style has changed. My early days as a duty officer were hallmarked by approving everything and trusting petty officers beyond what was healthy. My resulting pain has taught me to question everything. I take this a step further by exhaustively reviewing every single book and requirement put in front of me. I call the ENG to resolve even the most minor question, and if I find any problem, I stop the work immediately. This knee-jerk response earns me the name "Work Stoppage Machine" and divisional work managers begin to schedule work around my duty days because they know I'm so petrified of failing that I won't take any risks at all. The Chiefs understand my viewpoint, but they express flashes of emotion when they're trying to get important things done that happen to fall on my duty days.

Chief Gradwell's style infuriates me and fascinates me at the same time. He corrects me constantly and is quick to tell me when I'm being idiotic. He tells me that my best talent is writing messages, briefing the ENG and CO, and leaving him to do the actual technical work. EM1 Robinson is my leading petty officer, and he has the devotion and respect of the whole division. We fall into a routine where I handle paperwork and message writing, the Chief handles the technical problems and troubleshooting, and EM1 handles the day-to-day personnel management and work tasking.

Chief Gradwell also teaches me about communication and when officers are just better off dragging the Chief along with them. He lectures me about unclear communication and how it dooms many junior officers to failure.

"Sir, you just can't do that. You listen to me, you hear what you want to hear, and then you go tell the ENG something completely wrong. He asks you questions and you make assumptions. Those assumptions are briefed to the CO, and then when something else happens, everyone is confused. It's like the telephone game you played in grade school. I say 'cow,' and then you go to the ENG and say, 'The caribou killed the ham sandwich on Tuesday.' You can see how this gets annoying for me. So this is going to be our code. Whenever you're not listening to me and I need you to focus on what I'm saying, I'm just going to say, 'The caribou killed the ham sandwich on Tuesday.'"

Though his attitude and abruptness sometimes anger me, I can't help but like Chief Gradwell. I listen to him and ask him questions about almost every situation I encounter. Other petty officers begin to seek out Gradwell when I'm doing something boneheaded and need to be corrected. We spend so much time together that we don't even have to talk anymore, and he is so incredibly competent that his performance protects me from further pain. We both try to help out the other divisions, especially the mechanics, who are dealing with intense scrutiny from on and off the boat.

I'm on duty one night when a Naval Regional Maintenance Depot worker comes onboard for a tour of the ER. My Engineering Duty Petty Officer is the Mechanic Chief, who has just emerged from the seven weeks of work on the troublesome alteration. M-Div has finally finished and it looks like the curse may be shaken. The shipyard worker comes into Maneuvering about twenty minutes into his tour and asks me to come with him to look at something. The same alteration that's caused us so many weeks of problems looks like it's incorrect. I'm shocked, but I look at what the monitor is talking about, and I have to agree that it looks like something's wrong. I call the ENG and he agrees that we'll have to repeat the work again. It's a kick in the teeth that we've screwed up something so many people worked so hard on correcting. This sets us back four more weeks, and the Mechanic Chief yells and screams behind Maneuvering. As he gets over the denial and accepts that something is wrong, he sits on the floor with his head in his hands.

"Are you OK, Chief?" I ask. I'm seriously concerned about his welfare.

"I'm ducky, sir, just ducky." He sits on the floor, rocking his head back and forth, repeating the word "ducky." I talk to the ENG and we get him relieved. The EDMC and ENG decide that he'll be driven home. He's a suicide risk, and we call his wife to warn her to watch him carefully. I shake my head as I leave the Chief's quarters and call Adam to tell him that his Chief has freaked out. It's the last thing we need right now.

The Mechanic Chief doesn't come to work for two days, and when he does return, he's a broken man. He doesn't want to do the job and is transferred off the ship. This situation puts the Navy in a tough spot. He could be taken to mast for dereliction of duty, but he's also seen a psychologist and is in the process of being disqualified from the submarine service. Sub life is so hard that there's a special category of non-specific "personality disorders" that basically mean you can't handle being on the submarine anymore. The loss of the Chief makes life even harder for the mechanics, and Adam Johnson takes up the slack even as his best operators are still under punishment. A new Chief, Tom Rierson, waits at Squadron to come down to our ship. Squadron leadership won't let him come onboard because they don't want his reputation tainted by the failed alteration; they're going to hold him until he can get a fresh start.

We finally complete the alteration, the corrective actions, the punishment, and the personnel resolutions in September. We've been in port since May, and the fleet commanders are screaming to get use out of this boat, which hasn't done anything to justify being forward deployed in Guam. We go on a short underway to establish our proficiency with heavy squadron presence watching us carefully. I pass my one-year anniversary on the ship, and now I'm officially behind in qualification. Officers have one year to complete all watchstation qualifications and be awarded their dolphins for submarine qualification. I'm not qualified OOD, and I still have a major school to go to in Hawaii. I've just completed DOOW qualification, but the CO shows no sign of trusting me or allowing me to continue any further. The knowledge I have doesn't matter; if the CO doesn't trust my judgment, he won't qualify me. I still study hard, but I know I'm waiting on something that may never come.

Another problem rears its ugly head for the first time since it was brushed aside on the way out of Virginia. We've been operating for a year, replacing every easy-to-swap component, but the ship still makes too much noise. The ENG, sonar technicians, mechanics, and Naval contractors keep saying something's wrong. They've been repeating this since Virginia, but it's been explained away by the CO/XO and people higher to try to get us on the Guam Train and prove that subs based in Guam can work. The interim year has made this noise very hard to ignore, and other American submarines begin to take note of the noise in exercises and report it. We're still being pushed to get to a few more exercises and determine whether we're ready for mission certification. The denial of our noise problem is strong because only one option is left – dry-dock. Guam has no dry-docks rated for nuclear submarines, which means a trip back to the mainland and months of mission time wasted. The powers that be aren't ready to accept this eventuality.

My tardiness in qualification means that I'll get out of an underway and go to Hawaii for a week of school, much to the chagrin of the other officers. I watch from the pier as the ship leaves Guam for an exercise, leaving me with the XO's car and a few days off. The Captain had told me twenty-four hours before that I'm "broken as a leader and he did not know how to fix me." I'm deep in thought as I drive home.

I fly out of Guam for the first time on Monday morning on Continental Flight 001 to Honolulu, landing in Oahu on Sunday afternoon. I check into the military quarters and drive down Ala Moana Boulevard to Waikiki. I sip a "Tropical Itch" on the beach at Duke's while watching the soothing sunset behind surfers and families on vacation, and I can't help feeling happy. The school is way too short, and I have more fun in that one week than in the four months before. Old friends make me wish I'd been stationed in Pearl, and I meet a few Commanding Officers whose personalities are an incredible contrast to Lovpock's.

Back in Guam, I spend a week working for Squadron as we wait for an opportunity to meet the boat. Craig and I get plane tickets to Okinawa to meet the ship in a break between exercises. We arrive at the airport to learn that we are traveling with a new radio petty officer named White, Senior Chief Eyor from Squadron, and our old friend Captain Ginda. Captain Ginda is flying out to the ship to evaluate our readiness for the mission certification scheduled in Hawaii after the current exercise is over. Senior Chief Eyor is flying out to help our new Fire Control (FT) Chief train his divisional personnel and watch how our FTs work on an everyday basis. Good FTs can make or break a ship on mission, and if they're not ready for a high contact density, we can't go. The flight to Fukuoka is much shorter than the one to Hawaii, and we arrive in Okinawa early in the evening. We have one night at Kadena Air Force Base before catching a tug in the morning

The Kadena Officer's Club is a large, single-level cinder block building with a full restaurant, dance club, fast food court, and bar. We go there on a Friday night and find a line of Asian women in mini-skirts out the door and around the building. We walk to the door and discover that active duty military can walk right in, but Japanese nationals have to wait and pay a cover charge. The club is evenly divided between men (and a few women) in flight suits and Asian women on the dance floor. Craig and I are both boggled by people who would wear their work clothes in a bar at night. No submariner would ever be caught dead wearing a poopie suit in a bar. We only have a few beers since we have to be on a tug at 0530, but it's clear from those few minutes that being a pilot is very different from being a submarine driver. The joy these people have in their job drives both Craig and me to question the decision to join the submarine force.

The trip to White Beach happens while it's still dark outside. We board the boat with a Captain from the Pacific Fleet who will be evaluating a portion of the exercise. Captain Ginda becomes worried as our tug arrives because the Pac Fleet rider has not shown up. The San Francisco is already on the surface heading toward us, and stops in Japan are very hard to arrange. The U.S. Navy goes to great lengths to be respectful and considerate to all agencies of the Japanese government. The new focus on Asian security has made the U.S.-Japan relationship the most important regional alliance the U.S. can maintain. Every time a sailor gets drunk and comes on to an underage Japanese girl, it becomes harder and harder to keep Japanese public opinion from going against us. In this case, asking for another stop in Okinawa in such a short period is pushing our luck with the Japanese authorities. Finally, the tug is leaving and we have to board it or we'll miss the submarine. Captain Ginda looks very tense this morning, and it seems to get worse as we approach the San Francisco.

I've never boarded a submarine this way before, and I see many familiar faces topside as they maneuver the ship to create a leeward side for the tug to come alongside. Our bags are thrown over and Broomfield smiles his devilish grin and welcomes me back aboard. I go below to check out the berthing bill and throw my bags in my rack. It's as if I'd never left, and I find Henry in one of the staterooms and ask him what's going on. He shuts the door and whispers to me, "Alex, something bad happened yesterday. We were coming up to PD and Sprocket was driving. When he did his first sweeps with the scope, he saw an American destroyer that he thought was too close and called emergency deep. The Captain was watching the video monitor from the scope and didn't agree with the emergency deep call. As we were coming down, the CO flipped out and started yelling at Martin right in the control room. He was screaming nonsense and the only thing anybody understood was 'Now I have to send a fucking message because you called an emergency deep.'

"As soon as Sprocket got the ship back to 150 feet, the CO ordered him to clear baffles and come back to PD by turning toward the contact Martin thought was too close. The CO was swearing all over the place. Martin turned the ship back around and we drove right underneath the destroyer. We got way too close. We violated the safety rules of the exercise by breaking the range rules, and now Squadron has to investigate to make sure there was no damage to either ship. Captain Ginda got the call last night that he's the investigating officer."

Henry's story explains why Ginda seemed more worked up in the morning. Now, instead of evaluating, he'll be investigating a safety-related violation of exercise rules. Though it may seem minor, any violation is treated the same as a wartime failure. The good part is that things are very well documented. When submarines participate in exercises, we record everything and send it off for the reconstruction. These recordings include the voice record from the open microphone of everything that happens in the control room, including the CO's screaming session. I talk to the Sonar Supervisor at the time, and he confirms Henry's telling of the events.

The next day, the XO comes to me and tells me that Captain Ginda needs my help. Since I'm the only officer who wasn't onboard at the time and I'm a good hand with the ship's computer systems, Ginda wants me to take the navigation and fire control records from the time of the incident and help build a reconstructed plot of the events. Senior Chief Eyor and I spend hours rebuilding the event from surface ship position records and our navigational readouts. I can see exactly what happened and how the closest point of approach (CPA) occurred. It's hard work, but I'm fueled by the absolute horror on Martin Sprocket's face when he learns I'm doing the reconstruct. He is legally liable for the failure since he was the Officer of the Deck at the time, and now the key record that will help visualize his guilt or innocence is in the hands of the one person he's been tormenting mercilessly for an entire year.

I fantasize about painting Martin as an absolute incompetent failure, but I'm too professional to do that, and the data points to a different interpretation. The Captain of a submarine is accountable and responsible for the actions of everyone onboard. This is one of the few cases where the blame can be placed squarely on an order of the CO. His order for Martin to turn the ship back toward the destroyer after the emergency deep was the direct cause of the close CPA. The voice records from control confirm exactly what happened, and Captain Ginda puts together his report over the week of exercises that follows. I'm standing EOOW and don't see much of anyone after completing my portion of the investigation.

We pick up the Pac Fleet rider in Okinawa a few days later and complete our other tasks without further incident. We are now due to transit to Pearl Harbor for our tactical certification, but in a meeting with all the officers, the Captain tells us that our noise problem and level of proficiency won't allow us to continue. We're not ready for mission certification, and our schedule has been delayed again. The CO expresses clear frustration, and even though we're happy to be heading back to Guam sooner than expected, the crew is beginning to feel like the crippled child of the Pacific Fleet submarines. Failure, or lack of success, is a bad feeling to have for a year straight. Our certification timeline hasn't been updated because it's apparent from the messages we're getting that no one knows what comes next.

We pull back alongside the Frank Cable to find a new officer waiting for us. Josh Chester is a thin, wiry man with dark hair and angular features. He graduated with honors from Georgetown, and he's been driving my car for the few days since he reached the island. My apartment is in good shape thanks to the typhoon shutters holding through two tropical storms and one close pass by a typhoon. The ship begins doing frantic troubleshooting to try to find any solution to our noise problem other than dry-docking.

The focus on the ship is not on me, so I'm able to stay off the radar for work control problems by being extremely conscientious and slow moving. I spend nights sitting in my beautiful and huge apartment, where no one ever comes. The loneliness becomes unbearable, and I ask Dawn and Alan to set me up with any of their single doctor or nurse friends. The night we take Josh out to the strip clubs for the first time, Alan calls me on my cell to tell me he's out with a nice, single doctor who'd like to meet me. This is how I meet Sonja for the first time. Sonja is a 5'8" Indian woman with delicate features, bright eyes, and a smile that fills the room. She's also incredibly intelligent, forceful, opinionated, and one of the three Navy OB-GYNs on the island. We talk for a few hours over billiards, and I decide that I definitely want to see her again. I enjoy having someone to talk to who's not on the boat but understands the military.

I have duty the next day, a Saturday, and after finishing the normal morning evolutions, I'm sitting in the wardroom doing paperwork. I notice that all the department heads are onboard but not doing anything in particular. The Captain comes onboard and the duty officers jerk in surprise and run from the wardroom to meet him. I begin to wonder what's so special about this Saturday. A few minutes later, I hear the distinct call from topside: "Submarine Squadron Fifteen, arriving." The Commodore is here on a Saturday. This is weird. Even on an operational ship, it's strange to have every single senior person in the command onboard at 1000 on a Saturday. Twenty minutes later, the Commodore leaves, and then the Captain leaves. The NAV rushes into the wardroom and shuts the door with an excited look on his face.

"He's out. The Captain is getting relieved. The Commodore told him that he's lost confidence in his ability to command after hearing the tapes from the close CPA during the exercise. The new CO who was headed for the City of Corpus Christi has been reassigned. He'll be riding us next week and then relieving in a month. Lovpock is fired; he's done."

I'm puzzled, then in shock, and then ecstatic. Martin Sprocket is rotating off the boat this week and now the Captain is being relieved a year early. He's not officially being fired, but he will never again command a submarine and he will not advance further in the Navy. Matt Priests agrees that it's the best thing that could possibly happen for me personally; I'll get a fresh start with a new CO to rebuild my reputation. All I need to do is get off on the right foot, and I can complete my qualifications and gain the trust of a new leader. This will be my second chance.

Lovpock cares less and less as the days march onward. Phone calls for evening and turnover reports become easier and less thorough. I make the error of trusting a senior first class petty officer and not being thorough enough on a duty day, and we both end up removed from watchstanding. It's a testament to how little energy the CO has left that he only removes me from watchstanding and orders the ENG to draft a third letter of instruction. He'll let the new guy deal with me. I go on leave three days before the change of command and never say goodbye to Paul Lovpock. My first trip home in three years is filled with hope, as I pray that I'll get a clean slate with this new leader. He's a young, energetic man named Kevin Mooney.

Chapter 8: Second Chance

The Guam experiment is now in its fifteenth month, and we have little show for it: one ship on mission and one ship with a fired CO that just cannot stay at sea. The idea of basing submarines in Guam was debated and accepted largely because of the operational days saved by the ability to transit to and from Hawaii and San Diego. The Admirals and bureaucrats with careers on the line have been watching as money is poured into the San Francisco and Guam, and the results are not coming. The material problems after the overhaul and the personnel problems related to rebuilding the crew are causing frustration at all levels.

The crew feels this frustration most of all. We all signed on to go to Guam so we could be on an operational submarine doing the job, and all we have so far is a series of failures and long repair periods. The ship still isn't ready to go on mission, and everyone seems to be looking for someone to blame. The crew just wants to succeed; we want to be ready and able to serve our country, not trapped at the pier by material problems. People whisper that the ship is cursed, jinxed, broken, and stricken with bad luck. The officers often talk of gremlins hiding in the ship, breaking things at the most inopportune moment. Despite science and technology, sailors come from a very old profession populated by the most superstitious people in the world. We are not that far from the world of King Neptune and Davey Jones, so saying a ship is cursed is a very serious thing.

This is the environment Kevin Mooney faces when he comes to the San Francisco. He's a hard charger in the Navy, at the top of every school he ever attended and a rising star. He exudes excitement and energy in everything he does, and it's immediately clear he's very different from Paul Lovpock. He's been given the task of fixing the San Francisco and getting us on mission, no matter what it takes. Rumor spreads that the Commodore has given him a blank check to fire any officer or chief to clean out the dead wood. More is on the line here than one ship's performance, including the whole Guam experiment and an operational concept that needs proof to justify billions of dollars of expenditure.

We are all at the center of this drama as the Navy desperately tries to salvage the San Francisco situation. The first sign of this is the flood of personnel. Guam is not a popular assignment in the Navy, so we've been getting the last choice of people coming out of schools for the past year. People who get good grades generally get their choice of assignments, which leaves the lower performers at the detailer's mercy. We've been filled with only non-qualified nubs for the past nine months and none of the experienced second and first class petty officers that carry the practical experience of the submarine force.

The bad performances of the past year have finally convinced the submarine force that we need help. The flag goes up to the detailers to send us only top-half people until the situation improves. New chiefs and second class petty officers get orders to the ship, but it's still hard to clear these experienced people for duty in Guam. The overseas screening requires examination of medical records for the whole family, financial records, criminal history, alcohol treatment records, and anything else that could give the Navy trouble. Once you get past the dislike of Guam, the overseas screening, the poor infrastructure, and the rumors spreading about Guam boats, it's clear why the detailers have to strong-arm people to get them to this island.

I return from leave to find two new junior officers, Alec Beeker and Eric Braken, living in my apartment while they search for housing. Sonja picks me up from the airport and I come home to my crowded apartment, still relaxed after being on leave. It's December 23, and I have duty under-instruction on Christmas Eve with Matt Priests. I get word that I have to prove myself able to stand watch, and then the CO will re-qualify me. I'm filled with resolve and eager to use my fresh start. I work extremely hard on my duty days and finish my requalification just in time to have duty on New Year's Eve. That day, Commander Mooney comes in to sit down with me and talk about where I'm going on the ship and what he expects from me in the future.

I enter his stateroom and immediately see how different he is from Lovpock. He calls me by my first name, asks me to sit down, and puts me at ease. He is a shorter, athletic man with light brown hair and a face that seems to convey constant energy. A file on the desk contains my three letters of instruction, the last one written and signed after my most recent removal from watchstanding. He regards me cautiously as he begins to talk.

"Alex, you've had a tough time on this ship. I'm not going to tell you what Commander Lovpock said about you, but I know from the XO and the ENG that you're a smart, enthusiastic, hard-working guy. I like that; I like your energy. You're excited and upbeat, and that's exactly the kind of person we need to take this ship on mission. I know you're a mining wizard, and you seem to make good decisions on watch.

"So, here it is. Between you and me, there's a clean slate. I know you've had trouble in your past, but I have no prejudices. My opinion of you will be based on what you do from this day forward. I'm re-qualifying you Rig for Dive and EOOW/EDO. I won't have a member of my wardroom who's crippled and unable to do his job. We have an underway and TRE coming up, and I want you to finish your qualifications, get your dolphins, and be a fully functioning member of my wardroom. On that day, we'll come back here and tear up all these LOIs. They will cease to exist, and all the bad things that've happened will be wiped away.

"Alex, I'm on your side, and I want to see you succeed. Show me what you can do." He ends with a handshake and sends me out to start my year. I'm so thankful and excited that I can barely stand still. I'm working for a man who appreciates and values me and who will give me a chance to start over. Kevin Mooney is my professional savior, and at that moment, I'm prepared to follow him into hell.

He gives us all more instructions on his style in the week that follows. There will be no more "request permission to do this or that"; he wants us to evaluate the situation and make the best decision. During officer training on January 2, he tells us his reasoning.

"I'm training you guys to be the COs of your own submarines. I want you to choose the best path, support your point with evidence, and tell me what you intend to do. You should convince me that your way is the best and safest way to go, and I'll tell you if I think you're doing anything wrong. I'm here to train you to make decisions and be the CO of your own boat. I don't want you reliant on me for positive reinforcement."

We also find out that we're leaving in less than a week for the inevitable Tactical Readiness Evaluation and an evaluation of our noise problem in Hawaii. We're told to pack for two months at sea and bring enough clothes for a week in Hawaii. We don't know exactly what the resolution will be, but we should be able to get back to Guam and get the ship on mission relatively quickly. I'm still seeing Sonja, and we're both disappointed that I'm going to have to leave in the middle of our budding relationship. But that's the Navy; you go where they tell you without arguing. It's like being unmoored from life, moving around and unable to make any long-term plans or commitments.

A new attitude carries us away from the pier only a few hours late on January 4: we are warriors. The CO relates this to everything he says, and he's trying to convince everyone that we are warriors on a war-fighting machine. We're now deep into Tactical Readiness Exam (TRE) preparations, which involves study and practice in every area of submarine operations. This helps me because mining makes me look like a duck in water, and I'm the only junior officer who really understands it. The XO is great at strike warfare, and his knowledge carries us through. The ENG and NAV have incredible skills driving the ship in all situations, and we begin to look like a cohesive unit.

One day, the ENG calls me forward and tells me I'm being moved off the EOOW watchbill. The COB needs to stop standing three section watch so he can prepare for the examination, and I'm the only qualified and proficient Diving Officer of the Watch (DOOW). This watchstation is in the control room, responsible for maintaining ordered depth, ballasting the ship, maintaining stability at periscope depth, and controlling surfacing and diving evolutions (Note 12). The regular DOOWs are Chiefs, but I've expressed an interest in doing it, so I go on the forward watchbill and begin to learn – fast. The first time I drive the ship to periscope depth (PD) and control the weight and distribution correctly is like having sugar, caffeine, and nicotine rushes all combined with an orgasm. I can do it. I can really put it together and get the job done. I have only a week to spin up, but the Chiefs tell me I'm doing as well as any of them in their first watches.

I'm also driving the ship to PD as the OOD under-instruction so the Captain can see me work and become comfortable with my ship driving skills. I begin to get comfortable and grow more experienced in the control room, and I participate in all the battle stations and tactical evolutions. We do drills every other day, and these are like playtime as we practice fighting fires, flooding, hydraulic ruptures, and other fun stuff. I'm the XO's phone talker, always right behind him rushing to the scene of the casualty. We repeat so many basic drills with the same reports that Rick Bonner and I develop a shorthand, and if he forgets to say something or make a report, then I just make it anyway. I'm getting positive feedback and learning for the first time in a long time. The crew is growing as well, feeling like warriors, and Kevin Mooney's attitude is infectious. His passionate streaks of anger are more than eclipsed by his everyday verve.

I still make mistakes, but now, when I report those errors, the CO asks me what I've learned and how I'm going to prevent it from happening again. He focuses on how I'm going to fix it and keep fighting as opposed to punishing me for what I have done. He does fly off the handle about some things, but I feel like I can take risks, and I'm not petrified of screwing up. We also get indoctrinated to a new way of thinking about everything called "operational planning." We've done this practice to varying degrees, but the recent CO training courses have focused more and more on the construct of total ship planning and risk management. The creation of operational plans and tactical overlays consumes the rest of our life outside of watch.

We continue like this all the way to Pearl Harbor: training, drills, strike, mining, planning, walk-throughs, watch, submerged attack, surfaced attack, and on and on. The officers spend all waking hours not on watch preparing operational plans and "ready-to-use" briefs for every possible situation that the TRE team could create. We pore over old comments and lessons learned from other ships until we can barely keep our eyes open. Despite the pain, the "warrior" attitude is taking hold from the lowest ranks, and everyone is ready to succeed, no matter how much it takes. We are a competitive and intelligent bunch, and we're tired of being the crippled orphan of the Pacific Fleet.

I'm getting a different viewpoint on life and learning from MMC Hager (A-Gang), STSCS Miller (Sonar), FTCS Stevens (Fire Control), and the other Chiefs who rotate through DOOW with me. They teach me more about the boat than any book or officer. I'm working with the NAV, the best OOD onboard, and his backup keeps me out of trouble while I watch his style and learn what kind of officer I want to be.

The outlook in the wardroom is cautious. We know that we're doing well and learning fast, but we can do only so much in a few weeks. Captain Ginda is riding and seems to be as pleased as we've ever seen him, but this manifests itself as only a medium amount of painful comments and random tasking. On the last night of workup before picking up the team, Mike Vasquez and I finish our final walk-throughs for Submarine Qualification. We must be examined by the Commodore or his representative. We also do our oral examination boards with the CO and department heads, which go smoothly. I'm certain that, if I can get through TRE and show my competence as DOOW and Mining Officer, I will have earned the Captain's trust. My competence grows, but I still feel like I'm catching up when we surface south of Honolulu and head inbound to pick up the examination team.

We meet the tug south of the dry docks at Pearl Harbor Naval Shipyard and turn around after the TRE team comes onboard. The team is a Captain and a number of Chiefs and officers from different tactical areas. At 0900, we turn around and head south, out into the open ocean. The exam starts with a review of the records stored in hundreds of binders that prove our certification and training. The junior officers mostly rest or try to get rest before the insanity to follow. Very little random tasking is done in the first few hours, and I get some time in the rack with my shoes off and poopie suit on but unzipped before the drills in the afternoon.

The food always gets a little better when examination teams are onboard, so I wake up for burgers and hot dogs. We begin our first drill period after lunch, and I have an emergency air-breathing mask and a set of phones glued to my hands. The practice in the last few weeks has taken us through every major scenario, and the actual drills go very well. The crew responds as a team, and the XO and I can communicate with the slightest hand signal and facial expression during drill communications. A fire in the galley, a hydraulic rupture in the torpedo room, and flooding in the ER keep us busy. I'm so exhausted I can barely stand, and my poopie suit is soaked with sweat. I change quickly before the evening watch as DOOW.

Controlling a submarine at periscope depth is one of the most difficult things we do. It involves precisely maintaining the periscope a few feet out of the water. If we get too high in the water, it becomes easy to see and detect the scope on radar. If the scope dips too low, the person looking through can't see anything, and it may dip under the water. In the worst-case scenario, we lose control of the ship and get sucked up so the sail and rudder come out of the water in a "broach." This risks counter-detection and makes us about as stealthy as a large brick building.

On the other extreme, we could drop away from periscope depth and the scope optics sink below the surface of the water. This is called "sinking out." This means we can't track contacts or see anything that's going on until we get backup. Then we start to "yo-yo" up and down until we completely lose control and have to surface or go deep. Hopefully, the helm and planes don't overcorrect and we can steady back out again. These are the worst things that happen when the DOOWs don't know what they're doing, and this is my fear.

The evening trip to periscope depth goes well, though I'm nervous. The ballasting of the ship is close enough that the helmsman and planesman can compensate while I move water around the ship to catch up. The TRE team has no comments, and the evening message traffic confirms our tasking to shoot exercise weapons the next day. We'll be chasing a surface ship in the morning and then mining a harbor in the afternoon, just as our plans have briefed us. We finish up at periscope depth at 2300 and come down, turning all the lights back on as we lower the periscope. MMC Hager relieves me and I grab a few chicken nuggets from Midnight Rations before working on my mining brief and tactical overlay for the next day.

The TRE team has already gone to bed, but all the department heads and junior officers are putting final touches on plans and briefs for the morning. I collapse into my rack at 0300 and get some fitful and interrupted sleep because an electrical component fails and the messenger routes me paperwork every half-hour. Reveille is called at 0600, but I roll over and sleep until the CO calls "Man battle stations – Torpedo" at 0630. I'm the secondary computer operator providing independent solutions for the problems we face that morning. We secure from battle stations after shooting four exercise torpedoes at our quarry and chasing around the exercise area for four hours. I run down to the wardroom for lunch, but I have no time to sit down at the table, so I grab some food from the crew's mess and scarf it down while standing in my stateroom.

The other officers seem just as harried as I am, and the mining is up next. I head up to control to finalize my preparations. I relieve as the afternoon DOOW for twenty minutes until we hear "Man battle stations – Mine" and the COB relieves me. At periscope depth, we approach the mine area as I type in my final calculations with one of the TRE team standing over my shoulder. The exercise lasts all afternoon as we shower an exercise harbor with mines and deal with several tactical problems and drill weapons malfunctions. We finally finish at 1600, and I get to be DOOW again until turnover at 1730. We finish our first day on the range and spend the evening in briefs about peacetime safety for the submerged attack scenarios that await us the next day.

The Electrical division is fighting several minor problems, and the Engineering department is just trying to stay out of the way for this tactical evaluation. Chief Gradwell takes care of everything and sends people to me only when it's absolutely required. I sleep from 2300 until 0430, when the messenger wakes me for the morning DOOW. We spend the early part of the morning doing surveillance of a simulated target, and despite sinking out for a few seconds at a key time, I manage to hold it together for the rest of the intelligence gathering. We make a quick transition to submerged operations and I'm back on the computer for the torpedo attack. We hit our target, and we have a cautious feeling that things are going well. Battle station watches take us into the late afternoon, and then we're up at periscope depth getting communications again. The message comes down that we have an urgent strike to launch in the morning very far to the south.

We go deep and fast and begin planning and briefs for the missile launch. The brief ends at 2100 and we all try to get to the rack since everyone feels strung out and exhausted. The officers are running on fumes after two days of non-stop activity, and all we want to do is sleep until we get to the strike location in the morning. Suddenly, we hear "Hydraulic rupture in control" on the 1MC and we begin to rise upward at an

84

intense angle. I'm the off-going DOOW, so I rush to control to relieve Chief Hager, who will be involved in any hydraulic problem. Our control surfaces have suffered a simulated casualty and we're being forced to control them manually while we attempt repairs.

We finally get the problem under control and come up to PD to report our status. We'll be unable to make the strike on time because of this problem. As soon as our antenna clears the water, we get a message canceling our strike tasking; apparently, it was just a test to assess our planning skills and establish the initial conditions for our drill. The CO gets on the 1MC at 2200 and congratulates us on our effort. The TRE team has completed their evaluation, and we have one last night at sea before heading to Hawaii in the morning. We eat pizza in the wardroom, the traditional meal on the night before returning to port. Exhaustion amplifies the laughter and joking, and I have the midnight watch as DOOW.

We move toward Oahu and bring the ship up to PD at 0300. It's my best ascent ever; the ship just steadies at 58 feet with no hiccups at all. I'm proud of the team and myself as I drink coffee at a faintly alarming pace to stay awake. We surface at 0430, and by turnover, we're driving toward the harbor at full speed. The feedback from the team is very guarded, but everyone feels like we've done well. I sleep in my rack with my clothes on for half an hour before we wake up for the maneuvering watch. The CO and the Senior member of the TRE team are on the bridge, and I'm Control Room Supervisor as we head past Hospital Point and moor on the shipyard side of Pearl Harbor. Aside from the TRE, we have a short-notice screw change in the next few days.

We throw the lines over, and the very smelly and tired crew begins to filter topside to see the sun and make cell phone calls. The steep green mountains of Oahu, dotted with the pink color of the Tripler Army Medical Center, rise above us as the sun warms the dark metal of the submarine. I smell horrible, but I turn around to see that the crew is flooding topside. The TRE team has left, and the CO has called a quarters on the pier. I stand in the front line of the Engineering Department, and the first thing the XO says is, "Lieutenant Fleming, front and center." He grins even as he gets the words out.

I step out of formation and stand in front of the Commodore, who is attending the ceremony. He steps in front of me as I hear words that warm my heart as much as the sun warms my sweaty, smelly jumpsuit.

"Today we welcome another submariner into our midst. Having gained a thorough knowledge of submarine construction and equipment, having an in-depth knowledge of damage control and operations, and having my full confidence and trust, I hereby certify that Lieutenant Junior Grade Alexander C. Fleming is qualified in Submarines, this 24th day of January, 2004. Signed K.G. Mooney, Commanding Officer, USS San Francisco." I have never been so happy to hear the XO's voice.

The Commodore pins the small gold submarine flanked by two dolphins above my left breast pocket. It's a strange thing to see something there after so long with nothing but fabric. The call for Lieutenant Junior Grade Vasquez finds that he is on watch in the ER, and he is called up. Once Mike has his dolphins, the CO calls for us to break formation and gather round. He is a short man, and he climbs up on a concrete pylon to address the whole crew.

"Good morning, San Francisco." The crew erupts into spontaneous cheers. "It's been a long month, and we've covered a long way. You have given your heart and soul in the last few days, and it has paid off in what we've shown to the TRE team. I had a meeting with the team this morning, and they told me that the USS San Francisco has been rated ABOVE AVERAGE."

It's as if a bolt of lightning has struck every man present. The excitement is overwhelming, and the hundred men crowded around me begin to cheer and jump up and down. Finally, our efforts have paid off. Finally, we are a success and the pain has been used for something good. Officers and enlisted man are giddy as Commander Mooney quiets us down.

"I'm so proud of every one of you. You spun this ship up in less than a month and proved that we are warriors. We're going to take down every target in the Pacific Fleet and show them what the San Francisco is made of." Kevin Mooney has tears in his eyes as he addresses us, and every man there is proud to be onboard the ship. I walk down the pier after we are dismissed. I'm congratulated and saluted with enthusiasm by over

85

thirty people. I walk to the end of the pier and let the sun warm my face, looking at the dive tower, surface ships, and cloud-shrouded hills behind them. I crouch behind a concrete power box, looking at the gentle waves in the harbor, and feel tears of relief in my eyes. I feel like my chest could crack open with joy, and I stay there for a while.

I finally head below after a quick call to my parents and discover that the officers are meeting in the wardroom. I come in late as the CO reads the grades from each area of the exam: Basic Submarining – Average, Strike – Average, Ship Handling – Above Average, Mine Warfare – Excellent... My heart stops I'm so happy. The TRE team thinks that we're better at mining than most of the fleet. Since mining is my baby, I'm ecstatic. The CO finishes the comments and tells us about the areas we have to work on, but for today, we're going to celebrate. He says again how proud he is, and we head out of the wardroom to tie up loose ends and get out of here.

I don't have watch for the shutdown, so I throw some clothes in a bag and flee the ship as fast as I can. We find our way out of the shipyard and emerge on the surface side of the Pearl Harbor Naval Base. Luckily, we have rooms in the quarters on this side of the base, and the Supply Officer has the van so we don't have to rent cars. The first thing any person thinks of after getting off a submarine is a long, hot shower. The experience of letting the hot water run over you is something you miss a lot underway. We head to the mini-mart and get beer, wine, liquor, and munchies to help us get to the evening when the celebration starts. The enlisted guys are starting at Hooters in the Aloha Tower Market Place, but we have many hours of celebration ahead before then.

The alcohol flows as we gather in one of the rooms and begin to unwind from the underway. There is wrestling, cell phone calls, screaming, destruction, and general insanity. The sun slowly drops, and people get dressed to head out on the town. We pile into the government van, and I sit shotgun as a fight club develops in the back seats. A brawl breaks out across seats and out windows as we drive down H1 to Aloha Towers. We have dinner at Gordon Biersch and then find most of the crew at Hooters having wings. Everyone is well on their way to drunkenness, and we're kicked out of Hooters as I try to chug a pitcher of beer with my dolphins in the bottom.

The guys are giddy and proud of our accomplishments. All the officers and crew not on duty end up in an Irish pub doing Irish Car-bombs and telling the Captain how much better he is than the last guy. The screaming and yelling reaches a fever pitch as the night becomes fuzzy. All we know, all we need to know, is that we can succeed.

Chapter 9: Broken

The euphoria lasts for a few days, but reality has a way of grabbing you in the submarine force and destroying whatever happiness exists. The Finite Happiness Theory rears its ugly head on a gargantuan scale. After we've been happy for a while, someone senior to us comes and takes our happiness away again. Our two days of happiness end abruptly when the report on our noise problem comes from Pearl Harbor Naval Shipyard.

We've exhausted all of the cheap options; only two components are left that could be causing our problems: the screw and the shaft. Both are massive and expensive components that can't be replaced; they must be taken from other submarines that don't need them. Luckily, the USS Bremerton is just going into dry-dock, and we're stealing her screw along with a bunch of other components. This "cannibalization" is actually a very common thing in the submarine force, where so many parts are no longer made. If the Navy supply system can't find any spare parts, the part is removed from another ship.

The Navy is very frustrated because we're now one step closer to tactical certification, but the material condition of the ship won't let us go on mission. Every day we're not on mission is a waste of taxpayer dollars and further proof that the Guam experiment isn't working. Pearl Harbor proposes one last-ditch effort to replace our screw and then conduct testing to determine whether that miraculously fixes the problem, though visual inspections have shown no irregularities. If it doesn't, we'll have to replace the shaft, which means docking the ship.

Only a handful of dry-docks in the country can handle submarines, and the schedules for those docks are decided years in advance. The options for the Pacific Fleet are very limited, and there's only one dock that could be available for us quickly, but it's in San Diego. The cost of getting us there and putting us in dock is in the neighborhood of $20 million, and the Navy will do anything to avoid it. Our delays are now affecting the schedule of every submarine in the Pacific Fleet.

My first duty day as a dolphin-qualified officer comes on the day of the screw replacement, and I make my way into the shipyard area in the faint glow of morning twilight as crickets chirp. I grab a sausage, egg, and cheese sandwich at a small food truck before heading down the pier to the ship. There's something very peaceful about going to work before the sun comes up; it seems like you have a head start on the day and time to yourself. There's no one on the streets or sidewalks since all the reasonable people are still in bed at 0515. The divers are already on the ship and ready to go. I check the safety requirements and get them in the water as fast as I can. There's a large crane on the pier just to support our screw swap, and the work proceeds at an expected rate.

The day also brings a new Chief of the Boat, who flies in and is handed the keys to the ship as our old COB heads off to his next assignment. The turnover lasts about 45 minutes as the old COB lets his disdain for the San Francisco show. The new COB is a second-tour Master Chief named Billy Cramer from Submarine Squadron Seven. He stays only briefly before heading off to finish moving his family. He'll have plenty of time to make his impression on Monday.

The end of the day finds our screw off and the new one temporarily in place. My first night as duty officer is blessedly quiet. The following morning starts with the divers working again, and I am relieved just as the Dive Supervisor from Marine Diving and Salvage Unit 1 comes to the wardroom to talk to us. He looks nervous as he breaks the news that the new screw is going well, but in looking at the old screw, they were surprised to discover that we didn't have the right propeller for our class of submarine. He doesn't know what kind of screw it is, but it's not one for a Los Angeles class. It hits me and the oncoming duty officer with the force of a train wreck: **the workers at Norfolk Naval Shipyard installed the wrong screw and nobody caught the mistake.** Mike and I sit stunned as we listen, but we pass the word along to the Captain, and he is strangely calm. <u>We are beginning to discover that Norfolk Naval Shipyard gave us the cheapest and most inadequate overhaul they could possibly get away with for $200 million taxpayer dollars.</u>

The new screw takes another day to go on as the officers and crew live it up in Pearl Harbor. The day of the Super Bowl comes, and I find myself in Kaneohe Bay at the house of a friend when I get a call from the duty officer.

"Alex, one of your guys is missing. He didn't show up for duty and we can't find him on base anywhere. We have guys out looking for him now, but you know he's been having a tough time lately. If he doesn't want to be found, we're not going to find him." I take this news evenly. The electrician in question has been having a tough time, and the guys apparently have him convinced that things won't improve. I know he's into branding and crazy rave parties. Hopefully, he hasn't done anything to hurt himself.

The Captain is at the Super Bowl party with me, and he talks to me briefly about my missing man before I go back inside for the half-time show. I watch as Justin Timberlake rips Janet Jackson's top off, and I turn to the guy next to me.

"Dude, did he just rip her shirt off?" We shrug as we forget about the incident. Late in the afternoon, I get the call that my wayward division member has been found drunk in a tattoo parlor in Waikiki, and the Chief is bringing him back. I shake my head in amazement. I'll deal with it on Monday. The party goes fine, and I spend another day relaxing before moving back to the boat. The first muster day is a Monday, and the crew comes to work expecting to head back to Guam and get on mission, though some of the officers know that there's another possibility. We have packed only a few weeks of clothes, so most of the crew is thinking about getting back to wives and girlfriends.

The culture shift Billy Cramer brings immediately and strongly felt. He's a walking firestorm of energy, correcting formality, uniforms, communications, and every other aspect of life onboard. He hits me on out-of-uniform sunglasses as I walk onboard, and I discover what a submarine COB is supposed to be like. He's in every meeting, critique, and discussion and has an enormous wealth of knowledge and experience. I can tell immediately that the crew and Chiefs love him because the discipline and standards are welcome. It's also apparent that he and the CO have been talking because, despite the 45-minute turnover, it's like they're working on identical play-books and scripts. This quality now seems so obvious that I understand that it should never be any other way.

This shock is rippling through the crew when the CO gets on the 1MC to tell us that the sound report from our last underway has been analyzed, and it's been determined that our ship will need a shaft replacement. The final analysis of our noise after the screw swap will occur as we leave Pearl on the way to San Diego. The ARCO floating dry-dock is preparing to dock us as soon as possible because the urgency behind this repair is coming from the highest levels.

The Captain says we're going for a "quick dry-docking," but the officers sitting in the wardroom are already thinking it through and we know better. The best-case scenario we can come up with will take six weeks from the time we get into the dock. That already puts our return to Guam in late April or early May. Everyone is thinking that the week's worth of civilian clothes is probably insufficient for the time we're going to spend in San Diego. Now we're under the gun to get out of Pearl and go as fast as we can to California. There is training to be done on shipyard procedures and a hundred pieces of paperwork to do to get us into dock. Lifting a submarine out of the water is one of the most dangerous and intricate evolutions that occurs in the force, and we have to prepare for it in the short time it takes to steam from Hawaii to San Diego.

The feeling of being frantically behind takes over the ship again as we prepare for underway. Pre-underways involve a binder with a massive checklist for each division that has certain items to complete every twelve hours before the underway time. Management of these massive checklists falls to the duty officers, who have to make sure that everything gets done. Divisions spin up their equipment as fast as possible, and we start up the following morning to push away from the pier and head out. It's always sad to leave Pearl Harbor, a place that has so much more to offer us than Guam in every respect. But we have more on our plates now than anyone can imagine, and the free hours of the underway fill up quickly as we run as fast as we can. The messages start pouring in describing the preparations we need to get done.

The officers become overloaded quickly, as I find out that my next career transition will be out of ENG DEP to be the Sonar Officer. Matt Priests and I both feel that I need some distance from engineering matters to fully regain my confidence, and the WEPS needs some help. I've completed my required year to be eligible for the Engineer's exam, so as soon as we get into dock, I will turn over Electrical Assistant to Alec Beeker. I'm actually disappointed because Chief Gradwell and I have become comfortable with each other and get things done efficiently. I'm also excited to be working on tactical concerns since that's where my passion and interests lie.

The ship is not allowed to have weapons onboard for the dry-dock, so the WEPS is gearing up to offload the entire torpedo room, which will take at least two days of work by the entire department. Mike Harven is the Ship's Diving Officer and by tradition the Dry-docking Officer. He's in charge of making sure the ship meets the stringent conditions for docking. This is much easier said than done, and I see him sitting at the cramped desk in his stateroom, swearing at a massive stability spreadsheet for three hours a day. I stand my first underway watches as Officer of the Deck as we steam for San Diego. We haven't been here since Thanksgiving of 2002, and we definitely did not expect to be coming back this soon. Driving as fast as possible is pretty boring for a ship's control party and for Sonar since there's nothing to track. I quickly discover the boredom that comes when you try to read "Jane's Fighting Ships" and "The American Practical Navigator" to stay awake on a quiet watch. I'm still very inexperienced, so the Chiefs are keeping a close eye on me to keep me out of trouble since they've heard from the engineering guys that I need a lot of guidance when I'm green. My time standing DOOW during TRE means that I understand ship driving better than many junior officers, so I do pretty well. It's thrilling to take the ship up to periscope depth alone, with just the Captain watching, and get things done as the sole person in charge of the ship.

My seniority is rising as more and more of my antagonists leave the ship. This does not mean I'm more experienced; it just means that fewer people are bugging me every minute, and I now have time and space to learn on my own. Kevin Mooney is very clear that he does not want requests. He wants me to make a safe plan and then propose what I'm going to do and why. I should make the decision on my own and only look to him as a reinforcement of my own judgment. I make mistakes, and he makes me learn all the lessons from them and tell him what I will do better next time. His leadership style invigorates and empowers me.

I remember the smell of San Diego, but now it's freezing cold. We pull into Point Loma Naval Base on Thursday afternoon, and most of us have not felt a temperature under 80F since we got to Guam. The 50F wind gusts make us shiver and run back to the boat to look for our warm clothes. It occurs to me that I didn't bring any long pants in my civilian clothes, or jackets or sweaters for that matter. This is going to be a problem since it looks like we're going to be here for at least a few months.

We have quarters on the pier as soon as the ship is tied up. Everyone shivers uncontrollably on the stark cement pier as the sun goes behind Point Loma to the West. The Captain jumps up on the highest object in front of us in his usual "short man" act. I wonder briefly whether Napoleon had to do the same thing to address his troops. His speech begins quickly.

"Good afternoon, warriors. It's amazing what's happened since we left Guam and all the effort that every one of you put in to get us to this pier in San Diego. I'm extraordinarily proud of all of you, but it's not over. It is just beginning. The Navy needs this boat out on mission, and our job is to get it there as fast as possible. This dry-docking is going to be tough and long, and we are far away from our families, trying to get home. We are like an army forced to make a very long march, and I'm the General, trying to push you the hundreds of miles we have left to go. I know this situation is bad, but I need the best effort from every one of you to get the shaft fixed and get back out to sea. This is a long march, but there's no choice but to get through it."

The speech is good, but most of the people around me are focused on the fact that we're freezing our butts off. Men shiver left and right, and contrary to all logic, I want to go back down into the submarine. Quarters ends and I check out with the ENG, who sends me away because I don't have the shutdown. Mike Harven is surrounded by a crowd of people from ARCO, the floating dry-dock. The scheduled docking date is less than a week away, and he's already buried in a mountain of paperwork to get the ship exactly positioned. I grab my backpack to go see where I'm living for the next few months.

The CHOP gets us rooms in the small bachelor officer quarters near Point Loma lighthouse, and I walk into the industrial room with cheap furniture that will be my home. The bed is low and cheap with a weird hole in the mattress. The wall coverings are a study in pastel with a horrible watercolor painting of birds above a lake. The small bathroom has plastic fittings and water pressure so low that showering feels like someone is, in Rick Bonner's words, "pissing on your head." Mercifully, there is a TV with cable and a microwave/refrigerator combination. I open the window to look down on the back deck and the Pacific Ocean. My small consolation for being stuck here for months with only a week of civilian clothes is that I have a good view, and the liquor store is right across the street, so I can buy all the alcohol and microwave meals I can handle. I run to get a six-pack of Michelob Ultra and sip the first one as I sit in the shower. I dry off and sit in my towel on the windowsill. I glance at the small bag of things I brought with me and then stare out at the ocean and Coronado across the bay. This is really going to suck.

I don't sleep well because of the beeping. The Point Loma light is a navigation aid that also has a sound signal for ships during fog or other low-visibility conditions. My room looks out on the beautiful ocean, but it's also 300 yards from the incessant beeping noise that keeps me awake the first few nights. The bed, though strangely padded, is better than my rack on the submarine. I begin to get used to sleeping on shore as the events on the submarine speed up at an astounding pace.

I'm the incoming Assistant Weapons Officer, so WEPS wants me to observe the offloading of our torpedo room to help me qualify as a conventional weapons handling supervisor. The movement of weapons is governed by a very clear and concise procedure called the OD44979, which has massive checklists for every possible thing one could do to a weapon. Any deviation from this procedure requires the Captain's permission, and the process of taking all the torpedoes and Tomahawks out of the ship is painfully slow. The weapons offload starts every morning for three days with a 0600 safety briefing and continues until dark, with the breakdown of equipment taking until 2000. The ENG is busy, but he already expects Beeker to be the representative of Electrical Division, so I'm free to help the WEPS.

Mike Harven gets the worst of the pain because he has to establish the conditions for the dry-docking. There are two kinds of dry-docks: floating and in-place. In-place dry-docks are nothing more than holes in the ground next to the ocean. The hole is filled with water and the ship is floated into the dock. The dock shuts its gates and positions the ship before slowly pumping the water out of the hole. As the water line falls, the ship drops down until it rests on massive wooden blocks. The Navy still uses wooden blocks because they're stable and don't damage the hulls of ships. Floating dry-docks have some of the same principles, but they work in a completely different way. The floating dry-dock is a ship in itself that is normally pumped free of ballast and floats on the water. ARCO is the unit in San Diego, though its technical name is ARDM-5, which stands for Auxiliary Repair Dry-dock – Medium, number 5.

ARCO is shaped like a massive rectangular bathtub with openings at the front and rear. Looking at it from the end, it is shaped like a U. The two walls on either side are called the "wing-walls." The floor is the dry-dock "basin." Two massive cranes can move the wing-walls up and down, and several hydraulic cranks are used to pull ships into and out of the dock. To get a submarine into dock, the ARCO must fill its massive ballast tanks with water, causing it to sink so that only the very tops of the wing-walls are visible. Then the submarine is pulled into place by tugs and the line handling crews on the wing-walls. Once the ship is centered, the lines are replaced with steel ropes that are tightened to yank the ship exactly center. When you're dealing with hundreds of tons of steel, it needs to be balanced within inches or the ship will tip over and fall off the blocks.

The night before dry-docking is the Navigator's duty day, but Harven is a permanent feature of the ship now. The submarine must be positioned so that it has zero list (port and starboard) and zero trim (fore and aft). Normally, submarines ride with zero list, but this changes slightly during the day as water is pumped from one side of the ship to the other. Even 100 gallons of fluid in the wrong place can put the ship into a port or starboard list. Trim is the difficult thing to achieve because normally a submarine on the surface rides at an up-angle. The only way to get zero trim is to let air out of the forward ballast tanks until the ship is level, called ballasting down. This procedure is dangerous because, any time you let air out of the ballast tanks, there's a chance that you'll screw up and sink the ship at the pier. The night before the dry-docking, ARCO officials tell us we're not close enough to zero list and trim, so Harven and the NAV have to spend until 0200 ballasting down the forward tanks to achieve that condition.

The day begins for some of the crew at 0200 as they board the ARCO. The ARCO must begin flooding down at 0200 to be ready for us at 0630. I get to the ship at 0330 and supervise the shifting from shore power to the temporary topside diesel generator. The ship's reactor can't be operating when we get into the dock, and we can't run the ship's diesel because the divers need to swim near the ship and verify its position on the blocks. This small temporary diesel is the only power the ship will have for the eight hours of the docking. We offload normal shore power and verify the removal of all services for the docking, such as potable water, the drain connection, and the sanitary connection. By 0500, we are independent and ready to offload the personnel walkway. I'm not assigned to the Maneuvering watchbill, so I decide to go to the bridge to observe the procedure with the OOD. The WEPS is glad to have me, and there's plenty of space on the bridge because of the massive amount of scaffolding that has already been installed.

The fiery California sun is rising over downtown San Diego and Coronado as we attach the tugs and cast off the pier lines. The submarine crew is merely a spectator for most of this procedure since two tugs are pulling us away from the pier and transferring us to the dock. The light allows us to see that ARCO is almost completely underwater and waiting for us. I'm fascinated by the docking procedure; lines of people wait to bring us, bow first, into the dock. The tugs push us only so far, but then our bow lines are pulled by a hydraulic capstan and five teams of line handlers on each of the wing-walls. We are completely at the mercy of these handlers as the ship slowly moves into position. It is 0800 before we are roughly in position. The steel lines are installed and the ARCO docking officer begins to tightly position the ship at the centerline of the dock. Once we're in position, the last of the wooden blocks are pulled into position under the ship.

Then the really boring part begins, as ARCO slowly pumps water out and lifts us out of the water. There's a slight bumping jolt when we settle on the blocks, and then the divers verify that the ship is centered and in solid contact with the blocks. The ship slowly emerges from the ocean like a hulking giant. We are lifted higher and higher as more services are installed to support the shut-down reactor, and finally only six inches of water are left in the basin. The Captain and the Dry-dock CO put on large rubber boots and walk around the bottom of the ship to inspect the hull. The Captain discovers that a chunk of metal is missing from the leading edge of the rudder, the lowest point of the ship, indicating that we may have "rubbed" the bottom of a harbor sometime in the past few years. The other officers and I exchange a look when we hear about this, but we keep quiet. This is no time to drag up ghosts from the past.

There's something very peaceful about my walks to work at Point Loma. I rise in the oddly padded bed to hear the sound of the ocean and the whistle of wind over the cliff line. Since I'm already on base, I can throw on my poopie suit here, get my boots and hard hat, and leave everything else in the room. I walk across two parking lots and past the concrete block high-rises that house the enlisted men. The gym on my right looks like it was built in the fifties and has a softball field where the ship's team plays in the spring afternoons. I come around to enter the industrial part of the base, where the expanse of parking lots gives way to piping and hardware. A barbed wire fence protects the wide concrete pier, which much cleaner than ours in Guam. A few small craft are in the harbor and a four-story white building stands on the pier. I walk slowly, savoring the time outside the ship, but then I come past the building and see the ramp down into the dry-dock.

The sight of the San Francisco out of the water still shocks me. The cleaning crew is halfway done scrubbing and painting the hull a shiny black. I return the salute of the gate guard, who looks so young that he ought to be in grade school, and the M-16 rifle he holds looks awkwardly too big for him. The metal ramp slopes down to the dock. A rusted chain prevents people from going under the ship without hardhats. I always take a moment to look at the boat, standing free on a line of concrete and wooden blocks. No matter how many times I see it, I still think it's going to tip over since all the steel lines have been removed. I sigh and begin the long climb; the only way up to the ship is to climb the eighty-seven steps up to the wing-wall and then walk over the catwalk. I begin counting steps as I have done many times before. I'm heavier now, weighing almost 220 pounds, and the beer is not helping. I'm winded as I reach the top, and I take a moment to watch the sunrise over Coronado Island, the runways shining in massive geometric patterns. I eventually turn to look at the clean grey paint on top of the wing-wall and cross over to the ship, which is shrouded with scaffolding.

The week after we go into dock, work begins on the shaft repair. Initial estimates say it will take six weeks to replace the shaft, but we also don't yet know where our new shaft is coming from. The only 688 shaft in the Navy that isn't being used is in Norfolk, VA, but the real challenge is getting it to us (a challenge that interests me, in retrospect). The work proceeds without much influence from the crew. We get a disturbing message from the head of Navy Nuclear Power telling us that they've decided to include a major nuclear repair in this dry-docking period. This repair will involve us getting into an irregular condition and include conducting sensitive repairs of one of our most important reactor components. The ENG sees his boring dry-dock period disappear before his eyes as this repair is drop-kicked into his lap. Squadron Fifteen also wants us to do a pre-deployment workup for the combat teams. The Navy is putting incredible pressure on us to get on mission, so some clever soul decides that, since there's "nothing else going on" in dry-dock, the officers and forward personnel can devote most of their time to trainers and simulators up the hill at the San Diego Detachment of the Naval Submarine Training Center.

So now our lives are torn among support for the shaft repair, the nuclear repair, and our pre-deployment workup. This all comes on top of our normal training regime, paperwork, administration, and getting people off the ship to go to shore training schools. The XO is the one who must coordinate this and make sure that there are minimal conflicts between each activity. The ENG is in the worst position because he has to coordinate a dry-dock repair period and a major nuclear repair, but he's expected to be one of the OODs in every mission simulator, which sometimes takes four hours out of his day. I stand watch mostly as EDO, but because of simulators, I have to turn over the watch multiple times a day, which makes it very hard to keep work moving as new officers are briefed on procedures and try to make sure they're done safely.

The pace begins to take its toll on the crew. We're thousands of miles from our families, so the married people are getting pressure from wives and children. We've been gone for three months now with no end in sight. The crew lives like bachelors in hotel rooms, and the drinking and partying begin to increase as frustration with the pace and being away from home take hold. The Captain does his best to keep everyone focused and motivated on the mission, but it's hard to imagine being on mission when you're wearing a hardhat and boots every day and climbing seven flights of stairs to get up the dry-dock and onto the ship.

I decide that I want to lose weight, so I begin drinking one Myoplex shake for breakfast, one for lunch, and then a sensible dinner. The problem is the two six-packs of beer after dinner. I begin feeling very tired and unhealthy. I'm qualified but still junior, and the nuclear procedures we're doing now are subject to the most intense scrutiny the Navy can impose. The shipyard Test Engineers are stationed in Maneuvering at all times and watch the duty officer's every move. The pressure on the junior officers is relieved by massive partying sessions on Fifth Avenue in San Diego and with trips down to Tijuana. Some of the officers even buy cars so crappy that we can park them in Mexico and not worry about them being stolen.

This pace continues for six weeks, and then we get the report from the shipyard crew doing the shaft repair. I'm exhausted, and everyone tiring of being in the dock. They've discovered serious problems with our propulsion train related to the improper installation of the shaft in overhaul by Norfolk Naval Shipyard. The sound we first heard leaving Virginia has come back to haunt us. They tell us that the problems are so bad that they're going to have to cut a hole in the hull to replace components. It's the worst possible news, and the ENG begins to laugh as he reads me the report. The QA paperwork and testing involved in cutting a hole through a submarine hull is enormous. They tell us this hull cut will extend our dry-docking by at least six more weeks. The crew is crushed. It's now April, and we're going to be in dry-dock until May at the earliest. There is no choice, but the despair runs deep. Even the Captain's optimism seems to be faltering. The work continues.

The nuclear repair is now approaching the key portions, and the dangerous state it poses means that we have to do 24-hour shifts to get it done. This means ENG DEP is going into shift work. The department is split into three sections that work in eight-hour rotations. The EDMC makes a schedule that allows everyone weekends off, but it doesn't help the disrupted body clocks. I find myself standing day watch EDO for the first portions of the repair. The repair has been pushed up a few weeks, so it ends up happening partially when the ENG is on leave to see his family. This means that Lieutenant Sheklund is the acting ENG while we're in the really sensitive portions.

The scrutiny from the shipyard and the test engineers is microscopic. Work is stopped at any sign of trouble. Procedural compliance and formality standards are insanely exacting, and we get through the first week smoothly. Problems emerge at the beginning of the second week; guys are getting tired and small things start to appear sloppy. The CO and EDMC decide that the best thing to do is stop production work on the midwatch and continue with the key portions only during days and swings.

I'm shifted to midwatch EDO, and my stated job is to get all other routine daily evolutions done and prepare the Engine Room for work the following day. The first night of mids, I come into work at 2100 and we have our daily briefing with a PowerPoint slideshow that most of the workers could recite from memory by now. I walk onto the ship and begin turnover with Adam Johnson, who is supervising one of the key retests from the repair. RC Division comes in and wants to continue a procedure into the midwatch. The Division Chief, Chief Harbin, is on the midwatch with me, and I'm comfortable letting them continue, but we can't do this without the Engineer's permission. Adam Johnson calls the Acting ENG at 2330 and asks permission to work past midnight on RC division procedures. When Adam comes back to Maneuvering, he tells me that Sheklund gave permission but didn't sound fully awake at the time. We don't call the CO or EDMC because, in this case, the approval of the ENG is all that's required. The shipyard monitors have gone home for the night, and we continue work.

We get the job done and around 0530, we reposition some of the last valves to get set up for the next step, but I don't update the valve status board in Maneuvering with the new position of these valves. It's my fault, and I turn over to Mike Harven with these two valves in the right position but not updated. I collapse in my hotel room with incredible exhaustion. I get a call during the day asking about these valves, and it's clear something has gone wrong. I feel the sinking in my stomach, but I'm so tired that I turn over and head right back to sleep. It's Friday, and I get up at 2000 for my next midwatch.

I come into the ship to find the XO briefing the next duty section. I've been removed from watchstanding as EDO again, and the duty officer explains what happened during the day. The reactor was safe, but my failure to update the status board clued the shipyard and the test engineers on to the fact that we were working on the midwatch without their knowledge. Adam Johnson stands up for me and confirms that we had ENG's permission. But that's not enough; the XO tells me I should've known better. Lieutenant Sheklund is fired and now the XO is Acting ENG. The Senior Supervisory watch is now stationed twenty-four hours a day to provide experienced monitoring of the reactor plant. I'm frustrated, but I see what I did wrong. I talk to the XO, who tells me to come back in the morning to talk to the Captain about my upgrade.

I walk away from the ship at 2300 on a Friday night, wide awake with nothing to do. I'm frustrated and angry with myself for screwing up again, but I'm angrier with Sheklund because I feel that he put me in this position. There's nothing to do but go downtown and have a few drinks.

I find the Captain the next day walking down the pier, and I approach him in the style I know he prefers.

"Sir, I'd like to talk to you about what I did wrong on Thursday and how I'm going to fix it."

He smiles a little and replies, "Ok, Mr. Fleming, shoot."

The conversation goes well, as I'm getting better at the harsh self-criticism that's expected in nuclear power. The Captain listens to me and then says, "Alex, I understand what you 're saying, but I'm still disappointed by your judgment. I want you to go up and observe the end of the repair. The situation is really intense right now, so I can't let you stand watch, but just help us get through this and I'll reinstate you in a few days." Kevin Mooney is positive even as he tells me about his decision. The pressure the test engineers are putting on him doesn't allow him to bring me back to watchstanding before the end of the test procedure. I understand his position, and I find myself respecting the man and his position even more. He goes on to say, "Mr. Fleming, I want you to go up there and help Mr. Johnson finish up this test procedure however you can since you were around the last time we did this portion. I don't want officers who are perfect and never make mistakes; that's unrealistic. I want you to work hard and learn from your mistakes. If you do that, then I will always forgive you." He ends with a pat on the back and continues down the pier.

Despite my status as "removed from watchstanding," I find myself deliriously happy to have Kevin Mooney as my CO. I would do anything for that man, and the worst thing in my life would be to let him down. I decide at that moment that I will be the best officer in the wardroom and that I will make Kevin Mooney proud, no matter what it takes.

The repair ends a few days later, and we are down to the last month of dry-dock. The hole in the hull gets patched up and things begin to go back together. Rather than relief, we all feel more frantic as the squadron pushes us to do a mission workup at the same time as our repairs. Then we get the news that we will have another engineering inspection before we reach Guam. We're late on this procedure, and the ENG can't push it off anymore.

So our days are occupied by all three sections working in the attack center, which is a massive simulator of a submarine control center operating at periscope depth. The full watch sections of fourteen people work three four-hour shifts per day with "hot swaps," which means we do actual turnovers to the next section while the simulator is still running, just like what would happen in real life. The squadron personnel from the local Squadron Eleven and our Squadron Fifteen in Guam come to monitor these sessions. The critiques are harsh and painful as we try to shove months of operational experience into one week of a busy dry-docking. The only relief comes when the computers crash periodically, allowing us to rest and regroup. The guys whisper that the XO has an emergency method to crash the trainer before we make absolute fools of ourselves if things get really ugly.

We're also putting the ship back together as the new shaft is finally installed. The ENG and EDMC become engulfed in preparations for the upcoming inspection, the first one for the new Captain and the first one that reflects on this ENG since he was very new during the last one. Mike Harven is running around like a crazy man again preparing the ship to undock since there have been significant changes to the trim and list conditions, and the WEPS and I are swamped in preparations to load all the weapons back on, including four exercise mines. Squadron Fifteen tells us at the last minute that they want us to do a mining certification in Hawaii on the way back to Guam. This is a rare procedure that requires very specific preparation.

The undocking procedure is almost exactly the opposite of the docking. We button up the ship, clear the dry-dock basin, and begin flooding down back into the water at about 0300 on a crystal-clear morning in May. Our natural state is in the water, so getting us back down allows us to remove many temporary services and operate as normal. It's a relief to everyone. The only drama occurs as the tugs attach and begin to pull us out of the dock before we've removed all the lines from the ARCO. We hear a singing noise, and then a sound like a gunshot as one of the forward lines parts and snaps back. The new sonarman, Chief Akorn, knows what's happening and gets all his men out of the way. Snap-back from parted lines has been known to sever limbs, but miraculously, no one from the ship or the ARCO is hurt.

We're free and floating in the water again, and the excitement can be felt in every corner of the ship. The COB breaks down the ugly scaffolding from topside as fast as possible, and by the time we get to the pier, we almost look like a submarine. The three months living in hotels has treated us all badly; I've put on twenty pounds of beer weight. The WEPS and I spend the next four days loading all the weapons back into the torpedo room. It's an even slower process since we're all out of practice, and we have to load the four exercise mines at the end. These weapons are so old that they actually have components made of wood.

Everyone is scrambling to move out of the hotels and get all their stuff onboard. We're scheduled to head out on sea trials the following morning, and the Captain warns us to move out now because, if sea trials are successful, then we'll be underway for Hawaii the next morning.

We leave San Diego with a large complement of test engineers onboard. The first time a ship is underway or submerges after a repair period, a lot of retests and observations need to be done. The WEPS is working frantically as the QAO with piles and piles of paperwork to ensure that the ship is safe for underwater operations. We also have to do a deep dive to test depth to ensure that all the holes in the ship can hold back the full force of the ocean. The procedures go smoothly, and the sound problems with the shaft are gone. The sonar operators are so surprised by how quiet the ship is that they can identify many other sounds that need to be corrected that they couldn't hear when the shaft was rattling. These problems are minor, and we can fix them all after we leave.

The Navy is back in the Guam Train mentality. We barely touch the pier after two days of sea trials before we get the messages sending us across the ocean to Hawaii. Squadron Fifteen is intent on getting us on mission this year, so in mid-May, we leave San Diego for the last time. Many men have relationships with women in this area, and our time away has distanced us from everything going on in Guam. We can't speculate on how the families have dealt with our absence.

I find myself standing OOD again as we speed across the ocean. It's becoming a joke on 711 that we only have two speeds: All Stop and All Ahead Flank. The ENG and EDMC are deep in drills and training to prepare for the engineering inspection when we get a message that Squadron Fifteen would like to do a quick tactical evaluation while we're in the Hawaiian Op Areas. It's hard to prepare for the inspection alone, but now we have to do a Mining Certification, a strike exercise, and a practice run through an underwater minefield while we're there. The CO and XO are livid at the confusion we're enduring.

The main problem is that we don't have enough time. When submarines move across the ocean, they're in a very tight imaginary box called a SUBNOTE, which tells us how fast to go and where to drive. It we get outside of the SUBNOTE, we are not allowed to submerge and we have to surface. So the entire life of the ship is focused on making distance down track and staying in the box. The problem is that most training drills and evolutions involve the ship slowing down, which causes us to fall even further behind. So the ENG is trying to do his evolutions to prepare for inspection, while the WEPS and the NAV are trying to do tactical evolutions to prepare for the tactical evaluation. The OOD is trying to do all this and still get the ship down track while not falling behind the SUBNOTE. Since we have a new reactor plant, our SUBNOTE gives us a very fast speed of advance, so every minute we're not going as fast as we possibly can, we're losing ground.

We make it to Hawaii and don't even get to stop at the pier. We do a BSP in the outer portion of Pearl Harbor, pick up the Squadron riders who are evaluating us, and head back out to begin the evaluation immediately. The ship has to make multiple trips to periscope depth to trade messages about tactics and communicate. This is when I make one of my most important discoveries as an OOD. It's very different to be in charge of a ship underwater driving straight than it is to coordinate operations during tactical situations. I'm the officer of the deck as we transit to the training minefield while conducting tactical communications and preparing for a Tomahawk strike exercise. It's my job to balance everything that's going on while also driving the ship safely with at least two trips to periscope depth each watch. My inexperience begins to show when I get so distracted by everything that's going on that I allow the ship to get five miles away from where the Captain wants it to be. We are still in our operating area, so it's not a problem off the ship, but I've still violated the CO's Night Orders, which govern what happens on the ship from watch to watch. I'm removed from watchstanding pending a navigational upgrade, which is a blessing in disguise. Now I'm free to focus my efforts since I'm the AWEPS, the Mining Officer, and the Strike Officer. The fact that I'm not standing watch for a few days allows me to focus all my energy on getting the tactical evaluation done.

We are a fantastic success. The exercise mines work great, we complete the strike exercise, and Squadron seems satisfied with our level of proficiency in periscope depth (PD) operations after five months in port. I'm reinstated as we head back to Hawaii with an admonition from the CO and NAV on paying attention to the position of the ship and the CO's Night Orders. We spend one night in Pearl, hardly enough time to have one drink at Duke's Canoe Club, before we leave to return to Guam. The ENG and EDMC now have full control of the ship's schedule as we prepare for my second major engineering inspection on 711. I'm standing OOD and not getting any drill sets to prepare, so I'm very happy to stay in the front part of the ship and not be a direct participant.

We head back to Guam at full speed, and we have drills every single morning, which is exhausting. We enter a schedule called Vulcan Death Watches, which means that the ship runs three sections but in five shifts per day. The six-hour evening and midwatches are normal, but during the hours from 0600 to 1800, each watch section gets a four-hour drill watch (0600-1000, 1000-1400, and 1400-1800), and a specific drill team puts the entire ship through Engineering drills to practice responses to casualty situations. This very tiring schedule puts a strain on the whole crew because no one gets to sleep during the day, so everyone becomes more and more tired.

After three days of this, I'm trying to get small cat-naps in the hour between drill sets. We've just finished a fire drill, and I'm sweaty as I strip off my poopie suit and crawl into my rack. My eyes have barely shut when I feel the movement of the ship change. I hear fans coasting down because some portion of the power system has gone off, and the 1MC blasts out "Fire in the Engine Room; rig the ship for Fire and General Emergency!"

Chapter 10: The Tip of the Spear

I leap out of my rack in disbelief and feel the adrenaline pump as I throw on my uniform and head back to the ER. I find myself in a cloud of haze that smells like a campfire, and I see that way too many people are already there. I head forward to get out of the way and find the OOD in control with a puzzled look on his face. We can smell the smoke in the front of the ship as well, and half the power is off. The OOD has executed his actions and is bringing the ship to periscope depth. The Captain comes in and tells us to surface the ship so we can ventilate and get the smoke off. All procedures are more complicated since half the power system is still off to isolate the damage.

A few moments later, the electrical division Chief and the ENG come to control to brief the Captain. I miss the beginning of the conversation but inch closer to hear the last part.

"...of the breaker just exploded inside the switchboard. It doesn't look like there's any damage outside of the component, but it's going to take me at least 48 hours to pull the breaker and clean all the muck off the inside of the switchboard. If we reenergize the busses before that, we're just asking for grounds and another fire."

"So what does that take away from us?" the Captain asks.

"The starboard busses and parts of the evaporator; we're not going to be able to make fresh water until we get them back..." the Chief continues, but I'm already walking forward to the OOD to inform him about the evaporator. We have two mostly-full tanks of potable water, but we're also five days from Guam, and if we're going to make it with enough drinking water, we need to take action now.

Fresh water conservation is one of the most important things done on a submarine. Even though we have an evaporator, sometimes we can't run it for tactical reasons, and the capacity of the onboard storage tanks is fairly small. No one on a submarine lets the water run any longer than required. A "submarine shower" involves wetting yourself down for thirty seconds, turning off the water, soaping and shampooing, and then rinsing yourself off for another thirty seconds. The total elapsed time is four minutes if you really stretch it. The other thing onboard that uses an enormous amount of fresh water is cooking and washing the dishes, despite the rage of every galley chief telling his cooks to conserve water.

These facts drive the OOD's first orders after I inform him of the situation: "Chief of the Watch, Secure showers. To the Galley Watch Captain, go to paper, secure the laundry. Inform the COB that the evaporator is down, and I'm securing showers and laundry and putting the galley on paper." The WEPS knows exactly what to do.

The Chief of the Watch gives a verbatim repeat back, sends the messenger off to find the COB and post signs on the showers, and begins to make calls on the powered phones. Since the casualty is still in progress and the rig for fire and general emergency has not been secured, the NAV sticks his head into control from the CO's stateroom, which doubles as Damage Control Central during casualties.

"Officer of the Deck, the ship is ready to emergency ventilate the engine room with the blower; DC central intends to commence emergency ventilating." The request flows quickly and competently since we've been practicing these procedures every day for a week.

"Very well, NAV," the OOD replies.

"Commence emergency ventilating." The 1MC announcement follows. The low rumble of the low-pressure blower begins slowly, like a wolf working up to a full-fledged howl, and immediately the air in the ship begins to clear. Things slowly return to normal as we secure the rigs and return everyone to normal watchstation. I'm sweaty and smelly, but I realize that I can't do anything about it except wash my face and neck. I head for my stateroom and change into clean underwear, but I still feel grimy. I climb exhausted into my rack, not getting under the covers because I don't want to get them dirty.

After two days of no showers, one hundred twenty men in tight quarters get really smelly. I have watch every eighteen hours, and I get slimier until I can barely stand my own body. The electricians are hard at work trying to restore power to the other half of the ship, but it's a slow process. Every time a crewmember sees an electrician not on watch, he asks why he's not cleaning up the switchboards so we can all take showers. We are submerged and moving again, but the Captain sends us up to PD to ventilate once every six hours just to get rid of the smell.

Three days later, I'm the OOD when the EOOW calls forward with a long-awaited announcement.

"Conn, Maneuvering, the starboard AC busses are restored." I smile and sigh with relief. There are muted cheers from the control room watchstanders.

"Maneuvering, Conn, aye. Maneuvering, Conn, start up the evaporator and fill potable."

The EOOW gives me a verbatim repeat back that tells me he was anticipating this exact order. No one's had a shower for fifty hours. I call the Captain. I want to wait until we have a little water coming until I open the showers, but he tells me to restore showers. He makes a 1MC, congratulating the electrical division on their hard work and telling everyone that they stink. Laughs can be heard through the decks.

We arrive in Guam a few days later to a hero's welcome, which seems ironic to many of the crew. It's June 3, and we've been gone since January 4. The island hasn't changed, and the families are excited to see us. But the excitement is tempered by the inspection team that's waiting for us. We make quick overnight repairs, and I have duty, so I don't even leave the ship. We are underway the next day for the inspection. Once again, I'm not chosen as one of the participants that the team will observe. Being the OOD during an engineering inspection is quite boring, and you spend most of your time executing simple immediate actions while keeping everyone out of the team's way.

The inspection team takes over the wardroom, so officers have to eat standing up in the staterooms. Otherwise, as the Sonar Officer and AWEPS, I'm bored. I catch up on my sleep, respond to all the casualties as the XO's phone talker, and try to help in any way I can. The XO and I have had so much practice that I can pretty much read from his facial expressions what reports he wants to send, so we work like a well-oiled machine. The facial expressions of the engineering department become more pained as the days go by, and I can tell that things aren't going as well as they should.

I don't know how badly until we return to port two days later and the CO calls the officers to the wardroom. We have again performed below fleet standards. This is a very bad thing for the CO and ENG. A ship with recurring problems is a big red mark on the Pacific Fleet roster, and we're now going to be getting "special attention" to help us improve. This only means bad things for the Engineering Department, which will face the brunt of the "help" (micromanagement) from the squadron. I'm immune to some of this, being AWEPS, but the pain will be felt by all. The only saving grace is a private comment that the Senior Board Member made to the CO. He said that we have all the pieces; we just haven't been implementing them long enough to let them work. The CO is confident that we can fix ourselves, and that's why we didn't get a worse grade.

I gather my green canvas sea bag and walk topside. The day is hot and humid, and I stand for a moment, taking in the hills and breeze. I feel like I've lived a lifetime since we were last here. We've been gone for six months and I hope my apartment is OK as I walk up onto the pier. I loaned my car to the girl I was dating when I left in January, and I'm looking forward to seeing her again. I get a friend to drive me to a flower shop and then to the hospital to find her. Sonja is a Navy OB-GYN, and I find her office with little trouble.

She smiles and thanks me for the flowers, but she offers no hug or kiss as she invites me to sit down. I can see that something's wrong, and I prepare for the worst. My car is fine, but it turns out that, during the six months of my absence, she'd met another man, it got serious, and now she feels committed to him. I'm shocked but not angry since we weren't exclusive. I ask her why she didn't tell me this when I called her from Hawaii and San Diego, and she tells me it didn't feel right doing it over the phone. I think for a minute and she goes on to say that she likes me a lot, but she knows I'm not ready for a long-term relationship. I try to remain outwardly calm, but inside, I'm just mad at myself and the submarine lifestyle. I'm never going to have a normal relationship if this keeps happening. I ask to meet this great guy, and she replies that he was only here for a few months, and now he's in North Dakota.

I'm frustrated and done with the conversation. I ask her where my car is and if she could please give me the keys. I make my goodbyes and leave the hospital, picking up my car at her apartment building and heading home. My apartment is fine; the typhoon shutters protected the place from any serious damage, and one air conditioner kept the mildew away. I stand on my balcony overlooking Agana Bay and sip a beer, trying to figure out how I'm ever going to lead a normal life while working in the U.S. Submarine Force. I get a call a few minutes later from Mike, who asks if I want to come out drinking, and I can think of nothing better to do.

Mac and Marti's is the only popular bar that's not a strip joint, and we begin there. It's a polished nightclub with a large walk-in humidor and plenty of pool tables. After a few screwdrivers, we move on to some of our favorite places in Tumon. The dancers in Guam haven't changed. There are a few new faces, but mostly the dancers are happy to see the San Francisco sailors back in town because we're big spenders. Mike and I hit The G-Spot, Tourist, Crazy Horse, Club USA, and many other joints as we stumble up and down the strip. We end up closing down Crazy Horse at 0400 and the dancers invite us to have breakfast with them at one of Guam's many after-hours clubs.

The after-hours clubs get really packed about 0430, and the place is full of dancers just getting off work and their boyfriends or guys who want to take them home. The group I'm with is eating Chinese food when one of the dancers, Tanya, starts stumbling around the room yelling, followed closely by her large Samoan boyfriend. She's in pretty bad shape after dancing for eleven hours and having guys buy her drinks all night. I try to ignore her and talk to the other girls with us, but then Tanya grabs a barbeque lighter from the owner's pocket and starts lighting things on tables around the restaurant. The owner, a small Korean man, is used to her antics and just smiles, but I turn as Mike gets the bottom of his t-shirt lit. I turn back to my beef and broccoli when I feel a tingling on my arm. I turn to see my polyester shirt burning my left arm. I try to swat it out, but it doesn't work, so I revert to the "stop, drop, and roll" advice of my childhood.

I get up very angry as a huge second-degree burn begins to form on my left arm. I yell at Tanya, but she breaks down in tears and her Samoan boyfriend gets in my face and tells me to back off. The whole thing is incomprehensible to me because this drunken girl has just lit my arm on fire. I decide that I've had enough fun for one homecoming night, and I head back to my apartment. The next morning, I wake up with a two-inch by one-inch blister on my left arm. I'm going to have to live the rest of my life with a stripper burn scar. I put my pounding head in my hands and think in despair, *Only in Guam*.

Our homecoming relaxation period lasts exactly one day, and then we get back in high gear preparing for mission. We'll be underway for a week to do more training, then back for a week for simulators, and then underway and back when there is a material failure. The mission date looms only two months away, and the new Commodore makes it clear that we're going to make it or die trying. The officers can see that the Captain is under incredible pressure to get this boat fixed and operational. We are now eighteen months into the Guam experiment with not one operational mission day out of the San Francisco. The Commodore also has some help from his new senior deputy, Captain Ginda's replacement.

I'm on duty on July 4 when a Danger/Caution tagout system violation occurs because of a misspelling on a danger tag. The error is minor, but there's no such thing as a minor tagout problem. When you're dealing with ship and personnel safety measures, any error is major. Tagouts are a zero-fault system. My previous failures in the tagout process mean that I know exactly what needs to be done, and I start the investigation and call in all of the relevant Chiefs and department heads, holiday be damned. The Captain agrees with convening a critique and reminds me to invite the new Squadron Deputy, whom I have never met.

At 1415, I hear "Commander, United States Navy, arriving" from topside, and I rush up to the command passageway ladder to meet the guest. This is the duty officer's responsibility when any VIP arrives onboard. I get to the bottom of the ladder and hear a massive voice holler, "Down ladder." This guy moves fast. I get out of the way as a bear of a man descends into the Forward Compartment Upper Level. He is 6'3" with broad shoulders and short black hair with hints of grey at his temples. His arms look like sledgehammers and he has a slight belly that strains his belt but doesn't fold over. He looks me over quickly and then pushes me aside.

"Hey, duty officer, critique in the wardroom, correct?" he says, even as he is already going down the ladder to the middle level.

"Yes, sir," I say as I scurry after him. "Is there anything else I can get for you?"

"Nope." He smiles at me and enters the wardroom, shutting the door in my face. I'm puzzled and stand there thinking about the encounter. I don't know whether to be offended or amused by his manner. This is my first encounter with Andy Hale.

Commander Hale becomes a much bigger part of our lives in the following weeks. He has just returned from a tour as CO of the USS Santa Fe, and his job is to train the Captains in the squadron and be the Commodore's eyes and ears. The best second-in-command officers are those who make things happen and take care of management so the Commodore can focus on decision-making and public affairs. Andy Hale is a ball of energy that immediately pushes Squadron Fifteen to a higher level, and he makes it his personal mission to get us trained and out on mission. It will also be Hale who eventually decides whether we're ready to go out into operational situations. He makes it clear that we're smart, but we have a long way to go.

It becomes clear to me that Kevin Mooney and Andy Hale have worked together before because they seem to be friends, but that doesn't make things any easier. The officers are engulfed in lectures, attack centers, simulations, visual ship recognition drills, and periscope practice. The forward personnel barely have time to get routine maintenance done with all the operational training. We have to overcome problems getting our mail in Guam, which hasn't been coming to the right ship since we left Virginia. Computer systems are not yet operating and the attack center in Guam is barely getting on its feet.

We head out to sea to practice again in late July, and many people are sad because we're going to miss the biggest party day of the year in Guam: Liberation Day. Guam does observe the 4th of July, but it's only really celebrated by the military people. The locals pay very little attention because they're preparing for the massive three-day festival that surrounds July 21. This is the anniversary of the day that the U.S. Marines came ashore in Guam and ended the brutal and bloody Japanese occupation of the island in World War II. Some locals still remember the concentration camps native Chamorrans were taken to during the war. Several Guamanian families sacrificed deeply to hide American service members during the occupation, and the atrocities inflicted on the island's population were comparable to what the Nazis were doing in Poland.

Liberation Day shuts down the whole island as families camp out for days on the parade route that goes almost half the length of the island. The traffic is so bad that many Navy people are happy to be gone, but I've never seen the parade. So I'm sad when the CO tells us that we're heading out for another week of tracking practice on live targets. The ships of the U.S. Merchant Marine based out of Guam are always happy to drive around like crazy terrorists to help the submarines train, so we find ourselves on Liberation Day afternoon tracking a merchant ship as loud as a freight train up and down the Marianas Island chain.

We discover another problem, as a hydraulic rupture causes our fairwater planes to jam at full rise, and we get a one-way ticket to the surface. This is incredibly bad timing because now we have a major problem with a vital ship's control surface and we're only three weeks away from our mission certification. We have to go back to port to fix the problem and possibly conduct extensive repairs, but because it's Liberation Day, no tugs are available to get us back to port, so we spend the night cruising at five knots on the surface twenty miles from Guam.

I get the midwatch, my first taste of a night watch on the bridge. The sea salt fills the air and a warm wind blows gently across the black of night. The ocean at night has a sound that's calming and eerie at the same time. When the few clouds block the moonlight, I'm plunged into shadows that seem to chill my mind. We're not going fast, so there is little roaring of waves, just a gentle lapping against the hull. It's a moment of peace in an insane summer. The lights from the buildings on Guam shine in the distance. Suddenly, I see a flash, and the sound arrives a few seconds later. I get to see the fireworks of Liberation Day after all, with a delayed sound track. I call down to control and tell the guys on watch to get on the periscope if they want to see it. I laugh at the irony since I'm getting my wish while everyone is cursing the material condition of the ship.

We head back to port and make another frantic set of phone calls to get a flyaway team from Pearl Harbor to repair the sail planes. The Commodore is livid and the CO feels even more pressure. The material condition of the ship is stopping us at every turn as we try to get and keep this twenty-five-year-old boat underway. Our three weeks in port allow me to return to the Hash and begin running around the jungles of Guam again, but my happiness is muted by my frustration with women. I guess I an much angrier at Sonja than I'd previously thought. I try to place the emotion, since maybe I'm just hungering for human contact outside the Navy. Dancers are not great dating material because many of them have serious psychological problems, and it's hard to reconcile hundreds of guys a night getting to see your girlfriend naked. I try to stay off that path.

My friends Henry and Alli invite me to an interesting party for a girl whose fiancé has just broken off their engagement and left the island. The woman, a former helicopter pilot turned public affairs officer, is named Arwen. She is beautiful and funny, and in my slightly buzzed haze, I think she may be interested in me, but this turns out not to be the case. Without logic, I become even more frustrated with women, especially since she is set up on a blind date a few days later with Josh Chester and they seem to hit it off royally. I take my anger out on Josh, and our personalities clash since we're in the same watch section. The XO and ENG quietly change the watchbill so Josh and I don't have to work together.

The repair is done in two frantic weeks of working twenty-four hours a day and duty days are becoming more and more intense. Every single thing that breaks is tracked to its final conclusion since no one is relying on the material condition of the boat anymore. The XO begins to write "FIX IT NOW" on the top of every single Plan-of-the-Day, the document that controls our lives and schedules from hour to hour. The Duty Officers must report any minor deficiency in any system, and we're expected to tour extensively and find things going wrong every day. If you call the Captain for your evening report and you haven't found and fixed at least three material failures during the day, you're in big trouble. If you find a problem and don't follow up on it to the end, you'll end up with a major screaming session during your turnover report.

Standing duty on 711 is slowly turning into a minefield, even as we try frantically to get through all the retests and get our planes back together. Training intensifies, and the moment the planes are retested, we are sent underway again for our last week of workup before Mission Certification. The watch sections begin to come together as the XO makes scenarios for us to practice. It turns out that I'm pretty good at tracking multiple contacts and managing the fire control party, and I'm also forceful in my recommendations to the OOD. I'm now standing a watch called JOOD, making sure that the picture of the tactical situation on our computers in control matches what's actually going on through the periscope. The OOD, JOOD, and JOOW split the time on the periscope because it's really hard to be vigilant for more than twenty minutes straight looking through one eye, especially in the dark.

The workup is fun for me because I've been chosen as the Surface OOD for the certification. This means I'll get a lot of practice driving the ship in and out of port, controlling tugs, moving in the harbor, driving the navigation training channel, getting underway and returning to the pier, and spending a lot of time in the sun. I'm also busy as the Sonar Officer because I have to work with Chief Akorn and Petty Officer Broomfield, the Sonar Chief and LPO, to revitalize the sound silencing program. Sound silencing is of paramount importance on an operational submarine, but it's one of those things left to get dusty in long shipyard periods and overhauls. Now that our shaft is quiet, we can begin tracking and correcting sound deficiencies. We do our best to bring the program back to life, and I grow closer to Chief Akorn and Petty Officer Broomfield as I realize how incredibly competent they are. I begin to listen to them more and do what they say, asserting myself only rarely. They are so good at training me that I hardly notice that they're making me a better officer until it has already happened. I'm protecting them, and I begin to notice that they are protecting me behind my back. I begin to have more supporters than just the Captain, and I'm assigned to help the weakest fire control section with the new WEPS as my OOD.

Chris Worley and I hit it off immediately. He's a short man with a good sense of humor who lets much of the stupidity on submarines roll right off him. We are now in the same watch section and spend almost every waking hour together on watch or doing reconstruction after watch. Alec Beeker joins us as the JOOW, solidifying our officer section. Two new officers arrive three days before certification, Jim Henry and Nestor Stevens, and we tell them to go home and pack their sea bags because we're leaving and not coming back until December. We leave in August for our final workup and head north toward Japan for more practice. Andy Hale is onboard and seems to be everywhere at once as we get closer to mission status. The excitement of being operational engulfs the crew, and the more days we are at sea without a failure, the taller everyone stands and the more pride I see in every job.

One minor hiccup arises when we find a problem with one of the masts. It turns out that a section of 2 x 4 wood was left in the sail after the plane repair, and one of our communications masts is broken and needs replacement. We take this in stride as we reach Yokosuka, Japan for our first real port call after almost two years in the Western Pacific. We approach the pier, and everyone is excited to get out and see Japan. We stand on a floating dock at Yokosuka Naval Base and the XO releases the crew but tells the officers and Chiefs that we can't leave until we get him a long list of missing administrative items and paperwork. The leaders are furious, and we head below to polish any paperwork we have and get it to him no matter how bad it is. We're in a foreign country for a port call for the first time and we're stuck on the boat until 1900 doing paperwork.

I become angrier and angrier until the WEPS lets me go at 1930, and I have to run around the Navy base to try to meet up with the NAV, Sheklund, and Rome (another new officer from the summer) so we can head to the New Sanno Hotel in Tokyo for the weekend. Many of the guys want to stay in the Officer Sanctuary on the base, which is basically a fraternity house for submarine officers, fully stocked with alcohol. The NAV used to live in Tokyo, so he takes those of us who want to go up to the real party section of town. We make the last train up to Tokyo and arrive at the New Sanno just before they release our rooms. The New Sanno is an American military hotel in the Hiro section of Tokyo that has been in our possession since WWII. We check in and then review our game plan for the night. We head for the best party section of town: Roppongi.

I walk down the streets of Tokyo in awe. Roppongi is a cross between Mardi Gras and the most insane red light district I can imagine. Bars line the street, and many embassies are nearby, so foreigners abound. We head to a few famous clubs, one multi-level called GAS PANIC, but the true destination is an underground bar called the Lexington Queen. I immediately fall in love. The Queen's business concept is an open bar and models get in for free, while men have to pay a $100 cover charge. If you want to sit at the VIP tables, you have to buy bottles of liquor for $100/bottle, but then you get to sit in deep seats with a perfect view of the dance floor and the whole club. I look around and can't see a woman in the place who doesn't look like a model. It's a long night, and we return to the hotel at sunrise. The next night, more of the officers come up from the base and we have another great night; this time we end up in the VIP section or dancing with models on the dance floor. I'm convinced Tokyo is one of the greatest cities in the world, and my ability to speak Russian comes in handy with all the Eastern European models.

We have one weekend free, and then we're all yanked back into reality. I have duty on Tuesday and it's time to land the racetrack (a circular platform that allows people to work on the top of the sail) and repair the communications mast. I'm immediately impressed with the work ethic and efficiency of the Japanese workers. They are far above and beyond the quality of shipyard workers in Guam or Hawaii, and our repair gets done in record time. The Japanese are still suspicious of nuclear-powered ships, so a small man on a bike comes every day to take water samples and make sure we're not polluting. Living in the sanctuary, though it isn't Tokyo, is still awesome because it has a full pool table, movies, foozball, shuffleboard, a barbeque, a deck, and every other amenity you could imagine. I buy a scale and find out that my weight is the highest it has ever been in my life. I've put on almost 80 pounds since joining the crew. I'm better at my job, but the lifestyle of eating and little exercise does not work for my body. I begin my quest to get my weight down, but it's interrupted as we get underway again.

The word has come down that Commander Hale thinks were ready for our mission certification. We head back to Guam at full speed to prepare for the final push. Adam Johnson has left us because his commitment to the Navy is up. We leave him in Tokyo on the way to climb Mount Fuji. I'm rapidly getting closer to being the senior JO, a scary thought for me on many levels. Mike Harven has transferred, and the only person left who is senior to me is Mark Sheklund. The only thing this means for me practically is that I get to sleep in a better bunk in the WEPS stateroom, a vast improvement from the 9-man. We speed to Guam underneath a typhoon, as we thank our lucky stars for being a submarine. We come up to 200 feet under the center of the storm just to see what it feels like, and we take twenty-degree rolls even at that depth. I can only imagine what it's like on the surface. We get back to Guam in late August, and it's time for certification.

The crew can't believe it's happening. I can't believe it's happening. Sailors are very superstitious people, and many of us thought the ship was never going to go on mission. Minor repairs go on constantly, but the Captain's FIX IT NOW mentality is winning against the age of the ship. There is some reluctance to be overjoyed, but we all feel like things are looking up. We've been home less than 25 days in 2004, but it seems like it may be worth it. We're beginning to believe in ourselves and to believe we can get the job done. This fundamental shift in attitude is so subtle that I can't see it when it happens, but one day I feel it right along with everyone else. My apartment is in shambles, my weight is up, and my personal life is a wreck, but the USS San Francisco is operational and going on mission.

Certification is exhilarating, tiring, and painful all at the same time. We know our jobs and how to get things done; it's just a matter of doing it all at the same time. I learn an incredible amount in the week of exercises, rehearsing every possible mission we could have. The only hard part is seeing my apartment building out the periscope every day, knowing that we're so close but won't be home anytime soon.

My life blurs into a cyclical routine: wake up, tour, check the message traffic, pre-watch briefing, eat, relieve the watch, operations, get relieved, eat, do reconstruction, fill out the mission report, do divisional paperwork, try not to eat before bed, shower, get three hours down, and then start again. I should add "get coffee" between each step. We constantly self-assess after every mistake. The CO and XO work as hard as anyone, and we have a post-XO from Seattle onboard who needs mission experience. He stands as Command Duty officer in a three section rotation with the CO and the XO. Commander Hale seems satisfied with our performance, but that doesn't stop his corrections and upgrades of every single officer. Commander Hale and the Captain seem to get along fine most of the time; other times, we can hear them yelling at each other in the CO's stateroom.

The two weeks pass in a blur, and in the end, we are certified. The Navy doesn't let the knowledge we've gained fade at all, and we have two days in port to do final paperwork and get ready to be gone for months. We get an awkward reminder of our own mortality when a legal officer comes to update wills. We fill out the uplifting form that asks us if we want to know if a family member dies while we're on mission or if we want the Navy to wait to tell us until we get back to port. I have duty one of the days, so I barely have time to close up my apartment, pull the typhoon shutters, and toss my keys to my downstairs neighbor.

Completely appropriately, a typhoon forms just as we're about to leave. The most dangerous part of leaving Guam is large waves from heavy weather just outside the breakwater. So we decide on a minimal bridge rig, nothing but a blank sail and the basics. The lookout stays down in the enclosed area and there are no other watchstanders.

So, in the end, after nineteen months of pain, only Kevin Mooney and I sit on the bridge together as the ship prepares to get underway. I have a minute to think about where I am and what it took to make it here. I'm the OOD of a combat vessel, heading out to do its job. **We are the tip of the spear.** It is an emotional moment for both of us. Five minutes before our scheduled departure, everything is ready. I turn to the man I've come to respect and love as much as my father.

"Captain, sir, request permission to get underway."

"Officer of the Deck, get the ship underway," the Captain replies.

"Get the ship underway, aye, sir." I can't help but grin. I call the pilot on the bridge-to-bridge radio and tell him to stand-by; he's on the tug, so we don't have to transfer him off later. The tug is tied up at our bow, standing by at a 90-degree angle to pull us away from the pier. I shout down to the men standing topside.

"COB, CAST OFF ALL LINES."

"Cast off all lines, aye, sir." I catch the wisp of a smile on Billy Cramer's face from twenty feet below me. That's the way it should be. I turn to Petty Officer Christopher, my lookout, sitting by the whistle handle, ready to sound our underway signal.

"YN2, make it a good one." He nods, understanding my meaning.

"Helm, start the outboard." I speak into the microphone in my hand.

"Officer of the Deck, all lines cast off," the COB shouts. I turn to Christopher.

"Lookout, sound the whistle," I say. He pushes down the handle and the deep groan of the whistle seems to fill up the harbor and echo off the hills behind us. The ship is declaring to every person who doubted us that it is alive and it is a warrior.

I'm concentrating on the side of the ship so that we pull away evenly without hitting anything. We clear away from the pier and slowly rotate so we're pointing down the channel out of port. I order the tug cast off, but in my focus, I still hear the XO on the 1MC below saying, "The ship is underway, time five-seven." The cheers can be heard all the way to the bridge, and Kevin Mooney and I share a smile.

Being on mission is the most exhilarating experience of my life. We execute two operations vital to national security in the months that follow, and everyone is excited to do the job they were meant to do. Even the ship seems to be supporting us; almost nothing breaks down. The routine is tiring but satisfying. Routine communications are cut off, so nothing in the outside world can distract anybody. It is the greatest time of my life.

Despite the seriousness of the job, there are some moments of levity. Halfway Night is a series of ceremonies that allow the whole crew to relax in the middle of our trip. My watchsection thinks I'm such a hard-ass that they pay $700 to put a pie in my face. I'm in good company, though, since another watchsection pays almost $1,000 to throw a pie at the NAV. I learn that whipped cream mixed with tuna is very difficult to get out of your ears. Several interesting services are auctioned off, and one division pays $2,000 to get the officers to clean their portion of the ER during the next field day.

The highlight of Halfway Night is the drag queen beauty pageant to choose Miss San Francisco. The Captain judges as several crewmembers dance and perform in drag. It seems the COB's wife equipped him with a box of women's clothing to be used specifically for this purpose. There is a runoff between two Auxiliary Division members, Ashley and Funder. The Captain finally has to choose Funder (aka Leticia) because she's more "spunky" and did a better job stuffing her bra. I laugh so hard that I'm crying by the time the winner is declared.

We near the end of mission, and on the way back, we find out that we're going to be subjected to another engineering inspection. The Squadron Engineer has been riding us for the entire mission to "help" us prepare, and the ENG is eager to make up for the two previous performances but also nervous on principle. I won't be around for the inspection because I'm late for another part of my career progression. Each officer in the submarine force has to qualify to be an Engineer after eighteen months onboard. The process involves about two months of studying, several sectional exams on each part of nuclear power, and then a trip to Washington, D.C. for an oral exam at Naval Reactors. I'm late for this school, so I have to get started immediately once we return from mission. I'm excited because I'll get some time on shore, and I'm not sad at all about missing another exam.

The other officers are engulfed in inspection preparations by the time we hit the pier in Guam in early December. The return from mission party is a barbeque on the pier with all the wives and children present.

The crew dresses up in their best white uniforms, and the Captain, COB, and Commodore shake each man's hand as we walk off the brow. I don't have a significant other, so I say hi to a few people and then head down to the ship to change. There will be no partying tonight; we are mentally exhausted, and the crew has to be back at 0715 to continue inspection preparations.

I'm the first officer ever to do the engineer courses in Guam, so I'm pretty much on my own. I find the study room and begin working through hundreds of pages of questions. Most people study for the exam by trying to do every problem in the entire exam bank and hope to remember it all when they get the exam. I start with the Electrical section, and I wave goodbye to the ship as they head out for a week of inspection workup, followed by the actual inspection. I rapidly fall into a relaxed study schedule, finding my rhythm. The supervisors don't care when you study as long as you get your hours in and pass the exams. The worse you perform, the more supervision you get. I come into work at the lazy hour of 0930 and study until 1400. I work out from 1400-1600 and then study from 1600 until 2000. I live a quiet, academic, monk-like existence, which is a refreshing change from the boat. I feel more and more like a normal person.

I set up my Christmas leave plans, and I decide to head to Australia for some fun and exploring. The ship returns to port on December 23, and I barely make it to the pier before I hear the word: We've been given the highest possible score on the inspection. The ENG is freaking out. The guys are running around the pier screaming at the top of their lungs and the department chief smiles with quiet satisfaction. The year is complete. We got an Above Average on TRE, achieved Mission Certification and the best possible performance on the engineering inspection, and we finished two missions vital to national security. The CO and COB decide the new slogan of the San Francisco will be "The Best Damn Boat in the Pacific Fleet."

The whole department meets at Mac and Marti's to drink beer and tell sea stories. We bask in some well-earned success. The joke when I show up is that all the officers are excellent except for Fleming, who is below average. I laugh at that one a little bit, but it does make me feel bad for not being with them during the inspection. The CO sees my concern and pulls me aside.

"Alex, you know we're just screwing with you, right? You're my favorite JO and I know that you've stood behind me one hundred percent through everything that went on this year. I could not have done this without you, and I will never forget your support." Even though the Captain is feeling pretty good, I can tell that he means it. Hearing those words from him is better than any award the Navy could give me. We return to the crowd and the crew of 711 paints the town of Tumon that night.

I've been in Guam for two years and never been anywhere but Tokyo. I head to Australia on Christmas Day to stay in Sydney for New Year's. I stay in a hostel in King's Cross for two weeks and end up underneath the Sydney Harbor bridge for New Year's Eve with a few million of my closest friends. Many people are suffering because a tsunami has just struck Sumatra and Indonesia, but I'm living the good life in a beautiful city. I get a few days in Cairns and then reluctantly head back to reality on January 3. It's a good thing I didn't visit Sydney when things were going badly on the ship; I might never have returned.

I'm back for a teleconference training class called OpWaterChem, which I'm taking with an instructor in Hawaii. The time difference means that the class goes from 0500-1000 every day. It's annoying but part of the joy of the Guam experiment. The class is two weeks long and I have one duty day on the ship before they head off for their reward. Our successful mission means that the ship gets to go to Brisbane, Australia for a port call. The guys will get a week in Australia to party and find nice Australian women. It's the reward given to submarines that do a good job. I have just returned from that country, so I laugh and wish them good luck. I'm not jealous; they deserve it, and I'm getting a good deal by being off the ship at school.

I laugh as I am relieved on January 5, and I tell the oncoming duty officer, "Make sure you don't have too much fun." He just smiles because he knows they probably will.

I take my bag and walk off the ship as guys are loading supplies for the trip down south. The COB is bringing on materials for the "crossing the line" ceremony all Navy ships perform when they pass the equator.

I will miss that one as well. I cross the brow and pass a group of mechanics smoking on the pier. I smile and laugh at some gentle teasing from the group, which includes Funder, Senior Chief Hager, and Joey Ashley. I return their salutes and wish them good luck with the Aussie chicks as I continue down the pier to my car. It is the last time I see Ashley alive.

Chapter 11: Collision
January 8, 2005, 1142 hours, near the Caroline Islands

There is a low rumbling that sounds to some like "God crushing a beer can," and the ship slows instantaneously from thirty knots to four knots. The boat is well stowed for sea, so there are no projectiles, but every single person is thrown forward into the nearest vertical object. The people in the chow line end up in a huge pile in the middle level. Rome and Litty, on the starboard side of the Diesel in the lower level, land in a heap on the deck. The OOD is thrown out of control, shouting, "Emergency blow" even as he hits his head on a computer screen. The DOOW, Senior Chief Hager, is up out of his chair to update a status board and is thrown onto the ship's control panel, shattering a gauge. His chair is thrown forward, breaking his leg. The Quartermaster flies fifteen feet forward and lands on the stern planesman, breaking the back of his chair. The JOOD is thrown forward onto the fire control displays in front of him, hitting his head and neck. The men in the smoke pit land on the pumps directly in front of them, except for Ashley, who is thrown forward twenty feet and hits his head on a pump assembly. Every single plate of food is thrown all over the galley. In the wardroom, one officer shoves his fork through his lip, and the Captain watches as one of the mess cooks flies over his shoulder and lands on the flat-screen TV on the forward bulkhead.

The Captain is pinned in his chair but quickly recovers and runs up to control to find out what happened. He gets there after the Chief of the Watch has already thrown the emergency blow handles, but the ship is not going up. The DOOW is back in his chair, not saying a word about his broken leg, shouting out depths. The ship has a down angle, and it is clear from indications that something serious has happened to the forward ballast tanks. Matt Priests quickly recovers from being slammed against his stateroom wall and runs back to the ER as he hears an emergency report of flooding in the ER. He knows this is the most serious situation that a ship can have: underwater, doing an emergency blow with flooding in the ER. No submarine can get positive buoyancy with the ER filling with water, and for a moment, Matt is sure that they're all going to die. He quickly finds that the report was an error; the water is just a leak from a cracked freshwater pipe.

The Captain and Chief Hager in control are still watching the depth gauge, waiting for it to show upward movement. Finally, after almost a minute, the ship begins to rise, breaking the surface at 1143:52. The next forty minutes are a chaos of emergency reports, calls for the Doc, people trying to respond to ten different casualties, and people trying to care for injured shipmates. In shaft alley, an electrician named Brain Barnes doesn't know what else to do, so he holds Joey Ashley's hand and talks to him, waiting for Doc Akin to arrive.

It's about 1230 in Guam and 1130 in Japan when the following message is downloaded to every major Navy command in the world. It is the highest-priority NAVYBLUE message type that exists, ensuring that the senior leadership of the country will be awake no matter the time of day: "POSS GROUNDING. MANY INJURIES, ONE LIFE-THREATENING. SHIP ON SURFACE. NO HULL BREECH. NO DEBRIS SIGHTED. REQUEST EMERGENCY MEDICAL ASSISTANCE."

It is not much information, but it's enough to get everyone in Guam, Japan, and most of the Pacific Fleet going in hyper-drive to get to this remote location in the Caroline Islands. It takes a few hours, but every ship in the area is evaluated as a possible rescue platform. CSS-15 immediately calls the senior deputy, Andy Hale, who starts pushing the rescue. The Guam hospital is called and told very little except to send an ER doctor and nurse to the base as soon as possible. A small coast guard cutter called the Galveston Island can be ready to get underway in less than an hour. The Seal Team based in Guam is called and asked to start loading their gear onto a huge ship called the Gysgt Frederick W. Stockham, which is parked in Guam harbor. The Stockham can support a full Seal platoon and a helicopter. The local helicopter squadron is called and asked to provide an aircraft for possible evacuation and transfers to the submarine.

I'm a very long way down the list, but at 1700, I get a call from the Emergency Command Center (ECC) at CSS-15, telling me to report to Squadron immediately. The ECC has been activated to coordinate recovery efforts, and though I have no idea what's going on, I get a sinking feeling in the pit of my stomach when I see the parking lot full on a Saturday afternoon. I arrive at the ECC to find Chief Harbin and Ensign Savoca, both former 711 crew, manning the phones and computers. They tell me what's happened and we start a rotation in the ECC. I find a seat at a group of tables with eight phones. Three projection screens hang on the walls, and two televisions on either side of the room are tuned to cable news. The phones keep ringing, and the three of us race around the building since no one knows how bad it is and what we will need.

The USNS Kiska is underway south of Guam and directed to make best speed for 711, now limping north on the surface at about eight knots. Andy Hale and the CSS-15 Corpsman get underway on the Galveston Island along with an ER nurse and doctor, who board the ship still in their scrubs. The Seventh fleet in Japan sends a very short press release and assigns an On-Scene Commander for the response. P-3 aircraft out of Misawa, Japan are launched to monitor and provide coverage for the San Francisco. It will take two days for them to get home and the Admiral wants someone to be with them every step of the way. There are still the inherent problems of getting emergency medical help to a submarine, and as people begin to get reports about the nature of the critical injuries, a neurosurgeon is put on a plane from Okinawa since Naval Hospital Guam does not have one of its own. The next message from the ship at 1800 tells us that they need to Medical Evacuate (Medevac) the critically injured sailor.

That evening at 1945, the Stockham gets underway from Guam carrying a surgeon, an ICU nurse, four corpsmen, a doctor from the USS Frank Cable, and an entire Seal Platoon. We monitor and report this in the ECC, but now we have other problems. CSS-15 needs to contact the families of every single person onboard. This is easy for the families that live in the area, and we have a wives network in place to call everyone to a meeting. Robinson, who is now a Chief, is the senior enlisted man on land with me, and he begins to work with the wives to give them whatever information we can. The problems come with the bachelors, and that becomes my assignment. We have decent contact information for some, but some of the parents' phone numbers are outdated. It is now 2000 on Saturday evening in Guam and 0400 on Saturday morning on the East Coast, a bad time to try to get in touch with anyone. Between answering phones, monitoring the Seventh Fleet chat room where response is being coordinated, and making phone calls to the U.S., we're going to have a long night, but we're all thinking about what the men on the submarine are enduring.

Doc Akin immediately realizes that the focus of his attention needs to be on Ashley, who is in critical condition. The ship is on the surface now, and they're in voice contact with the medical officer at Task Force 74 in Japan. Luckily, Craig is a prior enlisted corpsman, so he and the other crewmembers trained in first aid set up a triage station to deal with minor injuries. He bandages almost forty people as the night continues, and the COB leads people in cleanup. The ENG and the Captain are mostly involved in assessing the material condition of the ship. The damage is extensive, and the ship is running the low-pressure blower continuously to stay on the surface. The bridge is manned, and the men can see severe damage to the bow section, with some stray pieces of metal sticking out of the water. The helmsman has to keep a port rudder on constantly to steer a straight course at eight knots. The officers know that the ship will probably have to go into dry-dock, so there are plenty of preparations to be made, and they send several material status messages to tell the fleet what is happening. People who are uninjured, not on watch, and not involved in repair efforts crawl into their racks and try to get a few hours of sleep. Nobody has any idea that the sub is the lead story on CNN and almost every news service in the world.

At almost 0200 in the ECC, the building is busier now than ever before. The Commodore is making personal phone calls to the family of every single crewmember, but there is one officer whose parents we cannot find. I'm exhausted, but I huddle with the Admin officer and we think we have a solution. I know where he lives, and he shares an apartment building with three other officers. If I can get the superintendent to let me into his apartment, I can find an address for his parents on his mail or something and then trace them through that information. I drive down into Tumon and reach the apartment building at about 0230. I call up to the wife of one of the other officers and I'm not surprised to find her awake. I talk to her for a few minutes to make sure she's OK, and then I explain the situation. She calls the superintendent and asks him to let us in to Chris Atkins' apartment. The super is understandably hesitant, but I show him my military ID and explain that we want to contact this person's parents before they see it on the news. He relents and lets me into the apartment, where it takes me about five minutes to find a letter from the Atkins family at a P.O. box in Florida. It's not the answer, but it's something. It takes me five minutes on the Internet to find the number for the Mail Boxes Etc., and I try to explain to the confused clerk what I need. She refuses to give me the home number for the Atkins, but I convince her to pass on an emergency message for them to call CSS-15 or me as soon as possible. I then call the Admin officer, who is still getting people on the phone for the Commodore, and tell him to expect the call. It is now almost 0400 and I head home to get some sleep before what I'm sure is going to be an even longer day tomorrow.

Just as I'm heading to bed, Commander Hale and the Galveston Island are closing to within twenty miles of the damaged submarine. Rain and fog cloud the night, but the San Francisco finally sights the Coast Guard cutter at about 0600. The situation is terrible because of the four-foot seas and seventeen-knot winds gusting through the area. This means that the submarine can't open any of the escape trunks, and any people who go on or off the ship have to come through the bridge trunk, a twenty-foot tunnel that goes from the upper level to the top of the sail. Andy Hale has been designated the On-Scene Commander (OSC) now, so he's in charge of the recovery efforts and any rescue attempts. He and the Captain discuss the situation and decide that the ship is too low in the water to attempt a small boat transfer, so the only option is the helicopters on the Stockholm, which is approaching at top speed.

Ashley needs to get off the submarine to a hospital, and a plan emerges to leapfrog a helicopter from the San Francisco, to the Stockholm, to the Kiska, and then to the Guam Naval Hospital. The trip is too long for the helicopter to make on one gas tank. The first priority is to get more medical personnel onto the submarine to help Craig Litty and Doc Akin, who have not rested or stopped moving since the collision. The helicopter hovers over the bridge around 0900 and lowers three Navy Seals (a doctor, a corpsman, and a rescue swimmer) onto the ship through a whirlwind of spray. The doctor evaluates Ashley and recommends immediate evacuation. The problem is that moving a stretcher around a submarine is hard enough, but getting it up the bridge hatch has never been attempted. Broomfield, also now a Chief, begins working surgically with a hacksaw to clear a path for the litter to move up to the bridge. This is made more complicated when Ashley stops breathing on his own and is given a breathing tube.

The crew attempts to lift Ashley vertically into the bridge trunk as the helicopter hovers overhead, but on the first attempt he has to be brought back down to control. Once he is stable again, they make another attempt to lift him up, but the litter cannot fit past the upper hatch. He is brought back down, and some people want to try again. Chief Broomfield offers to get a welding torch and cut a hole in the bridge hatch big enough for the stretcher, but Ashley's condition is deteriorating. The helicopter lowers the surgeon from the Stockholm to the submarine and then has to leave and refuel. Below, Ashley's condition is growing worse, and despite everyone's best efforts, Joseph "Cooter" Ashley passes away at 1311 on January 9, 2005.

I'm standing in the ECC with the Commodore, Chief Harbin, and Ensign Savoca when we hear the news. I'm strangely numb and dizzy, as if time has slowed down. A part of me tries to remember everything about Joey Ashley, but I can't decide what I'm feeling. The Commodore finishes the call with Commander Hale and puts down the phone. He turns to us.

"OK, no one says a word about this to anyone. There are notification procedures that have to be followed and we want his family to hear about this from us before anyone else. Inform me when notification procedures are complete." Arwen is standing to my left, doing an admirable job keeping her cool even though her boyfriend is on the San Francisco. She's the Public Affairs Officer for U.S. Naval Forces, Marianas, so she is responsible for the press releases regarding this event. She acknowledges and goes about her work.

Only certain people in the military are allowed to inform families about the death of a service member, and now the one in Ohio has a job to do at 0200 on a Sunday morning. The other injuries onboard are less critical, and our focus shifts to stabilizing the ship and getting everyone else off as soon as possible. I'm manning the phone in the ECC with the Squadron Assistant Navigator, who has the charts out for the area of the collision. We look over the two charts; one is labeled 81023 and the other is a smaller-scale "Echo" chart with more bottom contour lines. He plots the position of the collision and finds a small brown notation that says "Discolored water reported." We look at the Echo chart and find no notation for the same spot; it's just a blank piece of ocean. The discolored water spot was directly on the SUBNOTE path that the ship was supposed to take to Australia. I turn to the Chief and ask, "Chief, if you were driving in this area, which chart would you use?"

"The Echo," he replies with an even face.

"Do you think they looked at the 81023 and saw this?"

"I don't know, sir." He stares at the two charts with me.

"And another thing: where did this SUBNOTE come from? Have any ships passed through here before?" He has no answer for this either and remains silent. I turn to face the video of the broken bow being broadcast on the ECC screen.

"Chief, you know this investigation is going to take months and involve hundreds of people, but I bet that, in the end, it's going to come down to those two questions."

"Sir, you're probably right." He shakes his head and begins folding the charts.

The ECC now becomes a planning room for the ship's arrival. Twenty-nine people will have to be transported to the hospital as soon as they arrive. Engineers and Naval Architects are arriving tonight from Pearl Harbor to help assess the damage and stabilize the ship. A team of salvage divers from Virginia is in the air with all their gear, and they should arrive on Monday. The ship sends us a message describing what they want on the pier and how they would like to coordinate the transfer of injured personnel. The family support group is meeting to pass on as much information as possible, and the wives are understandably frantic to see their husbands. Chief Robinson and Summer Sweden, the ombudsman, do an incredible job keeping everyone calm and coordinated. The pieces needed to stabilize the ship and keep it afloat are staged on the pier. A quiet calm engulfs the squadron building as everyone does their job on Sunday evening, preparing for what will be an insane Monday. The Commodore schedules a meeting to go over the plan on Monday at 0900.

"People, today is about getting the San Francisco into port in a calm and respectful manner," the Commodore says to the standing-room-only ECC room.

"There will be no chaos on the pier, no rushed movement. We will be staging busses, ambulances, and other medical teams out of sight. The families will be kept at the end of the pier and will only be allowed down in an orderly fashion. Phone banks will be in place on the pier so single sailors can call their families. Once everyone has cleared out, we will remove Petty Officer Ashley. We do not know the mental state of the people on the San Francisco; they've gone through an incredible amount of trauma. Chief Robinson and Lieutenant Fleming are going to conduct training for the crew of the Corpus Christi (705) so that they can take over watches on the San Francisco if required. We want to be ready to help them in any way we can." The Commodore is in tight control as he explains the philosophy of the day.

I'm a qualified duty officer, and I've decided that, as soon as they get into port, I'm going to take the duty. I've been reading the material status messages and I know as much as anyone on shore about what's happening on 711. Chief Robinson conducts training for the 705 Engineering department so that they can be qualified and stand watches on 711. I sit down with seven engineers and architects, who discuss their initial plans for stabilization. Senior Chief Janowski, a mechanic from Squadron, will be leading the efforts because most of the senior mechanical Chiefs on 711 have been injured. I conduct training for the forward watchstanders of 705, telling them what I know about the material condition of the ship and reviewing what they should do when they encounter people who were in the collision.

"Don't pry for information. Be polite and courteous. Don't allow any 711 sailor to be issued a sidearm until he has spoken to a counselor. Listen if they want to talk, but remember, these people have been through something that we can't imagine, and we don't know how they're going to react. Remember the three basics to suicide prevention: Ask them if they're thinking about hurting themselves, don't leave them alone, and inform the Duty Officer and Duty Chief immediately." The message seems to sink in as I speak since all these sailors can sympathize with what is going on.

People start to assemble at Pier Sierra at 1600. A bus is arranged to take people to the hospital and two ambulances are parked in the wild, unkempt grass on the pier. The families are kept behind a barrier 100 yards down the road. The crewmembers of 711 who were on land are waiting to go onboard and take the watches. I stand with Chief Robinson at the end of the pier and watch as the Galveston Island comes into port, carrying Andy Hale and the CSS-15 Doc, who have been knocked around like crazy for two days on a very small ship. San Francisco rounds the turn into the inner harbor, and even though I know what to expect, I'm still shocked by how low she is in the water. Suddenly, I realize that every other submarine and ship in port has their crew topside and manning the rails. All flags are at half-staff, and each ship renders a solemn salute as the San Francisco cruises past. The U.S. Submarine Force is a small community, and we're all grieving for one of our brothers.

The two tugs pull the ship, which is still conducting a low-pressure blow to maintain positive buoyancy, up to the pier, where it is tied up. I find myself standing next to the Captain's wife, who is serene and collected. I see Kevin Mooney up on the bridge with another one of my friends as OOD. Avril Mooney whispers to herself, "God, he looks terrible." I look at the Captain and see that she's right; he is pale and the purple under his eyes makes him look like a skeleton. He has just been through one of the worst experiences a Captain can endure, so I'm not surprised.

Everyone stays out of the way as the brow is craned over, and the first person across is the 6'4" Doc Akin, who looks like he's about to fall over from exhaustion. He is embraced by the Chief Corpsman from Squadron, and the ambulance pulls up to take off the most seriously injured sailor, a mechanic who hurt his back badly when he was thrown forward onto a ladder in the ER. The ambulance pulls away, and then the bus arrives to take the twenty-nine other people who need to go to the hospital. Their wives come down the pier to greet them, and I begin to see my friends emerge with broken arms, broken legs, wrapped heads, and black eyes. I have to try very hard to keep a straight face, and despite my best efforts, I gasp as I see people.

Once the injured people are clear, I'm the first or second person across the brow, engulfed in a flood of people going on and coming off. My friends are surprised to see me, and they ask me about the news coverage of the event. I get to the crew's mess and find the WEPS, who asks what I'm doing here. I tell him I'm taking the duty. The Captain is right behind him.

"Sir, I've been manning the ECC for two days. I know the material status of the ship. I want to take the duty," I say. Kevin Mooney thinks for a moment and then just nods. I throw my bag on the WEPS rack and head up to control. The ship is a mess. It smells musty, different from normal. I see bandages and plastic wrappers on the floor, and I step back as I realize the dark marks on the carpet are blood. Cracked plastic is strewn everywhere, and pieces of metal walls are missing, hastily cut away with a hacksaw. The wide-screen TV in the wardroom is covered with a towel, and I lift it to see a crack with red spots in the center. Used medical supplies are everywhere and the whole place smells sweaty. I find Mike Vasquez in control and tell him that his wife is on the pier waiting for him. We do a quick briefing, and then I take the duty, announcing on the 1MC, "Lieutenant Fleming is the duty officer."

The hard part for me begins now. Some of the 711 crew is leaving and the 705 crew is coming onboard. The reactor is not being shut down, so the Engineering Department is staying. I tell a Chief from 705 to get surgical gloves on and start cleaning up the wardroom. The rest of our help begins scrubbing the walls and picking up trash, food, and all the other things that are lying around on the ship. The carpet is stripped from the wardroom because of the bloodstains that will never come out. I walk topside with the Duty Officer badge and immediately find myself in a crowd of shipyard engineers who want to get things done. I know that the biggest mistake we can make right now is being hasty and screwing something up, so I calm everybody down. Chief Janowski and I know what has to happen, and I tell him to go slowly and tell me when he's ready, that I will protect him from the frantic off-hull people.

But before we connect off-hull air, something else needs to happen. The sun has gone down and all the unessential people are gone when we begin to lift Joey Ashley out of the submarine. A single ambulance waits on the pier and a quiet descends as the people present line up. We hear only the crickets chirping as we wait, and the cloudy night obscures the moon. Arwen is with one of her staff, videotaping the ceremony for Ashley's parents. The men of his division, led by Craig, carry the black body bag over the brow draped in an American flag. The Captain and COB follow in their dress whites. The Squadron staff, crew of the 705, and crew of the 711 stand in two long lines stretching almost 100 yards down the pier. Each rank salutes as Joey passes, and there are many tears as we all face mortality. Once he is loaded in an ambulance, everyone remains at attention as they drive away, and then many are silent as we all contemplate our own lives.

I have work to do. The ship is low in the water and unstable, and the first priority is to connect off-hull air, which will bring the ship further out of the water and allow us to secure the low-pressure blower that's been running for three days straight. Chief Janowski is working on the procedure, and I have a meeting with Matt Priests and the engineers and architects, where I emphasize to them that we're going to move slowly and steadily and proceed only when we are safe and have an approved procedure. We're dealing with tired people and people who are unfamiliar with our systems in a highly abnormal condition, and I'm not going to screw this up by rushing. Matt Priests is oddly quiet for the whole meeting and turns to me after the engineers have left.

"Who the hell are you? Where did this come from? If you'd been like this as a watchstander last year, you would never have had any problems," he says.

I stop and realize that he's right. I understand why I've changed. I'm ashamed that I wasn't onboard with my friends in their time of need. I felt helpless for days watching the injury reports arrive. I could do nothing to help until now, and I've decided I'm going to be the best submarine officer in the fleet because that's how I can help my shipmates. It is my own unique manifestation of survivor's guilt. I have remade myself in Matt Priests' and Kevin Mooney's image. **I know what it takes to be a good submarine officer, I have learned it the hard way through trial and error, and I'm going to put aside my past and my personal feelings to do it.**

Things move slowly and carefully that night. I find myself on the bridge, coordinating the attachment of large air hoses that will pump air into the ship. The problem with this is that, if we don't get it right, the air could come out and cause us to sink at the pier. It is 0230 by the time we get the first set connected and tested, and we begin to lift the ship out of the water. There is a jagged edge about twenty feet aft of where the bow normally ends. We gaze in wonder as we realize that the metal forward portion of the ship is gone or crushed. The entire bow is compacted into a twisted mess. We get the ship only a few more feet out of the water before it stabilizes. We turn off the blower and do some testing that confirms the ship will indeed sink if we don't provide extra air. I call a halt at 0330 since the ship is floating and appears to be stable for now. The divers are preparing to enter the water in the morning, and the danger tags for that are being done. I get everyone to sleep and conduct a long tour to make sure everything is somewhat cleaned up for the morning. I get a fitful hour of rest in my clothes even though the phone keeps ringing every ten minutes with someone wanting more information.

I'm up again at 0600 for breakfast and to deal with more material problems. The 705 crew are doing a great job, and the 711 crew are quiet but seem in control. The WEPS comes in to relieve me at 0630, and I turn over the condition of the ship. I come to the Captain's stateroom with my bag at 0715 to give my turnover report since I have to head off to school. He looks very tired as I describe the events of the evening, and in the end, he speaks quietly.

"Alex, I can't tell you how much it meant to me that you were waiting on the pier for us and that you came down and took the duty. That was the act of a leader, leading from the front. I will never forget it."

I nod, humbled, and say goodbye.

My school keeps me busy the next few days, but it's clear that San Francisco needs to go into dry-dock. The ship is not stable enough to make it to Pearl Harbor alone, and Guam has no nuclear-rated dry-docks. The civilian Guam dry-dock is called "Big Blue," and it has never been used to dock a submarine. This is one of those times where things happen in a hurry, and the powers that be decide that we are going into the old, rusty Big Blue no matter what. The ship needs to be patched up before it can transit to its final repair destination. There is a lot of speculation on whether the ship is even going to be repaired, but that decision will be made by people much higher than we are.

The investigation teams begin to arrive. A safety center investigation is led by a Captain from Pearl Harbor. Their job is to determine what happened and how to prevent it from happening again. This is the Mishap Investigation. Another investigation, the official inquiry, could result in disciplinary action and blame for the people involved. Both of these begin at the same time, and people on the ship are testifying constantly. We all wonder what's going to happen to the CO because he was not relieved immediately when the ship got back to Guam. This situation is resolved a few days later.

I'm at the gas station on the naval base when my phone rings. It's the Navigator. He asks me where I am and tells me to be at the ship in ten minutes. I don't know what it's for, but I'm two minutes away, so I hurry over there. I come down below and see the XO, who says, "Oh, good, they found you; Officer Call in the wardroom now." I nod, hustle to the wardroom, and find myself seated at the table with all the other officers, waiting. The XO comes in to check on us and then tells one of the new officers that he doesn't have to be here because the Captain just wants to talk to the officers who were onboard before the grounding. Kevin Mooney comes in with a Diet Coke and a glass of ice. He puts his notebook down, crosses his arms, and doesn't look up for a few seconds.

"Men, the investigation committee has decided that there was enough information onboard the ship to prevent the collision. I'm going to be relieved this afternoon by Commander Hale. He will be the Captain by 1700." His voice cracks as he continues. "I know that this is going to be a hard time for everyone, but I want you men to remember the things I taught you. Remember that you are warriors, and stand tall." I listen to him, but I can't help being overwhelmed by sadness, and the words begin to wash over me. This man worked his whole life to be a submarine Captain. He turned a troubled ship around and took us on two successful missions. The crew loved him, he saved my career, and he taught me what it means to be an officer. I cannot believe that he is being fired. But I realize that, in the Navy, no matter what, the Captain is always responsible. He is taking responsibility, just as he told Ashley's parents on the day the ship returned: "I'm the one responsible for your son's death." I cannot imagine a harder test of character, and I know that Kevin Mooney will be with us all, even though he will not be in command of the San Francisco.

The speech ends quietly, and no one has any questions.

Chapter 12: Shattered

The first dry-docking of a nuclear submarine in Guam proceeds slowly and with many hitches. The damage to the hull extends too far back, so the plan for the wooden blocks under the submarine has to be changed. The Guam Shipyard personnel are inexperienced at best, and their crane operations during the dry-docking make everyone gasp in fear and check hardhats. The primary concern is that the San Francisco cannot achieve zero list and trim, which was so important during the San Diego dry-docking. The buoyancy changes make it physically impossible to even the ship, so the floating dry-dock has to be tilted to match the ship, lift the ship out of the water, and then level out. This all makes for a very long day for Craig Litty, who has to sit on the bridge for ten hours while the engineers and architects sort the mess out.

I drive down to the dock at noon and get lost on my way to the new location. Getting to Big Blue involves weaving past the identical cinder block Navy housing and down to the back end of the base. There is a marina with some nice ships, but others look like they have been sitting there since the Japanese invaded. I take a side street that stretches past long lines of swamp and reeds, eventually leading me to a rusted chain-link fence guarded by a tired-looking native with an oversized, sweaty uniform. His teeth are stained red from chewing the beetle-nut, which is popular among island residents. He smiles at my ID and waves me farther into the swamp. I continue past rusted equipment and old cranes, grown over with grass like an ancient junkyard, and I finally see the dry-dock. It is as much rust now as blue, nestled between two reefs in the outer harbor. It has a different view from Polaris Point; I can see the thin line of the breakwater leading to the commercial pier.

The parking lot is uneven, with a dozen rental cars and a new set of mobile homes constructed for office space. A hastily constructed shack stands at the end of the peninsula, along with a rough bridge leading to a catwalk out to the dock. I stop on a grassy ridge and look over the reef. Big Blue is much larger than our San Diego dock, and there are huge rectangular openings in the wing-walls that allow me to see the hull of the submarine. The ship does not even cover half the length of the dock.

I grab a hardhat and make my way down into the basin, looking with awe at the rusty holes in the bottom of the dock. The security guards are still unfamiliar with Navy personnel, so they stop me, but after I explain myself, they wave me through. I join a crowd of people standing in the basin looking at the front of the ship. The entire left side is buckled, the sonar dome is shattered, and the sonar sphere looks like a crushed volleyball. The bow of the ship has been bent to the right so that the whole thing is no longer straight. Nobody can believe what they're seeing, and I turn to the WEPS, who looks at me and says, "Alex, we should have died. It's amazing this boat made it to the surface."

I nod in agreement because I have no words to describe what I'm seeing. I can't help but remember the beautiful pictures of the smooth bow at the end of the San Diego dry-docking, right after we finished the hull cleaning. I feel terrible thinking it, but I cannot help but joke to the WEPS.

"You know, Dad is never going to let us borrow the car again," I say, and he laughs. Humor is sometimes the only solace for submariners in really bad situations. I go up to the ship to say hi to a few people and drop off some paperwork, but I really have nothing to do, so I return to studying. I have another month before my exam and I've lost time with all the attention on the ship after the collision. I pour myself into my studies, trying to ignore the hell I'm going to face when I get back to the ship.

As time goes by, several people develop post-traumatic stress disorder. Many never want to set foot on a submarine again. The Navy has these people talk to counselors but grants most of their requests. Nearly twenty people are removed from the San Francisco crew, but the rest of the men are still shattered. Everyone retreats into their own lives, trying to rebuild some sense of normalcy, no matter how frail. The whole Navy is worried about the mental condition of the people onboard, and the new Captain, XO, Navigator, and Assistant Navigator come into a situation where they are dealing with possible problems at every turn. Andy Hale is a known quantity for the crew, but the new XO is someone we're just beginning to understand.

Dana Niles is a tall, thin man with dirty blond hair. He is what the submarine force refers to as a "super-nuke." His technical skills are unmatched, and he spent his shore tour after being an Engineer as an officer in the Naval Reactors "Line Locker," a group of actual submarine and surface officers who provide reality checks and various other services to the Engineers at the center of nuclear power. He and I have a discussion after I introduce myself; I feel awkward because I was not onboard for the collision, and he has some of the same feelings. I ask him how he is dealing with it, and he tells me to do my job the best way I know how, and in the end, things will work out. The officers and I can immediately tell that Lieutenant Commander Niles is going to be an interesting and demanding XO. He's more thorough and comprehensive than I can imagine; he immediately begins using a "ship's tickler" and "action board" to ruthlessly track the hundreds of small administrative jobs on our plate. He's normally calm but not afraid to get angry, sometimes appearing to lose his temper at the drop of a hat. I don't think he's really angry; I think it's for show, but I don't know him well enough to be sure. The XO is supposed to be the taskmaster and disciplinarian, and I think he fills the role well.

I talk to him on the phone once every few weeks as I study, but most of my time is focused on nuclear power. I can take all the sectional exams in Guam, but I have to fly to Pearl Harbor to complete my last preparations and take the written final exam. The comprehensive exam is forty pages of questions that have to be completed in five hours. It will be graded by Engineers in Washington, just in time for me to fly there for an oral exam. I can't take it in Guam because even FedEx takes a long time to get to Guam, so my exam wouldn't make it to Washington in time. I'm happy to wrap up my notes and head to Hawaii again. The good part about this trip is that I'm staying in quarters on Pearl Harbor's submarine base, but the study office is actually on Ford Island, so that means I get a reimbursed rental car to drive back and forth.

I love Hawaii, and especially Oahu, so I rent a car anyway, but the Navy paying for it is just a bonus. I leave Guam on Monday morning and arrive in Hawaii on Sunday afternoon, one of the oddities of air travel across the International Date Line. I pick up my rental car, check into the quarters on base, and then head down the Nimitz Highway for one of my favorite drives. I pass the industrial area of Sand Island, the downtown area, Aloha Towers, and the Ala Moana Mall. I finally make the turn into Waikiki, and I feel like I'm home. I wonder what my life would be like if my first ship had been based in Hawaii. I guess I'd be sitting in my apartment, sad about those guys on the San Francisco out in Guam. I walk into Duke's Canoe Club in the Outrigger Hotel, which reflects my image of Hawaii with its dark wood and dried palm fronds. A band is playing on the deck, and the surf gently breaks as the sun drops below the horizon. I sip my Tropical Itch and wonder where the crew of San Francisco will go from here.

I complete the written exam and land in Washington, D.C. on a cold February day. I have been in Guam and Hawaii, so I'm wearing shorts, a t-shirt, and Tevas. I change into long pants in the airport, and I walk outside to find freezing rain. I curse the sky; I'd forgotten that freezing rain even existed. I make my way to a cab and wonder how anybody could possibly live in such a horrible place. The exam at Naval Reactors goes well, but it is tense for me because I keep getting called out of the room every twenty minutes. Everyone in the building wants to talk to an officer from the San Francisco and get a firsthand description of what's happening. I also meet Dana Niles's old boss, who questions me about my duty day following the collision and then thanks me for taking the time to come talk to him. The other students in the exam are convinced that I've failed because I keep getting called out. I pass in the end and call the ship to inform them. Nobody expected me to fail, but anything can happen in Washington, and I don't want to have to take the exam all over again. Dana Niles seems pleased, and I head back to Arizona for a few weeks of leave before returning to Guam.

Repairs are still just at the beginning when I return to the island. We've stolen every single welder from Pearl Harbor Naval Shipyard, stopping work on several other projects. They have cut off all the debris and reduced the front of the ship to a base for the temporary repair. Old steel domes for fast attack submarines are lying around somewhere, and we steal one. I return to the ship on a Monday to find that I'm going to be Matt Priests' assistant. The Assistant Engineer is a huge job and I'm worried because of my history, but Matt

115

tells me that all I have to do is be the person he saw on January 10 and I'll be fine. I take on the job with a passion, taking my absence as a chance to reinvent myself and change my interactions with the whole crew. I see what I did wrong early in my tour, and I have a new CO, a new XO, and plenty of new people in the department. I have a chance at a new life.

The crew doesn't have that much to do in this dry-docking. There will be no repairs and no nuclear work; the Admirals don't want us to touch anything. All we have to do is support the repairs to the front of the ship and make sure the crew is ready to undock and transit. We start to lose operational proficiency immediately, but the schedule is pretty good. Two days a week, we have physical training (PT) at 0730, and we don't have to be at work until 0900. The Captain sits us down and explains his philosophy.

"Gentlemen, this crew has been through a trauma and it needs time to rebuild. I know that, if we wanted to, we could generate enough work to fill each day until 1700, but I don't want you to do that. I want us to get done what needs to be done and send people home early. I don't want the LPOs and Chiefs driving people to the limit; I want people gone at 1500 if there's nothing to do. There will be plenty of days in the future to work long hours, but for now, this is a time for rebuilding. Here are my principles:

"1. Give people correct information. Right now, we don't know when the repair is going to be done, and we don't know when the ship is going to leave. There will probably be a change of homeport sometime, but we don't know when that is going to be. We don't know the final repair location. We don't know if the ship is going to be repaired. Don't speculate. Tell people only the facts and nothing else.

"2. Break up the routine and the monotony. That's why we're doing the PT sessions and that's why we're starting the command activity day next Wednesday. We will take each Wednesday afternoon to have something as a crew that will rebuild our camaraderie and get us off this ship when we really have nothing to do.

"3. Have something to look forward to. This is when you need to get guys doing correspondence courses, doing other things, playing with their kids and families. The command activity day is one of those things. Let people know that we're going to do things they like.

"4. Get guys qualified. We're not going to be at sea for months. Set up rides on other ships so guys can get their dolphins, get their practical factors, and get qualified. I don't care how bad the in-port watchbill gets; we need to keep people moving so they can advance in their careers. Push the ride program from the divisional level; don't make the XO do it.

"5. Get intrusive; ask your men about their lives. How are they spending their free time? Are they going home and drinking alone every night? What are they doing to move forward? ASK THE QUESTION. That's what intrusive leadership is all about. When you get passive, that's when bad things happen. I will start rewarding the ship with one day off for every thirty days that there are no alcohol-related incidents.

"6. Pull the string. If you see something wrong, follow it to its end. Don't just fix the symptom and ignore it. If you keep pulling the string, you might find the whole blanket falls apart right in front of your eyes. That is the only way to fix the big problems.

"7. Be a walking source of alternatives. The officers must know what there is to do on this island other than drinking. You should be able to tell sailors about snorkeling, scuba diving, hiking, fishing, and many other activities that don't involve alcohol. Start a tutoring program. Do community service. Get involved at a church, join a singing group, learn to salsa dance, and lift weights. There are healthy lifestyles out there and you as an officer have to be a champion of all of them."

The other officers and I write as fast as we can. This is a major change in outlook for us, and I'm already excited about it. I can also see the logic and how Captain Hale (he has just been promoted) is trying to let the crew put itself back together. I'm excited because I'm going to lead the crew on a hiking boonie stomp, one of my favorite things to do in the jungles of Guam. The exercise, command activity day, and light workload slowly begin to have an effect. The other officers and I agree that this is the best time we've ever had on an in-port submarine.

116

There are some tough moments. Joey Ashley's parents come to visit Guam to see the submarine and where Joey lived. They are shown the ship and the island, and many of the crew are unsure how to talk to them or what to say. It hits very close to home since Joey is a reminder to us all about our own mortality. The ship has a reception for them on a cliff overlooking the harbor, and every single member of the crew who was onboard before the collision attends. They look overwhelmed as each crewmember talks to them. I intend to introduce myself, but I can't decide what I want to say. I eventually walk up to Mr. Ashley and introduce myself, and the rest comes without thinking.

"Sir, my name is Alex Fleming and I'm an officer on the submarine. I just wanted to say that I trusted your son. He was an excellent worker, and if he told me something, I knew I could trust him with my life." Mr. Ashley nods and thanks me.

The end of the day has us all taking a picture with the Ashleys. They thank us for what we have done and tell us that they lost one son but gained 120. It is a very emotional moment for all of us as the sun sets at the Top of the Mar. I can see the dry-dock and the damaged submarine in the distance, always present.

Our working life is consumed with inspections. The San Francisco suffered the worst underwater grounding in the history of the submarine force that did not sink the ship. It was an unscheduled shock trial for the 688 class submarine, and our inspections reveal that it passed with flying colors. We inspect every single system and cabinet onboard the ship and find surprisingly little damage. There are obvious problems at the front of the ship, but it is thought that we can eventually cut off the bow and replace it with the front end from a submarine being decommissioned. Captain Hale stays with us as long as he can, but he is still the Squadron Deputy, so the Navy needs to assign another CO to take us out of dry-dock to our final repair destination. The chosen man is Kevin Brenton.

Commander Brenton has just finished a successful tour as the CO of another submarine, and his wife is a naval officer as well. He has been separated from his family for two years and now the Navy sends him across the world to Guam to take the San Francisco on the last leg of her journey. Kevin Brenton is a runner; that's my first impression of him as he walks out of customs at Guam International Airport. All the officers and Chiefs who are not on duty are there to meet him. He seems quiet and unassuming, but he has the air of incredible intelligence that you find in so many senior submarine officers. I will get a chance to spend a lot more time with him, but for now, he's observing us for a few weeks before taking command. The dry-dock schedule continues to be calm since we're still months away from completion and undocking.

One of my new duties, in addition to being the AENG, is something from my past. I'm also the new Ship's Diving Officer and responsible for the stability condition and drawings for the entire ship. The irony of having me in charge of Rig for Dive on the San Francisco is especially poignant. The ENG and I laugh about it for a long time, but he tells me that I know more about Rig for Dive than any other officer onboard. The main problem for me is that I'm the custodian of the ship's drawings, which are changing by the day. The schematics and drawings of a ship normally don't change at all for the life of a ship, though they are referenced for dry-dockings. The San Francisco has been extensively damaged and now we're getting a temporary repair that will change the stability condition greatly. Several systems are being changed or completely cut out. The drawings that reflect these changes are delivered to me, but I soon find that even the temporary repair is a work in progress. As the work is updated, the blueprints change, and I have to retain everything and keep the best status of the ship's condition. None of this has ever been done before, and it becomes clear that, with the different agencies working together, Matt Priests, an officer named Jeb McDowell, and I are possibly the only three people who have a real, accurate knowledge of the status of all the ship's systems. We are entering new engineering and architectural territory every day, and I begin to understand how much work there will be when we get to undocking.

The change of command from Captain Hale to Commander Brenton is a simple ceremony that occurs on the pier while I'm on duty. I'm getting used to adjusting now since this is my fourth CO in my officer tour. The normal is two, but the San Francisco is special on a number of different levels. One of my new duties is a combined set of night orders forward and aft that detail everything happening on the entire ship. They are different, but I can see their usefulness. The AENG is the one who ends up doing all sorts of interesting things during the day, and I find myself coordinating everything that occurs on the ship on a daily basis. It's exhilarating and tiring at the same time. I also volunteer to be the OOD for undocking; I'm just a sucker for punishment.

The command activity days, though they are loved, disappear as we get closer to undocking. It's now June, and it's becoming clear that, as soon as we get out of dock, the Navy is going to try to get us out of Guam as soon as possible. We have undocking, navigation certification, major nuclear testing, crew certification, sea trials, and then a change of homeport followed by a surface transit all the way across the Pacific Ocean. The days of letting everyone go early to rebuild morale are over. The Navy wants us out of Guam before the beginning of typhoon season in September, and the pressure is on us to get the job done.

Kevin Brenton sits the wardroom down and gives us his philosophy for command and a long memo on leadership to read.

"1) The Chiefs run the ship; the officers fight and drive the ship. 2) Standards are the same up and down, and what matters is how you act when nobody is looking. 3) There will be no punishment for honest mistakes and dumb decisions, as long as you learn from them. 4) There are no first names outside the wardroom between officers and no hanging out in the crew's mess. 5) Never lose your temper without a plan. 6) Officers make proposals and decisions; don't ask what to do. 7) Remain undetected in port; keep off the squadron's radar screen. 8) Don't drop things on people's desks; don't give anything to the Captain unless it has gone through the XO first. I have an open door, but don't abuse that privilege."

I can see why they sent this man to us. He's very impressive and clear. He is demanding and thorough, but he's not a screamer. As I observe him, I honestly believe that he never gets excited. He talks loudly with the enlisted guys for show, but with the officers, he never raises his voice or gets angry. I believe that I could walk into his stateroom and tell him the ship was sinking, and his only reply would be a calm "OK, what are you going to do about it?" I have learned so much from being exposed to several different leadership styles that I'm forgetting which quirks belong to which Captain. I like this man because he's consistent. I don't mind people who are demanding, uncompromising, short tempered, or any other characteristic as long as they are consistent and predictable. It's comforting to know that the CO is going to react the same way to similar things. That actually makes it easier for duty officers.

I feel myself making another transition in dry-dock. I'm going from US to THEM. It feels like there are two kinds of officers, those who are junior and "one of us" and those who are the disciplinarians and taskmasters, "one of THEM." I'm now one of THEM, and I have standards to uphold. I tell the XO and CO about this one day, and they just smile because they know what I'm talking about. I'm doing well in many things; the only problem is my weight. It is still high and a bad example to the enlisted guys. The schedule as we get closer to leaving prevents me from taking any big steps in that department.

The undocking starts one evening at midnight and I'm on the bridge until 1000. We clear the dock exactly as planned, despite some last-minute drama between the engineers and architects at the final meetings. It is strange for a 25-year-old officer when the most senior architect in the Navy who designed this class of submarine is telling you that he's pretty sure the ship is going to float but isn't quite sure how. The ship lifts off the blocks as planned, and we have a moment of terror as the inexperienced civilian line handlers nearly pull us into the dry-dock wall. We clear the dock and the COB again breaks down scaffolding as fast as he can. We are dirty and our nose is a little misshapen, but the ship is afloat.

The exams and certifications consume the next two months. There is also the problem that we haven't received our change of homeport certificate, so we can't move any of the families yet. We get within six weeks of the day they want us to leave and everyone starts to get a little tense. Things are tough at work as the pace continues to quicken. We have to be taught navigation all over again, which is ruthlessly enforced by the NAV and the XO. The training sessions are deep and teach us everything that the ship was found deficient in after the grounding and then some. We take exams every week, and by the end of the process, I feel more confident in my navigation knowledge than I ever was before. Then we are examined by Squadron on all the same things to determine whether our training has been effective.

The next thing on the plate is crew certification, which involves days of practicing evolutions, watchstanding, drills, and casualty response. This is all made more complicated by the fact that the setup of the ship has changed significantly, so I'm one of the people who has to retrain everybody on the new ship's systems. We also have to create new procedures for a status called "surface transit," which no submarine has ever done before. We get drafts of everything from the shipyard, but the ENG and I are the ones who have to put everything together.

Some major nuclear testing is thrown in that we can't put off, despite our best efforts to try. ENG DEP goes into shift work with me standing senior supervisory watch. We have to coordinate all the paperwork and preparations and still get this testing done without a hitch before we can leave. Then there are the cannibalizations. Guam is a remote port with very little part support, so if a submarine comes through on their way to mission and they need a part we have, then we have to remove it and give it to them, even if it means our system won't work. We have to give up parts every week until we are almost at the point that we can't get underway. Our parts priority has gone from the highest in the fleet to the lowest in the fleet since we're no longer a deployer or a mission-capable asset. We compare the transition to starting at the tip of the spear and landing at the very butt end.

Combined with all this, the crew has to prepare to move their families and possessions and cars away from the island of Guam forever. I don't get a change of homeport certificate because I have less than a year left onboard, so the only way for me to move off Guam is to wait for my resignation letter to be approved and then ship my belongings to my home of record. I will only be able to take with me on the submarine the things that fit, and that's all I will have for the nine months after we get to Seattle. I'm boggled by the idiocy of it. It is truly a situation that you can only find in the Navy. Luckily, my resignation from the Naval Service is approved with three weeks to spare, and I get my separation orders that allow me to move my household goods just in time. I'm also trying to take the GMAT for MBA admissions, which I have to skip once because of crew certification.

Sea trials are short since we're just trying to verify that the ship can still move and be safe at sea. We discover a few more people who have relapses of post-traumatic stress disorder when we get underway, so we have to process them off. There is another reason for sea trials: we have to find out who gets seasick. Normally, the ride on a submarine is very calm underwater and many people on the 711 actually get seasick on the surface. This isn't going to work very well as we transit across the surface of the entire Pacific Ocean at twelve knots, so we have to identify these people and get them off the ship as well. Once the CO and the shipyard engineers are satisfied that everything works, we return to port and have two weeks to get the hell out of Dodge.

I find myself incredibly sad because the most time I've had to make friends on Guam was after the grounding, and now I'm leaving. I take a week of leave and head up to Saipan and Tinian, figuring this is my last chance to see any part of the Marianas Islands. My apartment is strangely empty again, and I know that I won't see any of my stuff for nearly a year. Everything I have left has to go on the submarine or in the trash. I realize how much I've enjoyed the jungle, Hash, sun, scuba diving, and all the other little things about the islands.

I return from leave with five days left before departure and set about my task of helping our new Engineer. Matt Priests finishes his time on 711 after an ENG tour so difficult that would it make a strong man weep, but he does so in style and heads off to Washington. The new ENG is a small man named Andy Peskian, who looks like he's about fifteen years old. He is smart and able, but he's coming into an ENG DEP that's very tight knit and adjusted to each other. The EDMC and a few other chiefs provide a lot of support, and basically run the department. I'm still writing the night orders every day, a process I've become good at, but it's beginning to wear on my patience. There are a few parties before we leave, and I remark to a member of the

Guam Chamber of Commerce that I've survived three years on Guam without getting married or having any children. He laughs and proceeds to relate this to the entire audience during the presentation.

I get a ride back to the boat from Eric Braken, the last officer with a car. I've moved all my things to my stateroom on the boat, and all I have left is one visit to make. We drive up a winding hill into the jungle and along a dirt road near Ordot Dump. I ask him to pull over at a large concrete light pole on the side of the road. It's the spot where I totaled my Bronco during the worst time of my life in Guam. Grass has grown over the ditch and erased all trace of the hole my truck made in the mud. I look closely at the pole, and there is still blue paint from my car on the cool concrete. I touch it lightly, marveling at how much things have changed since then. We drive back to the boat, and I sleep fitfully in my rack.

I am rewarded for all my work with the gift of being the OOD for the last time we leave Guam. I'm experienced and confident now, and I go through the motions without much thought. A small party of people come to wave us off on the pier, and the same Guam Chamber of Commerce member jokes that two women at the base gates want me to give them money. It's a small amount of levity on a solemn day. One of the first boats of the Guam experiment is limping home after <u>only two months of mission operational time in three years</u>. The repairs to the San Francisco are going to cost the taxpayer around $200 million dollars, and what was it for? I take one last look at Guam harbor, the jungle hills, the squadron buildings, Big Blue, the Frank Cable, and all the things that have been part of our lives since we arrived in a federal disaster area three years before. We cast off on time, and I turn to look forward down track, never looking back.

We have an escort vessel, a small ocean-going tug, which will stay with us all the way to Seattle. I'm the midwatch cowboy Officer of the Deck, and I work from 2200 until 0900 every night. I get to sleep during the day when the new ENG is not waking me up to ask me questions. I quickly learn to love the ocean at night. It's warm and clear in the Western Pacific, and the crash of waves against the sleek black hull is soothing in the bright moonlight. It begins to get a little colder as we approach Hawaii.

We get a single weekend in Oahu, and I spend it crashing on Adam Johnson's couch in Kailua. He is out of the Navy and teaching at Pearl Harbor Naval Shipyard's nuclear power school. He teaches the test engineers who repair submarines, the same kind who tortured us for years. The officers relax and party, heading out on a pontoon boat to the sandbar in Kaneohe Bay for the normal Saturday afternoon gathering. As I stand in the warm sea sipping a beer as the sun sets over Oahu, I can't stop the feeling that this is all ending. The story of the San Francisco is drawing to a close, and it will be years before we get back to a tropical island.

We clear Hawaii to head north, and the sea gets much colder. I have to bundle up like crazy before manning the bridge at night. My favorite moment of the day is each morning around 0300 when the constellation Orion rises in the evening sky. The waves get bigger and frigid as we near the straights of Juan de Fuca. I'm on the bridge one afternoon when we start taking massive waves over the ship and I have to secure everything and shift the watch below decks. I stuff my ball cap in my pocket and frantically put away all the important gear, even as I get dunked in seawater, choking and gasping every few seconds. Christopher and I slip and stumble as we close the hatch, shaking water out of our ears and hair. We both take a deep breath as the ship lurches and we hang on in the dark bridge trunk, and then we head down the ladder.

We get to control to find the Captain, XO, and COB waiting for us. We've left only a few things on the bridge, as it's too dangerous to try to get them because of the wind and waves. I remain below decks, driving off the periscope until the ship makes the turn into the Straights. I've been up for twenty-four hours straight when I get relieved, so I miss the approaches to Seattle, sleeping as we come into Puget Sound. I only wake up for the maneuvering watch as we near Bremerton. A crowd of families stands on the pier waiting for us since we have been underway on the surface for nearly a month. It's raining, so we dress in khakis instead of whites for the arrival ceremony. The mooring goes slowly since it's being done with steel lines. Nobody thinks we'll be going anywhere anytime soon. We have no repair date, and even our dry-docking date is months away.

Once we are moored, I walk topside into a lovely Indian summer day in September. The evergreen trees of Washington are so foreign to me that I have to take a moment to remember them. Even though I've been told about it, I still gasp at the beauty of Mount Rainier, rising like a tower in the distance, and the

Olympic Mountains on the Peninsula. I can see the top of the Space Needle in nearby Seattle. I have no family waiting, so I walk off the brow and down the pier. The concrete here is lighter and smoother than that in Guam. A temporary tent has been set up with activities for the families and children, and a DJ is playing upbeat music. I look at the temporary bow repair, which is permanently misshapen, like a broken nose, but has carried us across the ocean without any problems. I look out across the water and a cold breeze makes me zip my jacket and cross my arms. I realize that I will probably never be the OOD of an ocean-going vessel again. The sea is a cruel master, but I've grown to love it and I will never see it the same way again. This thought fills me with great sadness, even as I hear uplifting guitar chords playing behind me: "The boys are back in town…"

Conclusion

The ship stayed at the same pier in Bremerton for the next eleven months before anything happened. It was clear to us as soon as we arrived that nobody had any idea what the repair plan was or when it was going to occur. I helped get everything shut down and stabilized for a long haul. The crew quickly fell back into a shipyard routine.

Many people transferred and retired in the months after we arrived. The people with career ambitions headed off to better assignments and others started to be pulled away on temporary duty to other submarines. The submarine force quickly realized that we were a source of well-trained, experienced bodies as well as parts. The cannibalization requests didn't stop for months. The ship was slowly being taken apart mentally and physically. Everyone told us that the repairs were coming, but it didn't materialize.

A few months after the arrival, I was sitting with Chief Broomfield in the gym locker room, talking about where we'd been. He and I were two of the four people still onboard who'd been with the ship when it left Norfolk in 2002. I turned to him and asked bluntly, "We're falling back into the shipyard mentality, aren't we?"

"Yes, sir, we're already there. We've lost everything we had on mission." He was sad as well.

"This whole thing is going to start from scratch again, and they're going to have to go through all the pain," I realized slowly.

"That's true," Chris Broomfield said, always the realist.

"Well, then, it's like the whole three years in between are gone, like it never happened." He had no reply to this; he just nodded and walked away. It was a sad thought to carry with me, but the more I saw, the more I knew it was true.

I decided to leave the Navy and finished my commitment the following year. I watched too many good people be destroyed and chewed up in the U.S. Submarine Force. I couldn't imagine doing it for fifteen more years until the minimum service time (twenty years) for paid retirement. There were some happy moments in Seattle. Matt Priests came to visit for Kevin Mooney's retirement. I gave Commander Mooney the flag that flew on the San Francisco's bridge for the surface transit, and we had some great conversations before he left. Kevin is now a very successful executive for a shipyard in San Diego, CA. Billy Cramer retired in 2014 after several more command master chief tours and lives in Ohio. Rick Bonner works in the energy industry in Dallas, TX. Josh Chester followed the engineering and intelligence career path and lives in Hawaii. Micah Stevens earned his MBA and then became a partner in a management consulting firm; his wife Natalie recovered from her illness and now works as an occupational therapist; they have several children. Matt Priests finished his work at the Pentagon and is a partner in the same firm as Micah. Mark Ginda became the CO of Naval Base Groton, CT; he retired from the Navy as a Captain and now works for Naval Intelligence. Andy Hale was chosen to be the Captain of one of the crews of the USS Ohio (SSGN), later left the Navy to join Naval Reactors as a Senior Executive, and then left the federal government and now lives in Vancouver. Kevin Brenton later commanded the squadron at Kings Bay, GA and was promoted to Admiral; he now works as a defense contractor. Craig Litty stayed in the Navy to become the Flag Lieutenant for the Commander, Naval Forces Marianas, and then he became the Engineer on the USS Buffalo. He recently completed his Executive Officer tour on the USS Albuquerque. Doc Akin made Chief and completed a tour in Japan for CTF 74. Many of the other officers and Chiefs have left 711 for other assignments, but some are still there. Wherever they go, their experience is respected because of what they learned.

The USS San Francisco repair was finished in November 2010, and the ship has since deployed twice to the Western Pacific from its new home base in San Diego, CA. It is scheduled to be converted to a Moored Training Ship to be used to train officers and enlisted personnel in reactor operations in Charleston, South Carolina.

My time on the boat taught me more about leadership and management than I ever thought possible, and the lessons of that time are still with me. The chance to observe five different Commanding Officers grapple with impossible situations gave me incredible insight into military leadership and humanity. The Navy's poor planning and execution of the move to Guam helped me understand organizational decision-making and how it can go horribly wrong. The results of the USS San Francisco's botched overhaul taught me what happens when established corporate relationships cause the military customer to accept an inferior product. The crew of 711 taught me the resilience and drive of ordinary men forced to negotiate extraordinary circumstances. The trials I personally faced taught me to persevere no matter how dismal life seems, and they added depth and breadth to my understanding of the world. I traveled deep into my own mind and emerged on the other side a different person. I'm still trying to figure out who that person is, but I have a loyal family and great friends to help me on the path.

The initial years of the Guam experiment were a failure. In the words of one XO, the Navy tried to move to Guam "on the cheap." The men of 705 and 711 made it work, but there was so much skimping on training resources and cutting of corners that something bad was bound to happen. What did happen was a surprise to everyone, and it came just when things were beginning to look up. U.S. taxpayers are now paying the price for these mistakes.

The men who found themselves part of this experiment did their best to get the job done. We paid for the poor support in blood, sweat, trauma, depression, broken families, and every other hardship a crew can endure. The people on 711 came through closer and stronger than any group of people I have ever known. The bravery I witnessed humbles me to this day. The San Francisco showed the submarine force the best of what a crew can achieve.

I hope the Navy can learn from our experience.

Alex C. Fleming
May 3, 2011

The Submariner

Only a submariner realizes to what great extent the entire ship depends on him as an individual. To a landsman this is not understandable, and sometimes it is even difficult to comprehend, but it is so!

A submarine at sea is a different world in herself, and in consideration of the protracted and distant operations of submarines, the Navy must place responsibility and trust in the hands of those who take such ships to sea.

In each submarine there are men who, in the hour of emergency or peril at sea, can turn to each other. These men are ultimately responsible to themselves and each to the other for all aspects of operation of their submarine. They are the crew. They are the ship.

This is perhaps the most difficult and demanding assignment in the Navy. There is not an instant during his tour as a submariner that he can escape the grasp of responsibility. His privileges in view of his obligations are almost ludicrously small; nevertheless, it is the spur which has given the Navy its greatest mariner: the men of the Submarine Service.

It is a duty which most richly deserves the proud and time-honored title of...

Submariner

Source: U.S. Submarine Force, Atlantic Fleet website

Afterword

The decision to publish this book was the most difficult one I have made in my entire life. The odd part about writing the story was that my purpose at the beginning was completely different from my reasoning at the end...

The idea of writing a book about the San Francisco first entered my mind in the months after the collision. We had a lot of free time in Guam, and one evening as I was eating dinner at my favorite Mexican restaurant, I grabbed an envelope and jotted down my first ideas for chapter titles. I called the idea "Letters from Guam," and when I reached home, I couldn't get the idea out of my head. I rolled out of bed that night, sleepless, and expanded the titles into the first outline of this work.

My drive at the beginning was anger and frustration. I was trying to come to grips with the experience I had just endured and the emotions I was feeling. The shock of Joey Ashley's death made all of us examine our mortality. I pored over the outline for two days, eventually typing it up, but then I put it in a drawer. We became engulfed in the preparations to leave Guam, and I didn't get back to the idea for almost a year. Our arrival in Seattle allowed me to interact with many old friends and officers from different submarines, and as we talked, I came to realize the strangeness of our experience. I began to think that if I could write down what had happened to me and why, then I would be able to get over it and recover something of the person I was before the Navy.

I got the chance to do this in February 2006, when my duties on the ship began to wane and I was able to go home earlier and earlier. I found a nice spot on my roommate's La-Z-Boy couch overlooking Puget Sound and began to write, interspersing the first-person narrative with long descriptions of the technical aspects of submarine life. These asides were rather dense, and if you're interested, you can find them in the endnotes. I also didn't realize the pain reliving the worst moments of my life could cause. I was depressed for weeks as I wrote the middle chapters, and I barely slept the night I finished the narrative of the car accident. I finished describing my qualification and our celebration in Hawaii, and I had to stop. I felt like I was getting too close to reality and that I had to let more time pass and distance myself from the rest of the story. Perhaps this was simply my way of justifying being mentally exhausted and needing to stop and recover.

I put the document away after soliciting input from a number of my Navy comrades. The initial response to the idea was very negative. People told me that I was trying to capitalize on the collision and Ashley's death, and they asked me what right I had to write the story of the San Francisco. I was just one person on the ship, and it was unjust of me to speak for everyone. These ideas made me pause for many months, and in the interim, I left the Navy and spent my first semester in graduate school. It was on Christmas vacation in 2006-2007 in Telluride that I returned to the book. I got into an argument with my mother about why I hadn't finished the manuscript, telling her the reasons above, and she got very angry.

"Why don't you have the right? You were there. If you don't tell it, then who should? Who would be better at telling the story?" she asked before ending the conversation.

I got a better idea then why I really wanted to finish the book: I wanted other people to understand what the crew went through, and my personal journey illustrated many of the key events in our three-year tour. I woke up the next morning, watched my parents leave for home, and then I started writing. I locked myself in the house for a week, typing from noon to 8 p.m. every day. I completed one chapter each day and then proofread the whole thing for the first time. Now the hard part began: Navy approval.

I did my homework, finding out which agencies of the government had to see my manuscript, and I mailed it off to them in early February 2007. For two months, I heard nothing, and then the fun began. I was called, in the same week, by the NCIS, Naval Reactors, and a Captain from the Pentagon I had never met. NCIS and Naval Reactors said they had some changes for my manuscript, and the Captain from the Submarine Warfare division wanted me to come into the Pentagon for some "feedback." Apparently, some officers really didn't like what I had to say and thought I should be "discouraged" from publishing. I spoke to Matt Priests and Kevin Mooney before going in, and we discussed the likely arguments:

1) This book would affect my ability to interact with the crew, and some of them, especially my antagonists, would undoubtedly be alienated from me if it came out.

2) The things I did as a young man, though they seem fine now, may be inconvenient if I were ever to occupy a high-profile position.

3) The act of writing the book may have been the catharsis I needed, and publishing it might not be that important.

4) I may affect the reputation and credibility of the submarine force by telling the true stories of things people would rather forget about since it's not often that Admirals and the public have to face the real-life problems of a junior officer.

My meeting at the Pentagon was cordial. Though there were some unique approaches, the key arguments were the ones we anticipated. I took Matt's good advice and said as little as possible, getting the meeting over with as soon as I could. The person I met with had not read my book, nor had any other person I actually encountered. My time at Naval Reactors editing the manuscript was, oddly, much more pleasant. The public affairs representatives politely and efficiently helped me get the approval I needed. As I sat on the D.C. subway with my approved manuscript, I stared at the anonymous faces and walls rushing past and I realized why I really wanted to publish this book:

1. The world needs to know the story of the USS San Francisco. The courage and sacrifice I witnessed on our journey have the power to inspire people everywhere, both inside the submarine force and outside. The reality of our struggle was unique and extraordinary. The Navy should learn all it can from these events, not try to ignore or suppress them, because, in the end, it can help the Submarine Force get better.

2. I want to help young people learning about leadership and management (especially future submarine officers). The lessons I learned the hard way, if presented to people still in training, could help them achieve greater success with much less pain and psychological anguish than I endured. If this book can help one person become a better leader in the Navy or the world and avoid my mistakes, then the writing was worth it.

I decided to change most of the names in the book to protect the people in the crew who do not want to be associated with this effort, but these are the ideas that drove me to complete the book you hold in your hands and give it to the world. I hope my story will help you.

Alex Fleming
November 17, 2015
Denver, CO

Glossary

1MC – The primary announcing circuit; speakers are heard by the whole ship

2MC – An announcing circuit heard only in the Engine Room

705 – The hull number of the USS City of Corpus Christi (CoCC)

711 – The hull number of the USS San Francisco (San Fran) (SFO) ("the Boat")

CHOP – (slang) Supply Officer

CO – Commanding Officer, Captain of the ship

COB – Chief of the Boat (usually a Master Chief)

Cone – (slang) Forward Compartment

Coner – (slang) Non-Engineering Personnel

CPA – Closest point of approach

Doc – (slang) Term describing the Independent Duty Corpsman

DRB – Disciplinary Review Board

EDMC – Engineering Department Master Chief

EDO – Engineering Duty Officer

ENG – Engineer Officer, Engineering Department Head (pronounced like "hinge")

ENG DEP – Engineering Department

EOOW – Engineering Officer of the Watch

ER – Engine Room

ERUL – Engine Room Upper Level

ERML – Engine Room Middle Level

ERLL – Engine Room Lower Level

FCUL – Forward Compartment Upper Level

FCML – Forward Compartment Middle Level

FCLL – Forward Compartment Lower Level

JO – Junior Officer, all officers below Department Head

JOOD – Junior Officer of the Deck, Assistant to the OOD

JOOW – Junior Officer of the Watch, Assistant to the JOOD

NAV – Navigator, Navigation-Operations Department Head

Nuke – Nuclear Trained Person, Engineering Department

OOD – Officer of the Deck

PD – Periscope depth

PIM – Position of intended movement

PNEO – Prospective Nuclear Engineer Officer School

QA – Quality Assurance

SANS – Sanitary tanks

SDO – Ship's Duty Officer

SOA – Speed of advance

SUBSAFE – Submarine Safety Program

WEPS – Weapons Officer, Weapons Department Head

XO – Executive Officer, Second in Command

End Notes

1 - My path to the Navy began in 1996, when I was informed by my mother that, after my parents spent a great deal of money on a private boarding school for high school, I would have to help them pay for my college education. My options were limited, but my family had a Naval Aviation tradition, and I had always kept my desire to serve in the back of my mind.

The Navy Nuclear Officer pipeline is the brainchild of Admiral Hyman G. Rickover, who built the program from the ground up through sheer force of will and political skill. His influence is seen in every part of our lives from initial entry into the program until we are finally "read out" of Navy Nuclear Propulsion Information. My personal interview with a four-star Admiral as a senior in college is a tradition that Rickover treasured. He saw every single officer who operated one of his plants and decided whether they measured up after a day of math and physics interviews. My meeting with Admiral Bowman in December 2000 lasted four minutes and was a relief after the horrible stories I had heard in preparation.

My physics background apparently satisfied the Navy because my interview ended with quick congratulations and then I was off to processing. The more important thing for me as a 21-year-old college student was the form that told the Navy where to send my $10,000 signing bonus. I remember thinking how awesome it was that I got so much money for doing so little. The Navy is a great equalizer; whatever good it gives, it takes back from you equally at the most inconvenient time possible.

The next step took me from Philadelphia after graduation to Charleston, South Carolina and the Navy Nuclear Power Training Center. This building was a model of form and function with one purpose, to stuff all the knowledge possible into young minds in the shortest realistic time. I spent six months there, and it was like drinking from a fire hose. Classes were from 0800 to 1500 hours with ten-minute breaks every hour. Each week held a new exam that ramped up from physics and math to heat transfer and reactor theory. We were required to study twenty hours a week outside normal class hours. My life usually began at 0430. I was at the schoolhouse by 0515. I would study until class began and then leave school immediately at 1500 to play golf or exercise. I returned to school at 1800 and studied until 2200, followed by a quiet drive home and then to bed by 2300.

Our classroom had no windows, and in retrospect, I guess it was training for the 23 men in my section on how to deal with people. There were women in other classes but, by random chance, not in ours. The nuclear power pipeline has many "unofficial" experiences that serve to weed out those psychologically unable to deal with the confinement and hard work. The people I met were some of the smartest I ever encountered, and that started a trend that would continue to this day. After building a basis of nuclear operation and enduring a grueling five-hour final examination in which we had to write every minute or lose points, we moved on to the next step.

My next step took me from the warmth of Charleston to Saratoga Springs, New York in the first week of December 2001. The classroom training is only the beginning of nuclear power in the Navy. The second part, perhaps more important, is prototype training. This is where the Navy lets students operate, under heavy supervision, a real nuclear reactor for the sole purpose of training. I put all the concepts I learned in school into use. The six months allows students to find out how the Navy works with actual nuclear operators and to learn how to work in the fleet. The real learning did not occur in the books but by operating the plant and going to the repair shops. The divisional shop was where the instructors worked in their divisions to keep the training plants running. I thrived at prototype because I'm outgoing and like dealing with people much more than books. I qualified first in my class and loved what I was doing and the culture of learning. I would have stayed at prototype for my whole tour given the opportunity.

Near the end of my time at prototype, I received my orders to Guam. The Navy had never based fast attack nuclear submarines in Guam until the City of Corpus Christi and San Francisco were moved there after refueling in 2002. The decision to make this move was the small-scale interpretation of a very large shift in U.S. defense policy. Many factors were moving toward Southeast Asia and the U.S. needed to have operators right there all the time.

2 - The USS San Francisco is a first flight Los Angeles-class attack submarine built by Norfolk Naval Shipyard and commissioned in 1979. The Los Angeles class was a design that kept America a competitor in the Cold War as Russia raced us for faster and quieter nuclear technology. San Francisco, hull number 711, was near the end of the first "flight" of the class, which is distinctive because it has fairwater planes (wing-like structures on the sail) and lacks vertical cruise missile launch capabilities. These characteristics in the submarine force make it a "four shooter," an informal term for a boat that can only launch four Tomahawks before having to reload. Some might see this as a disadvantage, but it actually makes our lives more interesting because we very rarely get trapped working for battle group strike coordinators, so we get more independent operations, which is the true passion of the submariner.

A fast attack is organized into three sections: the forward compartment, the reactor compartment, and the engine room. The reactor compartment and engine room contain a General Electric pressurized water reactor that heats primary water, which boils water in a secondary system in steam generators. This steam is used to generate electricity to power ship loads and to push the ship through the water. The people who work in this section of the boat are nuclear trained operators who are informally known as "Nukes" or "aft guys" since they spend most of their time in the back of the ship. All officers on submarines are required to be nuclear trained, but enlisted personnel volunteer for this path, and only about half of the people onboard are part of the Engineering Department (ENG DEP). A favorite joke directed at nukes hanging around in the crew's mess is telling them to "shut up, get in back, and push." This is very kind-spirited because every person on the boat knows that, without power and engines, everything else would be pretty useless. The Engineering Department Master Chief (EDMC), also known as the "Bull Nuke," manages the everyday operations of ENG DEP. The forward compartment is made up of three levels that hold all the working spaces for the forward personnel, sometimes informally known as "Coners," and the living space for the entire crew. The upper level contains the control room and attack center, which is the nerve center of the ship where all sensors and controls come together. This space contains the periscopes and the ship's control systems. The upper level also contains a ventilation room, radio room, CO/XO staterooms, and various computer spaces. The middle level of the ship is the crossroads for the entire crew. It contains the crew's mess, galley, wardroom (officer dining room), countermeasures space, two crew berthing spaces and crew's head, officer staterooms and head, a nine-man bunk room (spoken "9 man"), and the chief petty officer quarters. This level also contains the refrigerator and freezer (chill and freeze boxes) and the forward escape trunk. The lower level is made up of an auxiliary machinery space that contains the ship's emergency diesel, a smaller bunk room usually for first class petty officers, a smaller head, and the torpedo room. There is also a small shack in the forward end of the lower level that houses the supply personnel, though they have lockers all over the ship. The day-to-day operations of the entire ship are managed by a Master Chief Petty Officer called the Chief of the Boat, or COB. The COB is the senior enlisted advisor to the Captain on all matters affecting the crew.

When the submarine is in port, people usually access the ship by climbing down a ladder through the weapons shipping hatch into the command passageway, and then you'd better move or you're in the way.

3 - Everything that happens on a submarine begins with formality and procedural compliance. Formality means everything is done in a military manner, from uniforms to job execution. The most obvious interpretation of formality is in verbatim repeat-backs. Every order given on a submarine is repeated back exactly as spoken to the person giving it. This allows the person giving the order to make sure the order is understood. Giving orders without repeat-backs results in unclear communication and puts crewmembers in danger. It can seem cumbersome when you first hear long and involved orders, but it is just how business is done. Many of the operating procedures submariners obey are written in the blood of less careful men.

Procedural compliance means everything that happens on a submarine is written in a book somewhere. A sailor should never execute a single evolution without the procedure open in front of him. If there is no procedure, write one and have it approved by your chain of command. There is very little allowance for personal system knowledge, except in emergency situations. Enforcement of these two rules is religious and happens every minute of every day.

4 - The SUBSAFE (Submarine Safe) program is a way to control the materials, parts, and integrity of the parts and systems that keep the ocean out of the "people space" on a submarine. The program was created after a horrible accident that cost an entire submarine and crew. The Naval Sea Systems Command, which controls everything concerning the materials and design of ships, created a new standard of material and work control for all the parts that make up a submarine. Every bolt, valve, o-ring, and lubricant that goes into a submarine must be perfect, certified, and traceable to its origin. If any discrepancies exist, the piece will not be allowed, and someone has to have locked positive control of it for its entire "life." The Navy intentionally staffs QA jobs with the most uncompromising and disciplined people it can find. These people can stop any boat in its tracks if they find even the smallest documentation problem.

5 - Learning and qualification on Naval ships are based on a method of self-study and oral examination controlled for each job and watch station by Qualification Cards. Officers have some of the largest books. Each page has a number of topics with a signature block next to each. You progress by studying a topic until you have sufficient knowledge to satisfy whoever is signing the block and then go ask for a "checkout." Getting a checkout means going to someone with the qualification and asking them to examine you until they are satisfied. Officers and Chiefs can give qualification interviews, but usually for smaller systems and early stages, the senior people don't have a lot of time to sit around talking to NUBs. The people who do have time to give checkouts are the second class petty officers standing watch in the engineering plant and looking for ways to stave off the boredom that comes with taking the same logs every hour day in and day out. During a checkout, the watchstander asks questions, and the student must demonstrate knowledge until the examiner is satisfied. If you don't know certain answers, you get "lookups." The student then goes to find these answers and reports back to finish the signature.

Qual Cards also have practical factors, where the student must actually take a watch as "under-instruction" and perform an evolution under the supervision of a qualified operator. The end of each watch qualification has final interviews with Chiefs and Division Officers, an exam, and finally an interview with the ENG or CO. As a JO, I have an inch-thick binder filled with things to qualify, including Basic Engineering Qualification (BEQ), Battery-Charging Lineup (BCLU), Rig for Dive, Engineering Officer of the Watch (EOOW), Engineering Duty Officer (EDO), Contact Coordinator, Diving Officer of the Watch (DOOW), Surfaced and Submerged Officer of the Deck (OOD), Ship's Duty Officer (SDO), and Submarine Qualification. The whole book takes about a year to complete and rules every day of life until you finally put on your gold dolphins at the end. The dolphins are the symbol of an officer qualified in submarines.

6 - The "shipyard mentality" is an expression for everything that happens to a Navy crew in an extended overhaul period when the ship does not go to sea. Advancement in the Navy is based on one thing: operational experience. The people who are out driving, shooting, sneaking, and doing the job of real warriors are the ones who get every priority in the Navy. These ships are first in line for people, parts, training, money, and anything else they need to accomplish the mission. The budget cuts to the Navy have just made the disparity between the most funded units and the least more intense. Operational experience is also the major factor in advancement, which includes higher rank and more pay. The only way to move higher in peacetime military, for both officers and enlisted personnel, is to get operational experience, which will lead you to the front of the line when it comes to everything else about your career.

Unfortunately, the money crunch after the Cold War also means that there are fewer ships in the Navy and the remaining ships are getting older, so they need more and more repair periods to keep them running safely. When a ship goes into a long overhaul period, the first thing that happens is the crew loses operational proficiency and the sense of urgency that is key to military operations. The priorities shift from "get it done now" to "it will get done some time." The leadership goes from active to passive, and the military environment relaxes as you deal with more civilian contractors and fewer operational commitments.

Then there is a sorting of the people onboard. The hard chargers, the smart people, and the ones with advancement potential want to get off the boat as soon as possible. The shipyard doesn't advance any career; if you want to be noticed in the cutthroat post-Cold War Navy, you have to have front-line experience. The people who can get off the boat through normal rotations go, and the people who can find any excuse to get off the boat for any reason to go to an operational ship do so. This is in the best interests of their career, although it takes them away from their family. The people who remain onboard are there for four reasons. 1. They're not talented enough to convince the detailer to send them elsewhere. 2. They're new and don't have any experience or pull with the detailers. 3. They don't want operational experience and would prefer to be on land. 4. They're stuck.

The end of a shipyard period leaves a collection of people who have very little experience and seniority or do not want to be underway at all. The Navy tries to combat this with assignments of senior personnel, but it doesn't change the inherent truth of the situation. This is a challenging leadership situation for any officer because the lessons that every Naval ship must learn cannot occur quickly. The core of experience and operational competency on submarines is the sea-returnee second class and first class petty officers who get everything done day to day. Leadership can attempt to make up for deficiencies, but the battle is nearly impossible without some help from the ranks.

7 - Submariners crave independent operations, where we are beholden to no one except our squadron and fleet commanders who give a great deal of latitude in the ship's operations. During independent operations, we can communicate once per day to get our messages, but otherwise, we complete the mission mostly at the CO's discretion. Battle group operations are annoying to submarines because working for a boss on an aircraft carrier is a very different dynamic. Surface ship commanders are used to being able to talk to all their subordinates at any time without delay. New orders, procedures, updates, and news go out quickly at all hours of the day and require instant response and compliance. Submarines are not part of this instantaneous communications network, so they give surface commanders a headache, and they compensate by letting the subs under their command go deep for only short periods of time.

When submarines work with carrier battle groups, we come up to periscope depth (PD) at the command of the battle group and remain there until released. Surface sailors have no qualms about keeping us at PD for hours and hours on end, restricting our ability to get our job done, just to be able to talk to us instantly. Submarine officers are stationed on carrier group staffs to communicate this, but mostly they are overridden by the commander's desire to be in instant contact with all his assets. They know that, when we go deep, we are effectively gone from all communications until the next PD trip.

8 - The Cold War brought a new kind of prosperity to Guam as the U.S. Navy based a squadron of the new Polaris nuclear missile submarines on the island because of its range to Siberia. The crews and their families brought steady income to the island, which helped to build infrastructure for the tourist trade. The Navy's interest in the island began to wane as advances in missile technology allowed inflicted death from one side of the world to the other without even leaving the U.S. The missile squadron left Guam in 1981, and the Naval installation was allowed to pass into disrepair and stagnate. Some small commands remained, but the large activity for the island with a population of 150,000 people was at Anderson Air Force Base in the northern village of Yigo.

The year 2000 brought changes in U.S. policy and a refocus toward the growing power of China in the 21st century. It was decided that an integral part of U.S. strategy would be to base fast attack submarines on the "Second Island Chain." So the USS City of Corpus Christi and USS San Francisco would complete refueling and repopulate Submarine Squadron Fifteen (CSS-15). The return of nuclear submarines to the island brought money, people, and attention to a place where tourism was faltering in the post-9/11 era. The island economy was not doing well in 2000-2002 and the people of Guam were feeling the economic pinch. Two nuclear subs and the promise of more support staff, shore facilities, and all the associated people and their families injected billions of dollars of capital into the island economy. This will help the people in ways that government aid cannot.

9 - Wetting-down parties have been a tradition in the Navy officer ranks for as long as anyone can remember. When an officer is promoted to a new rank, it's a tradition that a party is thrown to wet down the new uniform with a requisite amount of alcohol. This tends to ruin new uniforms, but it's a fun tradition. Modern-day wetting downs are tamer, but it's tradition that the officer being promoted spends his first month's pay raise on the party. When a number of officers are promoted together, the combined money can be very significant.

10 - Personnel upgrade procedures in the Navy begin with a counseling session. This counseling is a conversation, sometimes recorded on paper, sometimes not, that tells a person how he is failing and what he should do to improve. Counseling sessions are the most basic form of correction, and they are recorded on paper only if the superior is trying to build paperwork for a larger punishment. The next step for enlisted personnel is a disciplinary review board (DRB), which has a number of chiefs that tell the person what he is doing wrong, try to find out why, and decide what upgrade is appropriate. If the DRB concludes that the seaman needs a more severe corrective action, he is written up officially for XO investigation of the occurrence. The XO assigns an investigating officer to determine what articles of the uniform code of military justice have been violated, and this report helps the XO decide whether to send the enlisted man to Non-Judicial Punishment. Non-Judicial Punishment, or Captain's Mast, is a trial where the CO can decide the outcome of a crime and give the member various punishments, such as restriction to the ship, reduction in rate, and even the "bread and water" punishment, which is still on the books. The member, if unhappy with the results of his mast case, can appeal to the Squadron, but this is generally never done because the punishments only get worse as you go higher.

11 - Communicating with a submarine is a continuing problem that defines a great deal of how all navies operate. The predominance of radio signals is defeated by the interference of even a few feet of seawater, and when a submarine goes under water, it's invisible to everyone. Despite extensive research in other areas, the most reliable way for a submarine to communicate is to come up to a depth right below the surface of the water and stick up an antenna, which is used to conduct communications. These trips to "periscope depth" (PD) are the most dangerous procedure we execute on a daily basis because it involves going from the deep ocean, where we are most comfortable, to a very unstable spot just below the surface of the water, where we are in danger of being run over by surface ships. Our sonar systems are some of the best in the world, but there is still uncertainty about contacts until the periscope clears the water and we verify that no one is in the immediate vicinity.

Staying at periscope depth is also annoying for a submarine because we have to worry about being seen by others, keeping a fresh set of eyes on the periscope, and keeping the ship's control party sharp. Wave action makes it a very sensitive procedure to balance the buoyancy of the ship right below the surface of the water, and we constantly fight against a "broaching," where the ship goes out of control and the sail comes out of the water, allowing anyone around to see exactly where we are. Masts and antennas can be hidden and lowered, but nothing can be done when you stick 10 feet of sail out of the water. We also constantly practice "Emergency Deep" procedures, which is how we get down from periscope depth when a contact gets so close that the ship is in danger. The order of precedence of anything that happens on a submarine is always 1) safety of the ship, 2) avoid counter-detection, and 3) mission accomplishment.

Made in the USA
Coppell, TX
17 September 2020

38124217R10080